OTHER BOOKS BY JANE WATSON HOPPING

The Pioneer Lady's Country Kitchen

The Pioneer Lady's Country Christmas

The Country Mothers Cookbook

The Lazy Days of Summer
COOKBOOK

The Lazy Days of Summer
COOKBOOK

A CELEBRATION OF SUMMER'S BOUNTY

Jane Watson Hopping,

THE PIONEER LADY

VILLARD BOOKS, NEW YORK
1992

Library of Congress Cataloging-in-Publication Data

Hopping, Jane Watson.
    The lazy days of summer: a celebration of summer's bounty/
Jane Watson Hopping.—1st ed.
        p.   cm.
    Includes index.
    ISBN 0-679-40336-1
    1. Cookery.   2. Summer.   I. Title.
TX714.H66   1992
641.5′64—dc20   91-31265

Grateful acknowledgment is made to the following for permission to
reprint previously published material:

Music Sales Corporation: Lyrics from "I Don't Want to Play in Your Yard,"
by H. W. Petrie, from *Everybody's Community Folksongs.* Copyright © 1935
(Renewed) Amsco Publications, a division of Music Sales Corporation.
International Copyright Secured. All Rights Reserved. Used by
permission.

Shawnee Press, Inc.: Excerpt from the lyrics of "The More We Get
Together" from *Everybody Sing Book,* edited by Kenneth Clark. Copyright
© 1935 (Renewed) Shawnee Press, Inc. International Copyright Secured.
All Rights Reserved. Used by permission.

Unity School of Christianity: "The Pleasant Ways of Home," by Frances
McKinnon Morton, from *Best Loved Unity Poems,* by Dorothy Frances
Gurney, published by United School of Christianity.

"On Learning My Mother Has Cherokee Blood," "Grandfield," "Cloud
Nocturne," "Summer," and "Jacksonville: Pigeons" by Alvin Reiss
originally appeared in the *Oregonian.*

Manufactured in the United States of America

9   8   7   6   5   4   3   2

First edition

BOOK DESIGN: BARBARA MARKS

♥

DANDELIONS, Dandelions, Like golden stars
    Are you,
Shining in the meadow-grass and sparkling
    With the dew.
Did you shine up yonder, dears,
    All the long night thro'
And then come dancing down with the sun
    Because the children all love you?

        —THE DANDELION
        Words by Alice C. D. Riley

A
NONSENSE CALENDAR.

JUNE.

In balmy June we may espy
The flittering, fluttering Butterfly.
He idles round in sunny bowers,
And whispers nonsense to the flowers.

The most superfluous of things —
He 's nothing but a pair of wings;
He cannot work, he cannot play,
He never has a word to say.

But every day in sunny June,
Especially in the afternoon,
He sits with lazy, happy smile,
And winks his wings once in a while.

He 's of no use; he 's only sent
To June to be her ornament.
And so we smile as we espy
The flittering, fluttering Butterfly.

Acknowledgments

AS I WORKED ON this book, I thought often about those whose skills have enhanced it. On a personal basis, I have the loving support of my family, who sustain me not only at the desk, but throughout the routine of my daily life. The love that I bear my husband of forty-two years, Raymond, and my grown children, Randy and Colleen, and my son-in-law, Mark, and the love that they bear me, often fill the well that is inside me.

Mother, who is now eighty-six and a bit fragile, still tells me tales of the past that I have never heard before, and refreshes my memory when I can't quite recall out of my childhood a family story that keeps haunting me. Sheila, my sister and best friend, contributes lovely decorative art that not only enhances the beauty of the book but adds to it a certain continuity.

I owe considerable thanks to my friend Alvin Reiss, who has contributed his own original poetry to the work, and who has, when I've been unable to find just the right piece for a special segment, written a new poem to match the text. I would be remiss if I did not express here my posthumous gratitude to the poets of the past whose lovely songs grace the pages of the book.

Also, much appreciation to the retired principal of Jacksonville Elementary School, Arthur A. Lockeridge, and to Elaine Reisinger and her third-grade class, all of whom made possible the use of several delightful pieces of children's poetry in this book. And many thanks to those at the Jane Rotrosen Agency, Meg Ruley and her able assistant, Julie Evans.

Last but certainly not least, I would like to express my respect and appreciation for editors Emily Bestler, Thomas G. Fiffer, and others at Villard Books who make considerable effort to show off my literary child.

Contents

INTRODUCTION:
'TWAS A SUMMER WARM AS WINE

xvii

♥

*O'er Happy Lands Where
Sunshine Lies*

3

SCHOOL'S OUT

4

*Sun-Ripened Strawberries Dipped in Sugar
Cinnamon Pie
Strawberry Pineapple Punch*

GRADUATION FROM THE
EIGHTH GRADE

9

*Aunt Sue's Chicken Croquettes Served with
Mustard-Horseradish Sauce
Aunty's Honey-Glazed Carrots
Grandpa's Grabbled Baked Red Potatoes
Mother's Red Cabbage and Spinach Salad
Dressed with Homemade Tomato French
Dressing
Ada's Rosy Rhubarb Pie*

THREE CHEERS FOR
THE RED, WHITE, AND BLUE

16

Aunt Mabel's Flag Day Cake

A COUNTRY BAPTISM IN COW CREEK

19

*Ruby and Butter-Crunch Lettuce Salad with
Herbed Vinaigrette
Ham with Baked Beans
Aunt Mae's Bath Buns
Yorkshire Country Captain
Ada's Poppyseed Pound Cake with Tangy
Lemon-Orange Glaze*

♥

*'Bout the Time Strawberries Melt
on the Vine*

28

PICKIN' WEATHER

29

*Effie's Strawberry Mousse
Young Martha's Strawberry Topping for
Ice Cream
Aunt El's Strawberry Pie*

OLD MISSUS UPJOHN'S HERB TEAS, HONEY,
AND BUZZIN' BEES

33

*Balm Melissa, Bee Balm, or Lemon Balm
Basil Tea
Geranium (Pelargonium) Tea
Goldenrod or Blue Mountain Tea
Old Missus Upjohn's Sour Cream Cookies*

♥

June's the Month When the Bobolink Sings

36

A FATHER'S DAY OUTING

38

Fried Spring Chicken
Mother's Potato Salad
Lemon Batter Rolls
Sweet-Cherry Crunch
Easy-to-Make Picnic Punch

A PICNIC IN THE RAIN

45

Pan-Fried Mountain Trout
English Pea Salad
Potato Butter Horn Rolls
Sour Cream Red June Apple Pie with
Butter-Cinnamon Topping

AUNT CLARY'S NINETY-EIGHTH
BIRTHDAY PARTY

52

Scottish Fancies
Wellesley Tea
Fannie Merritt Farmer's Gossamer Gingerbread

HEAVEN AND HOMEMADE BREAD

55

Anadama Bread

♥

The Pearls of Dew and Roses of June

59

A VINTAGE FASHION SHOW

60

Rainbow Cakes
Effie's Boston Brown Bread Tea Sandwiches
with Assorted Fillings

'MID STREAMING RAYS OF GOLDEN SUNSHINE

67

Chicken Salad with Homemade Curried
French Dressing
Deluxe Bran Muffins
Summertime Iced Cider Punch

♥

A Merry Fairy Dream

71

A KISS AS SWEET AS HEATED
HONEY IS

73

Bride's Orange-Blossom Cake
Groom's Cake with Creamy Chocolate
Butter Frosting
A Housewarming Cake

DRINKING ALL THAT LIFE HOLDS, LOVE

80

An Old-Fashioned Fruit Salad Platter with
Honey-Lemon Mayonnaise

An Old-Fashioned Ham Loaf
Garden-Fresh Green Bean Medley
Honey Rice Pudding

♥

He's the Goodest Man Ever You Saw

85

A SUMMER APPLE FESTIVAL

86

Ada's Apple Crisp
Aunt Mabel's Cider Applesauce
Easy-to-Make Raw Apple and Carrot Cookies

THE RUNAWAY BOY

92

Willie's Favorite Fruit Pockets
Uncle Bud's Favorite Dried Fig and
Honey Cookies
Old-Fashioned Hermits

WHEN GOD SORTS OUT THE WEATHER AND SENDS RAIN

98

Salmon with Tartar Sauce
Green and Gold Snap Beans
Golden Acre Cabbage Salad
Effie's Poppyseed Rolls
Marshmallow Bavarian Cream

♥

Up and Down Old Brandywine

104

A FOURTH OF JULY PICNIC ON THE AMERICAN RIVER

105

Aunt Sue's Salmon Macaroni Salad
Aunt Irene's Stuffed Tomatoes
Mother's Coconut Angel Cake

AN AFTERNOON RIPE WITH HEAT

110

Chilled Baked Salmon
Dilled Cucumbers and Sweet Onions in
Sour Cream
Garden-Fresh Grabbled Potatoes with Herbs
Vine-Ripened Red Raspberries Topped with
Chilled Heavy Cream

BENEATH A SILVER WILLOW TREE

114

An Old-Fashioned Cottage Cheese Apple Pie
with Butter-Crust Pastry
Economical Surprise Pie with
Vanilla Wafer Crust
Ada's Blueberry Pie with Double-Crust
Egg Pastry

♥

A Languid Atmosphere, a Lazy Breeze

121

AN OLD-TIME WILD BLACKBERRY SOCIAL

123

Wild Blackberry Pie with Flaky Lattice Crust
Deep-Dish Wild Blackberry Crunch with Vanilla
Wafer Topping
Wild Blackberry Cordial

THE ROADSIDE PRODUCE STAND

129

Poached Fresh Peaches
A Summer Garden Casserole
Effie's Jellied Cucumber Salad

THE BOY 'AT LIVES ON OUR FARM

135

Old-Fashioned Corn Pudding
Effie's Stuffed Red Bell Peppers
Eggplant with Tomatoes
Ann's Early Peach Ice Cream Shortcake

♥

A Country Growers' Market

140

OF STATICE AND OTHER BEAUTIFUL
SUMMER FLOWERS

142

Yellow Rose-Petal Sugar
Candied Red Rose Petals
Mock Capers
Nasturtium Salad

LEMON CUCUMBERS AND FOOTLONG BEANS

148

Lemon-Cucumber Cottage Cheese Salad
Hot Footlong Beans and Bacon Salad
A Medley of Watermelons

♥

The Crick So Still and Deep

152

A CHILDREN'S COUNTRY POETRY CONTEST

154

Summertime in the Valley
A Summer Afternoon
Summer
Climbing Trees, Catching Butterflies
Summer Evening Sounds

LOVING IS A TWO-WAY STREET!

157

Salmon Wiggle
Mid-Season Corn
Ada's Favorite Snap-Bean Dish
Blueberry and Almond Muffins

EFFIE'S GAZEBO

163

Effie's Watercress Sandwiches
Almond Wafers
Russian Tea with Preserved Strawberries

AN OLD-TIME ICE CREAM SOCIAL AT THE SCHOOLHOUSE

167

Old-Fashioned Peach Ice Cream
Luscious Frozen Strawberry Custard
Old-Time Soft Sugar Cookies

♥

Joyful Memories Revived

173

MY LOVE IS LIKE A WILD, WILD ROSE

175

Effie's Sweetheart Cake with Lemon-Flavored
Seven-Minute Frosting

SUMMER'S WANDERLUST

178

New England Hot Pot

MAGNOLIAS AND MOSS-DRAPED PINES

181

Georgia Belle Peach Cobbler

♥

Warm-Weather Pleasures That Last a Lifetime

184

THIS FUNNY LITTLE FRIEND OF MINE

186

Sand Tarts
Chocolaty Pecan Dollars
Slice-and-Bake Vanilla Walnut Cookies

YOU CAN'T CLIMB OUR APPLE TREE

190

Effie's Homemade Graham Bread
Apricot Nectar Ice Cubes

♥

Beneath a Chinaberry Tree

193

APPLE PIE SUNDAYS

195

Mabel Reiss's Apple Pie
Mabel's Luscious Divinity
A Boy's Favorite Peanut Butter Cookies

SUMMER SATURDAYS IN OKLAHOMA

199

Spice Drops with Creamy Orange Icing

KATRINA, KATRINA

203

Ada's Jeweled Cookies

A DAY AT THE BEACH

206

Aunt Mabel's Braised Chilled Chicken
Lima Bean Salad
Our Favorite Buttermilk Rolls
Orange Tea Cakes with Orange Butter Frosting

♥

On Bridges of Memory

212

OFF OLD POINT COMFORT

214

Oven-Fried Sea Bream

THE LAST BLACKSMITH ON NANTUCKET

216

New England Doughnuts
Apple Turnovers with a Simple
Powdered-Sugar Glaze

THIS SUMMER OF THE HEART

220

Easy-to-Make Potato Salad
Sliced Tomato Salad
A Simple Three-Bean Salad
Fresh Spinach Salad
Luscious Orange Sponge

A PINE BED UNDER THE TREES

227

WHEN YOU AND I WERE YOUNG

229

An Old-Fashioned Elberta Peach Pie
An Apple Brown Betty
A Ginger-Flavored Fig Cake

♥

Mountain Memories Music Festival

235

THE DARKNESS AND THE DEW

239

Ada's Harvest Salad
Easy-to-Make Dill Pickles
Country-Fried Sweet Potatoes
Sour Cream Swiss Steak
Aunt Clary's Plain Gingerbread

♥

The Span of Owl's Wings

246

HERMAN'S WOODEN SPOONS, MINIATURE ROCKING HORSES, AND OTHER LOVELY HANDMADE THINGS

249

Vera's Raisin Cake with Brandy-Flavored
Powdered-Sugar Glaze
Easy-To-Make Refrigerator Ginger Cookies
Sweet Buns with Fruit Filling
Cinnamon-Topped Oatmeal Muffins

FARING DOWN SOME WOODED TRAIL

255

A HUNTER'S MOON POTLUCK

257

A Hunter's Moon Venison Roast
Baby Beets in Vinegar
Our Favorite Chinese-Cabbage Salad
Baked Butternut Squash
Mother's Cloverleaf Rolls
Uncle Bill's Sour Cream Raisin Cake

♥

A Sudden Thought of Heaven

265

Index

267

Introduction:
'Twas a Summer Warm As Wine

Grandma (Elizabeth) White

IN its color, shade and shine
  'Twas a summer warm as wine,
With an effervescent flavoring of flowered
  bough and vine,
And a fragrance and a taste
Of ripe roses gone to waste,
And a dreamy sense of sun and moon and
  Starlight interlaced.

—From A WRAITH OF SUMMER-TIME
James Whitcomb Riley

FOR GRANDMA WHITE, THE lazy days of summer marked a time of celebration, a time of plenty.

She would get up at dawn and be out working in the cool morning hours long before I arrived to spend the day with her, visiting, and sometimes washing our clothes together. In July we would make jam from the sweet golden apricots off her trees. Later in summer, I would go to her house several days in a row to help her take the grey-green hulls off the almonds so that Grandpa could take them to market.

Now, years later, as I write this book, Grandma is often with me. I can hear her laughter and see her again at the kitchen table, eyes aglow, playing cards to win.

She loved to be with people and was always ready to go to a family dinner, a picnic, a potluck, or just shopping with her daughters. Whatever the occasion, she would arrive early to help with the preparations. And when that was done, she would convince someone to play cribbage with her or, if the young folk preferred, a game of hearts.

Kind and loving, all her life she sent get-well and thinking-of-you cards, never forgetting a birthday or a friend who was ill.

Out of such memories of her, and of family, friends, and neighbors, has come the inspiration for this book, which is about potluck dinners and games, gossip and baby talk in the park, grange and church suppers, a summer apple festival, a swimming party at the river, a late-night supper cooked and eaten in the light of a campfire, a fishing trip, and a ball game—family outings and feasting with loved ones.

For the most part, though, it is about good wholesome country food that is easy to prepare and for which the ingredients are not costly. The recipes reflect the seasonal bounty of summer . . .

Aunt Sue's Chicken Croquettes Served with Mustard-Horseradish Sauce
Yorkshire Country Captain
Ada's Poppyseed Pound Cake with Tangy Lemon-Orange Glaze
Sweet-Cherry Crunch
Deluxe Bran Muffins
Garden-Fresh Green Bean Medley
Aunt Irene's Stuffed Tomatoes
Effie's Stuffed Red Bell Peppers
Ann's Early Peach Ice Cream Shortcake

The chapters, which begin early in June and end as autumn approaches, are a celebration of the lazy days and playfulness of summer, the lingering memories of romantic interludes, remembrances of warm breezes, golden sunshine, heady blossoms, and sea breezes. Throughout, I have hoped that readers who partake of this richly blessed time of year will carry with them into the chilly blasts of winter a little bit of sunshine.

The Lazy Days of Summer
COOKBOOK

Raymond, Walter, and Marlene

O'ER
HAPPY LANDS
WHERE
SUNSHINE LIES

~~~~~~~~~

EVERY YEAR IN JUNE, a quiet joy comes over the countryside. It is almost as though the whole earth is pregnant. Deep-red strawberries hang in profusion on lush plants canopied under dark green leaves, and birds raucously argue over possession of luscious tree-ripened black sweet cherries. Hardworking country folk bask in the sun, or wander during the cool morning hours along the creeks through gardens, orchards, and pastures to listen to the sweet songs of birds and the sounds of wild critters searching for their breakfast in the underbrush.

School's Out

LONG BEFORE SCHOOL WAS out country children, accustomed to lots of outdoor activity, began to dream of summer, of hammocks in the shade, ice-cold lemonade, and hot ripe cherries. Some daydreamed about hidden berry patches, ripe and sweet, the fragrance so heady it made the head reel and the stomach growl.

No one, not even a teacher, could keep his mind off fishing holes and picnic spots, loved relatives who would be seen again after the long winter, watermelons lying thick in the patch just waiting to be thumped. Who could resist thoughts of streaming rays of golden sunlight, soft breezes, freedom to wander through the woods, along creeks, to sit on hilltops and watch the wind work its way through the trees?

I dreamed of trips to the country library, where I could pick out any book I liked, and of reading uninterrupted for hours in the shade of a giant tree; of spending more time with my family—Grandpa, Mother, Daddy, and Sheila—and of big family picnics, parties, and get-togethers. Aunt Mabel always asked me to stay with her for a week, and my cousins and I had great plans for staying overnight, sometimes even longer, at our house or theirs.

And yet, even with exciting summer plans afoot, I often felt a bit teary, that last day of school, a little nostalgic at leaving behind loved teachers, friends, classmates, familiar rooms, and the enrichment of books, paper, and pen.

ও

SUMMER

THE sun and the sky
And the birds and I,
   And the great, tall whisp'ring trees,
Are all as happy as happy can be,
   Out in the Summer breeze.

There is time to play
All the live-long day,
   For our holidays are here;
I'm free as the birds and happy as they—
   School's over for the year.

—Alden Arthur Knipe

JANE WATSON HOPPING

THE THRUSH'S NEST

WITHIN a thick and spreading hawthorn bush,
That overhung a molehill large and round,
I heard from morn to morn a merry thrush
Sing hymns of rapture, while I drank the sound
With joy and oft, an unintruding guest,
I watch'd her secret toils from day to day;
How true she warp'd the moss to form her nest,
And modell'd it within the wood and clay,
And by and by, like heath-bells gilt with dew,
There lay her shining eggs as bright as flowers,
Ink-spotted over, shells of green and blue:
And there I witness'd in the summer hours
A brood of Nature's minstrels chirp and fly
Glad as the sunshine and the laughing sky.

—John Clare

♥

Sun-Ripened Strawberries Dipped in Sugar

MAKES ENOUGH FOR 4 TO 6 CHILDREN

ABOUT THE TIME SCHOOL lets out, our children love to gather on the back porch and celebrate their summer freedom with a big bowl of huge, smooth, scarlet berries, sweet and chock-full of wild strawberry flavor, dipped in sugar.

2 quarts large vine-ripened
strawberries

½ cup granulated sugar, more
when that is gone

Set about 4 to 6 children down on the back porch. Put a large bowl of lightly washed, hulled strawberries in the center of a small table and place sugar nearby. Step back and enjoy the laughter, the strawberry-smeared faces and sugared fingers.

♥

Cinnamon Pie

MAKES ENOUGH FOR 3 SERVINGS

½ cup butter or margarine
1 cup all-purpose flour, plus flour
*   for rolling*
½ teaspoon salt

1 egg
1 teaspoon cider vinegar
3 tablespoons sugar
Cinnamon

Preheat oven to 425°F. Set out a 9-inch pie pan.

In a medium bowl, work butter or margarine into combined flour and salt until the mixture is coarse and has developed lumps about the size of peas. In a small bowl, beat the egg, about *2 tablespoons cold water (more if needed),* and vinegar to a froth, then stir this into the flour mixture. Form the dough into a ball and place on a floured surface. Handle only as much as is needed to form a smooth ball (which should not stick to the hands). Roll out the dough and line the 9-inch pan with it. *Sprinkle over the dough about 3 tablespoons sugar and a generous dusting of cinnamon, and a little butter if desired.* Bake until crust is golden brown (take care not to burn the filling), about 15 to 20 minutes. When done, remove from the oven and cool until the pastry can be either broken or cut into serving pieces for boys (or girls). Serve with icy-cold milk.

෨

CINNAMON PIE

WHEN you roll pie dough
to fill with sliced apples,
with sugar and cinnamon and butter
and immeasurable servings of love,
and you roll enough to cover,
always roll just a little more.
Spread it in a tin. Sprinkle
cinnamon and sugar
and a little butter.

These are not cuttings
to be discarded from the crust.
These are cinnamon pies.
When your son comes in from play,
treat him to a surprise.
He will remember you always
and love you forever.
I know this is true,
My mother did, and I do.

—Alvin Reiss

Strawberry Pineapple Punch

MAKES ABOUT 12 SERVINGS

THE FIRST DAY AFTER school was out, Aunt Sue would take her children and a few more down to the pond to fish. They never caught much, but just sitting on the grass beside the sparkling water, watching dragonflies and the wild mallard ducks that had come to stay, was enough.

For a treat, Aunty took jugs of Strawberry Pineapple Punch, packed in crushed ice, and a few plain cookies.

1 pint strawberries, hulled
½ cup sugar plus ¼ cup more
2 cups pineapple juice

Juice from 3 lemons
1 cup mild Orange Pekoe tea

In a medium saucepan combine hulled berries, 2 cups water, and ½ cup sugar; heat to just under the boiling point. Cover and cool; when completely cool, strain off the strawberry juice. Combine with pineapple juice, lemon juice, and tea. If desired, sweeten to taste with the *additional ¼ cup sugar*.

From ALL THINGS BRIGHT AND BEAUTIFUL

ALL things bright and beautiful,
All creatures great and small,
All things wise and wonderful,—
The Lord God made them all.

He gave us eyes to see them,
And lips that we might tell
How great is God Almighty,
Who hath made all things well.

—Cecil Frances Alexander

JANE WATSON HOPPING

Leone

Graduation from the Eighth Grade

WHEN MY SISTER, SHEILA, and I were in the second and seventh grades, respectively, our family, including Grandpa, moved from our beloved canyon home to Bowman, California, a very small community which boasted an old-time two-room elementary school.

In the smaller room a quiet, soft-spoken older teacher taught first, second, and third grades. In the larger room the desks were ordered in five rows, one for each of the upper grades. The teacher, who was also principal of the school, was a stern but kindly middle-aged woman who brought to her poorly equipped school all the enrichment she could muster. We had no music department, but we sang; we had no art department, but we were encouraged in many ways to be creative. We were taught that it is important to have principles and morals, to have ideals and dreams.

The following year, my eighth-grade year, there were only five of us in the graduating class. Much of our time was spent reviewing subject matter on which we would be tested before graduation. This meant that we boned up on history, geography, math, English, science, and anything else our teacher thought we might need a little extra practice on.

In early June the testing began, and when it was finished and the scores returned to us, my good friend Richard and I had tied for the top score, something like 98.5.

Our teacher asked us to stay in for a moment at recess. She told us that I had been chosen to give the Salutatory Address, a welcoming speech at the graduation ceremony; Richard had been chosen to give the Valedictory Address, a farewell speech at the end of the ceremonies.

From that moment, the entire school began to work toward the graduation. Younger children began to practice songs and short recitations. Parents offered their money and assistance. Women in the community promised flowers, cookies, and punch. Finally, all was ready; the big day had come.

Overnight, the larger classroom was turned into an auditorium of sorts. It was spotlessly clean, and there were ribbons and flowers everywhere. Parents, neighbors, and friends sat on benches and at desks. We of the eighth grade sat at the front of the room. When the graduation service began, I stood up and told our guests how pleased we were to have them with us, and how much we appreciated their support. The younger children sang and recited their pieces. Then our teacher and principal praised us and reminded us that while the high school was much larger than our elementary school, we had been prepared and would do well there. She then handed out our diplomas. Richard gave the Valedictory Address, speaking softly about our little country school and about the friendships we had made there and the respect we had for our teachers. When the ceremonies were over, coffee, tea, punch, and cookies were served.

Later, at home, my entire family came to our house to celebrate. All my relatives hugged or patted me, congratulated me, and told me that they were proud of me. My parents gave me a gold watch. Aunt Hattie and Uncle Floyd gave me a book, as did Aunt Mabel and Uncle Mope; Aunt Pauline and Uncle Arch gave me toilet water and book-plates; Aunt Irene and Uncle Ben gave me bath crystals and scented bath powder.

And then we had a potluck supper. My mother and aunts had prepared a feast of chicken croquettes smothered in mustard-and-horseradish sauce; Grandpa's earthy fresh red potatoes, baked and topped with Mother's fresh butter; red cabbage and spinach salad; and honey-glazed baby carrots, followed by Ada's scrumptious rhubarb pie.

JANE WATSON HOPPING

♥

Aunt Sue's Chicken Croquettes Served with Mustard-Horseradish Sauce

MAKES ABOUT 8 SERVINGS

UNCLE BEN LOVED THESE chicken croquettes covered with mustard-horseradish sauce. He and Grandpa would tease the women into giving them a sample to munch on while the food was being put on the table.

2 cups cold, cooked chicken (remove skin and fat, and chop while chicken is still warm)
1 cup Thick White Sauce (recipe follows)
1 egg yolk, well beaten, plus 1 whole egg, slightly beaten
1 tablespoon lemon juice, strained
½ teaspoon salt
1 teaspoon parsley, minced
¼ teaspoon paprika
Cooking oil, as needed for deep-fat frying
½ cup cracker crumbs, finely crushed with a rolling pin
1 cup Mustard-Horseradish Sauce (recipe follows)

In a medium bowl, combine chicken, white sauce, egg yolk, lemon juice, salt, parsley, and paprika. Cool at room temperature.

When chicken mixture is cool enough to shape into balls, set out cooking oil in a deep-fat fryer or other deep pot and heat to cooking temperature (375°F). Set out a large pan or platter and cover it with absorbent paper. Form chicken mixture into balls about the size of large eggs. Roll in cracker crumbs, then dip in the whole egg, which has been beaten and diluted with 2 tablespoons cold water. Dip a second time in cracker crumbs.

Fry in hot oil until coating is golden brown, 1¾ to 2 minutes. Drain on absorbent paper for about 2 minutes (turn over very carefully for more thorough draining). Serve piping hot or chilled, with Mustard-Horseradish Sauce.

♥

Thick White Sauce

¼ cup butter or margarine,
    softened at room temperature
¼ cup all-purpose flour

1 cup milk
¼ teaspoon salt
⅛ teaspoon ground black pepper

In a medium saucepan melt butter or margarine over low heat. Still over low heat, blend in flour and cook, stirring constantly, until mixture is smooth and bubbly. Remove from heat and stir in milk; return to heat and, still stirring constantly, bring to a boil. Boil for about 1 minute. To prevent sticking keep stirring while mixture boils. Remove pan from heat, and add salt and pepper.

♥

Mustard-Horseradish Sauce

MAKES ABOUT I CUP SAUCE

¾ cup mayonnaise
½ teaspoon dry mustard

⅓ cup prepared horseradish,
    drained, but not too dry

In a small bowl with a tight-fitting lid blend mayonnaise, dry mustard, and horseradish. Cover tightly and refrigerate until needed. (For best flavor, make this sauce not more than 15 to 20 minutes before using.)

♥

Aunty's Honey-Glazed Carrots

MAKES 6 SERVINGS

BY MID-JUNE, SMALL, tender carrots can be pulled from carrot rows in the garden without damaging those still growing. Aunty loved the flavor of these half-grown carrots and often glazed them with honey.

12 to 15 carrots, depending on size (allow enough for 6 servings)

3 tablespoons light honey (clover honey preferred)

3 tablespoons butter, melted

2 tablespoons parsley, minced

½ teaspoon orange rind, grated

¼ teaspoon salt

¼ teaspoon pepper

⅛ teaspoon thyme

Preheat oven to 375°F. Thoroughly grease a 1½-quart covered casserole dish. Set aside.

Brush young carrots carefully (skins are very tender). Leave whole or cut lengthwise and place in prepared casserole dish. In a small bowl, combine honey, melted butter, parsley, orange rind, salt, pepper, and thyme; mix thoroughly, then pour mixture over carrots and cover the dish.

Bake until carrots are fork-tender and well glazed with the honey mixture, about 1 hour.

♥

Grandpa's Grabbled Baked Red Potatoes

MAKES 6 SERVINGS

EVERY YEAR, GRANDPA PLANTED his red potato sets on St. Patrick's Day, so that we could grabble (dig out of the potato hill by hand) a few in early June. All of us loved the earthy flavor and waxy texture of his potatoes and baked them often.

6 medium red potatoes (or 12 smaller ones)

About 2 tablespoons softened butter for greasing skins of potatoes, more for seasoning baked potatoes

Salt and pepper as desired

Preheat oven to 425°F. Set out a medium baking sheet.

Scrub potatoes gently (peels are tender) and remove eyes and any blemishes. Take a little soft butter on your fingers and grease potato skins. Place on ungreased baking sheet.

Bake until tender, about 45 minutes to 1 hour. To test for doneness, wrap a dishtowel around your hand and squeeze the potatoes; they should feel soft. When done, immediately break open the skins to keep them from getting soggy and serve promptly with butter, salt, and pepper to taste.

♥

Mother's Red Cabbage and Spinach Salad Dressed with Homemade Tomato French Dressing

MAKES ABOUT 6 SERVINGS

WHEN PLANTED EARLY, THESE small, crisp heads of cabbage are ready for use in mid-June. Because of the rich blend of colors, Mother loved to combine finely shredded red cabbage with sweet, tender green spinach. Grandpa thought this was as good as his favorite greens—wilted lettuce.

½ cup Homemade Tomato French
*   Dressing (recipe follows)*
½ head red cabbage, finely
*   shredded*
1 pound tender spinach, washed
*   and torn into small pieces*

1 tablespoon green onion (1 tender
*   young onion)*
½ cup celery, diced (Mother
*   preferred the light-colored ribs)*

Make dressing, then chill while preparing vegetables.

In a large bowl, combine cabbage, spinach, green onion, and celery. Using a whisk, blend chilled dressing. Pour 3 to 4 tablespoons dressing over vegetables, toss, and serve.

♥

Homemade Tomato French Dressing

MAKES I CUP

½ cup salad oil
¼ cup catsup, homemade or store-
*   bought*
2 tablespoons sugar
¼ cup cider vinegar

1 teaspoon salt
⅛ teaspoon freshly ground black
*   pepper*
1 teaspoon paprika
1 teaspoon grated sweet onion

In a small bowl with a cover, combine all ingredients. Beat with a whisk to blend. Use ½ cup to dress salad. Tightly cover remaining dressing and refrigerate for later use.

♥

Ada's Rosy Rhubarb Pie

MAKES ONE 9-INCH PIE (6 SERVINGS)

WHEN I WAS GROWING up every lady had her favorite version of rhubarb pie. Early in the season, after the bland flavors of winter, the thick crimson stalks yielded up a luscious blend of sweetness and tartness—the flavors of summer.

*Double-Crust Flaky Pastry (recipe
  follows)*
*1 pound (3 cups) rhubarb,
  trimmed but not peeled, cut
  into 1-inch pieces*

3 tablespoons all-purpose flour
½ cup sugar
⅛ teaspoon salt
½ cup light corn syrup
2 eggs, lightly beaten

Make pastry and chill. Just before preparing the filling, remove dough from refrigerator, roll out half of it and line a 9-inch pie pan. Roll the remaining pastry into a rectangular sheet about ¼ inch thick for the lattice top.

Preheat oven to 450°F.

Into a large bowl, turn prepared rhubarb. Thoroughly mix in the flour, sugar, and salt. Add corn syrup and eggs. Using a spatula or a wooden spoon, blend ingredients together. Turn into pastry-lined pie pan. Cut the remaining rectangle of pastry into strips; weave strips over top of pie and crimp edges.

Bake in 450°F oven for 10 minutes, then reduce heat to 375°F and bake until pie crust is well browned and filling is clear and bubbly, about 30 to 45 minutes more. When the pie is done, remove from oven, taking care not to get filling on your hands, as it will stick and burn. Set pie on a wire rack to cool. Serve at room temperature.

♥

Double-Crust Flaky Pastry

MAKES ENOUGH FOR ONE DOUBLE-CRUST 9-INCH PIE

*2 cups all-purpose flour, plus ½
  cup for rolling out dough*

1 teaspoon salt
1 cup cold butter or margarine

In a medium bowl, combine the flour and salt. Using a pastry blender, two table knives, or your fingertips, cut in the butter or margarine until the mixture resembles grains of corn. Sprinkle ¼ cup cold water over the mixture and blend thoroughly with a fork until all particles cling together to form a ball.

Three Cheers for the Red, White, and Blue

WHEN Freedom, from her mountain height,
Unfurled her standard to the air,
She tore the azure robe of night
And set the stars of glory there!

—From THE AMERICAN FLAG
Joseph Rodman Drake

ॐ

WHEN I WAS GROWING up, children everywhere were taught to honor our country and flag. In those days, folks put the colors out on special patriotic days, especially Flag Day. School bands practiced songs like "It's a Grand Old Flag," "Columbia, the Gem of the Ocean," and "America." Small towns made plans for a parade.

We lived eight miles from the town of Auburn, California, but even so our mother and father made a special trip up out of the canyon to stand with us and with all of the rest of the family—aunts, uncles, and cousins—along the street to listen to the bands, watch the marchers, and see all the flags being carried by. They taught us right there to stand up straight and put our hands over our hearts as the flags passed by; they told us that to do so was the traditional and accepted way Americans show their loyalty and love for the United States, the nation's flag, and democratic principles.

After the parade, Aunt Mabel treated us to sodas at a real soda fountain, and she taught us about the origins of the flag.

She explained carefully that after independence had been declared on July 4, 1776, there was a desire among the people to have a national standard or flag, enough of a desire that a resolution was adopted in Congress on June 17, 1777, stating that the flag of the United States be thirteen stripes alternately red and white, with white stars in a blue field representing a new constellation. In 1782, when the colors of the flag were made part of the newly designed Great Seal of the United States, a spokesman for the Department of State revealed to the public the meaning of the colors:

THE red stripes would forever stand for hardiness and courage,
White stripes symbolized purity and innocence,
White stars spoke of liberty,
A blue field represented vigilance, perseverance and justice.

JANE WATSON HOPPING

♥

Aunt Mabel's Flag Day Cake

MAKES ONE 9-INCH LAYER CAKE

MY FAVORITE AUNT TRIED in many ways to make holidays special for us all. She usually invited our family, Aunt Hattie's family, Uncle Arch and Aunt Pauline, Uncle Ben and Aunt Irene, and a few extra aunties and uncles who were well loved, but not blood relatives, to her house to cap off the Flag Day celebration with a little visiting and this delicious cake and coffee.

2 cups cake flour, sifted	1/3 cup milk
2 teaspoons baking powder	1 teaspoon vanilla extract
1/2 teaspoon salt	Seven-Minute Frosting (recipe
2/3 cup butter or margarine,	follows)
softened at room temperature	2 cups sweetened coconut
1 cup sugar	
3 eggs, separated and the yolks	
well beaten and whites beaten	
into stiff peaks	

Preheat oven to 375°F. Thoroughly grease two 9-inch layer cake pans. Set aside.

Into a medium bowl sift flour a second and third time with baking powder and salt; set aside. In a large bowl, cream butter or margarine thoroughly until soft and waxy. Add sugar gradually, about 2 tablespoons at a time, and cream together until light and fluffy. Add well-beaten egg yolks and stir to blend. Then add flour mixture alternately with milk, a small amount at a time, beating until batter is thick but smooth and fluffy. Add vanilla; give batter a few final strokes to blend. Fold in stiffly beaten egg whites. (Do not beat after whites are added.) Turn into prepared pans.

Set pans in the center of the preheated oven. Bake until layers are well risen, golden brown, and firm to the touch, about 25 to 30 minutes. Cool 8 to 10 minutes in the pans, then turn layers out on a wire rack to cool thoroughly. Thinly fill cooled layers with Seven-Minute Frosting, then spread *remaining* frosting over top and sides of the cake. Sprinkle generously with coconut, covering both top and sides of the cake. Decorate with a dozen, more or less, of tiny American flags.

♥

Seven-Minute Frosting

MAKES ENOUGH FROSTING FOR ONE 9-INCH LAYER CAKE

2 egg whites, unbeaten
1½ cups sugar

1½ teaspoons light corn syrup
1 teaspoon vanilla

In the top of a double boiler, combine egg whites, sugar, 5 tablespoons water, and corn syrup. Beat with a rotary egg beater until thoroughly mixed. Heat water in the bottom pan to boiling. Set the combined ingredients over the rapidly boiling water; beat constantly with rotary egg beater while cooking until frosting stands in peaks, 7 minutes.

Remove pan of frosting from boiling water; add vanilla and beat until thick enough to spread.

Orvil and Mabel Porter

A Song for Flag Day

Out on the breeze,
O'er land and seas,
A beautiful banner is streaming.
Shining its stars,
Splendid its bars,
Under the sunshine 'tis gleaming.

Over the brave
Long may it wave,
Peace to the world ever bringing.
While to the stars,
Linked with the bars,
Hearts will forever be singing.

—Lydia A. Coonley

A Country Baptism in Cow Creek

WHEN SHEILA AND I were young, we attended a nearby Community Church. The building was old, built in the nineteenth century; the congregation, perhaps fifty or more in number, still sang out of an old-fashioned hymnal, and we younger ones learned choruses like:

> SUNLIGHT, sunlight in my soul today,
> Sunlight, sunlight all along the way;
> Since the Savior found me, took away my sin,
> I have had the sunlight of his love within.

By early spring the pastor began to talk to those of us who had not been baptized about the meaning of baptism and about plans for an early summer baptism in Cow Creek.

When the day arrived, we—adults and young adults—who wanted to be baptized wore our Sunday best to church, and brought old clothes for the baptism. That Sunday the pastor spoke to the whole congregation about John the Baptist, clothed with camel's hair, and with a girdle of skin about his loins, living on locusts and wild honey, who baptized in the wilderness and preached repentance and the coming kingdom of God.

He read to us about Christ's own baptism. Of His immersion by John in the Jordan River, and how straightaway as He came up out of the water, Jesus saw the heavens open and the Spirit of God, like a dove, descended upon Him. And of how a voice from heaven said, "Thou are my beloved Son in whom I am well pleased."

After the service, we changed into our baptismal clothes. Women left early so they too could change their clothing and could pick up food they had prepared for the picnic. Men hoisted huge fold-down tables and chairs into their trucks and transported them out to shaded spots along the creek bank where the baptisms were to be performed. Those of us who were to be baptized remained at the church.

About one-thirty in the afternoon, the pastor called us all together and spoke softly to each one, reminding each that complete immersion in water was symbolic of the washing away of sins and the acceptance of the Christian faith. Then, riding with different church members, we all went out to nearby Cow Creek, a clear, spring-fed stream, where the other members of the congregation were waiting for us. They had gathered along the creek bank to witness the baptisms. When we arrived and got out of the cars, the choir began to sing:

WHEN peace, like a river, attendeth my way,
When sorrows like sea billows roll;
Whatever my lot, Thou has taught me to say,
It is well, it is well with my soul.

After singing several hymns, the gathering listened to a few more words from the pastor. He then waded with each one of us individually out into the creek until we stood waist-deep in the water. After a few private words, spoken so softly that none but the one being baptized could hear them, he cautioned the candidate to close mouth and eyes and cover each nose, supported the person's head, and quickly dipped each one backward under the water.

Each one of us was immersed, one at a time, until the last baptism was finished and we all stood on a sandbar near the water's edge, drying ourselves. Older members of the congregation came forward with towels and, in spite of the dripping water, gave us hugs and good wishes.

When we had changed into dry clothing and combed our hair, the menfolk began to tease the women about whether or not we were going to have a picnic. The women told them to hush but began to move about more quickly, uncovering dishes on the laden tables and checking buckets of home-churned ice cream to see if it was ripened (firmed up).

Chairs were brought for the older folks, who looked tired from the day's activities. Young people found a place at a table or spread a blanket in the shade of a tree. After grace was said, everyone, hungry because of the late dinner hour, filled a plate and began to eat and visit.

All through the meal and into the late afternoon, old folks recalled other baptisms they had attended. Some, like Great-Grandma Holt, recalled her mother's baptism in the Platte River on their way west. Young people told simple tales of conversion, and everyone agreed that the baptism had been a success.

♥

Ruby and Butter-Crunch Lettuce Salad with Herbed Vinaigrette

MAKES 4 TO 6 SERVINGS

THIS DELICIOUS OLD-FASHIONED SALAD is easy to make. The leaf lettuces, which have been popular for generations, are packed with flavor, vitamins, and minerals.

1 head ruby-leaf lettuce, washed and torn into small pieces
1 head butter-crunch (Bibb) lettuce, washed and torn into small pieces
1 head black-seeded Simpson lettuce (an antique variety which is still available where garden seeds are sold), washed and torn into small pieces

1 large cucumber, peeled, halved lengthwise, seeded, and sliced
2 large tomatoes, washed, cored, and diced
1/4 cup green pepper, chopped
2 green onions, sliced diagonally
Herbed Vinaigrette (recipe follows)

Make Dill Vinegar at least two weeks before using to flavor the Herbed Vinaigrette.

In a large salad bowl, combine lettuces, cucumber, tomatoes, green pepper, and green onions. Toss to blend, then pour just enough Herbed Vinaigrette over salad to coat leaves, and toss again. Serve on a salad plate or in a bowl.

♥

Herbed Vinaigrette

MAKES ABOUT 3/4 CUP

1/2 cup salad oil
1/4 cup Dill Vinegar (recipe follows)
1 tablespoon thinly sliced sweet onion (Vidalia preferred)

2 teaspoons sugar
1/2 teaspoon paprika
1/2 teaspoon dry mustard
1/4 teaspoon salt

Measure salad oil, Dill Vinegar, 2 tablespoons water, onion, sugar, paprika, dry mustard, and salt into a pint jar with a tight-fitting lid. Cover and shake vigorously to blend. When thoroughly blended, pour into a decorative 1-cup bottle or jar that can be tightly sealed. Chill.

♥

Dill Vinegar

MAKES I PINT

1 cup fresh dill, dried (about
   3 heads)

2 cups white vinegar
2 small cloves garlic

Wash dill and dry well; snip into small pieces. In a screw-top jar, combine dill with vinegar and garlic. Cover. Let stand 24 hours in a cool, dark place, then remove garlic. Screw cover on tightly, set herb vinegar back in a cool, dark place and let it sit for 2 weeks. Strain and bottle.

♥

Ham with Baked Beans

MAKES 8 SERVINGS

UNCLE FRANK MADE THE best hams in our immediate family. He soaked them in a sugar-salt brine for a month or more, depending on their weight. For special occasions he would bring a whole ham in from the smokehouse, cut it into a butt piece and a shank piece, and take a thick slice, 1 inch or more, right out of the center for Aunt Sylvia's cooking.

A 2-pound slice of ham 1 inch or
   more thick
2 cups navy beans soaked overnight
   in enough water to cover by
   2 inches

1/2 cup light brown sugar
Salt to taste (use sparingly)
1/8 teaspoon freshly ground black
   pepper

Set out and lightly grease a large baking dish.

Place ham in a large saucepan or Dutch oven; cover with cold water and simmer for 30 minutes. Remove ham from broth to a large platter; reserve the broth. Drain soaked beans, discarding the liquid. Turn them into the broth and cook for 30 minutes over medium heat. Meanwhile, cut ham into bite-size pieces. Arrange about a quarter of the ham in the bottom of the prepared dish, reserving *remaining* ham for layering with beans.

When the beans have been cooking for about 15 minutes, preheat oven to 325°F.

When beans are done, sprinkle the ham that is in the baking dish with *a quarter* of the brown sugar and cover with *a third* of the beans. Repeat until all of the ham, sugar, and beans have been used, topping the dish with a layer of ham.

Bake in a 325°F oven for 3 hours. Serve piping hot.

♥

Aunt Mae's Bath Buns

MAKES 12 BUNS

ADA'S AUNT MAE WORRIED a bit about losing her family recipes, so she had them copied and shared them with all the young women in her immediate family and ours. Most of the girls refer to them now as Aunt Mae's Heritage Buns.

2 cups all-purpose flour, sifted
3 tablespoons baking powder
½ teaspoon salt
3 tablespoons butter
Rind of ½ lemon, grated
1 tablespoon sugar plus
    2 tablespoons for topping
1 egg, well beaten (reserve
    1 tablespoon for brushing
    tops of buns)

½ cup dark raisins
1 cup milk
12 small pieces of candied citron
2 or more tablespoons heavy cream
    (light cream can be
    substituted)

Preheat oven to 450°F. Thoroughly grease a medium baking sheet. Set aside.

Into a large bowl sift flour a second time with baking powder and salt. Using a pastry cutter, two dinner knives, or your fingertips, work butter into flour mixture until it resembles grains of rice. Add lemon rind, 1 tablespoon sugar, egg (reserving 1 tablespoon), raisins, and milk to make a soft dough that can be molded.

Turn out onto a lightly floured flat surface and knead a few times. Shape into a ball and pat out into a sheet 1 inch thick. Using a cookie or biscuit cutter, cut into 12 rounds, or mold into 12 buns of equal size. Stick a bit of citron in the top of each, then brush the tops with the *reserved* egg. Place on prepared baking sheet.

Bake in a hot oven until well risen, golden brown, and firm to the touch, about 12 to 15 minutes. Remove from the oven and brush tops with a wash made of *2 tablespoons sugar* and *2 tablespoons cream,* blended together. Serve piping hot.

♥

Yorkshire Country Captain

MAKES 6 SERVINGS

THIS RECIPE WAS POPULAR in the thirties and, for a while, women made it for every potluck that came along.

1 teaspoon salt
⅛ teaspoon freshly ground black pepper
¼ teaspoon curry powder
Flour, about ⅔ cup for dredging chicken plus 2 tablespoons for thickening gravy
One 3-pound chicken, washed, fat and giblets removed, and cut into serving-size pieces
¼ cup mild onions, minced
¾ cup salt pork, finely minced
2 cups Homemade Chicken Broth (see note)

1 tablespoon butter or margarine (melted) for toasting slivered almonds, plus 2 tablespoons for frying onion slices, and 2 tablespoons for gravy
Shredded almonds
2 cups fresh peas (frozen or canned peas can be substituted)
3 medium onions, peeled and thinly sliced
¾ cup rice

Shake the seasonings and ⅔ cup flour together in a brown paper bag. Put chicken pieces (all or a few pieces at a time) in the bag and shake to coat. In a medium skillet fry minced onions and salt pork together until golden brown. Add chicken and brown slowly over low to medium heat. Add broth, cover, and simmer until chicken is tender, 25 to 30 minutes.

While the chicken is cooking, melt the *1 tablespoon* butter or margarine and toast the shredded almonds to a golden brown (take care not to burn). Put fresh or frozen peas in a medium saucepan and add *about ½ cup water* and *a pinch* of salt if you wish; simmer until tender-done, about 8 minutes (warm canned peas just before serving). Then fry onion slices in the *2 tablespoons* of butter until clear throughout and lightly colored. Steam the rice. Set all prepared ingredients aside and keep warm.

When chicken is done, remove from broth and keep warm while making gravy: In a small bowl, combine the *2 tablespoons* butter with *2 tablespoons* flour, working the two together until texture is like fine meal. Bring the chicken broth to a boil. Stirring constantly, sprinkle the flour mixture into the broth; continue stirring until gravy is clear and has thickened.

While ingredients are still hot, arrange the chicken on a large, deep platter. Cover with hot gravy and garnish with cooked onion rings. Sprinkle with the toasted almonds. Spoon hot peas and rice around the chicken. Serve immediately.

NOTE: To make stock, put the necks, giblets (excluding the liver), and backs into cold, lightly salted water, with a small peeled onion and a bay leaf; simmer until the meat falls off the bone, about 45 minutes. Set off heat to cool.

ಶಿ

From A Vision of Summer

'TWAS a marvelous vision of Summer.
  That morning the dawn was late,
And came, like a long dream-ridden guest,
  Through the gold of the Eastern gate.

Languid it came, and halting
  As one that yawned, half roused,
With lifted arms and indolent lids
  And eyes that drowsed and drowsed.

A glimmering haze hung over
  The face of the smiling air;
And the green of the trees and the blue of the leas
And the skies gleamed everywhere.

And the dewdrops' dazzling jewels,
  In garlands and diadems,
Lightened and twinkled and glanced and shot
  As the glints of a thousand gems.

—James Whitcomb Riley

♥

Ada's Poppyseed Pound Cake with Tangy Lemon-Orange Glaze

MAKES ONE 10-INCH TUBE CAKE (12 OR MORE SERVINGS)

FOR AS LONG AS I can remember this has been a special-occasion cake, served at graduation parties, open houses, and baptisms. All the menfolk, and most of the womenfolk, agreed that Ada made the best poppyseed pound cake, and most of them thought she put in a secret ingredient.

1 1/4 tablespoons poppyseeds	1 teaspoon vanilla extract
1/4 cup milk	1 teaspoon lemon extract
6 eggs, separated	1/4 teaspoon baking soda
1 cup butter or margarine, softened at room temperature	3 cups all-purpose flour
	1 teaspoon baking powder
2 1/2 cups sugar	Tangy Lemon-Orange Glaze
1 cup buttermilk	(recipe follows)

Preheat oven to 350°F. Thoroughly grease and flour a 10-inch tube pan. Set aside.

In a small bowl, soak poppyseeds in the 1/4 cup milk. While they are soaking, assemble other ingredients: In a large straight-sided bowl, beat egg whites until stiff peaks form; set aside. In a second large bowl cream yolks, butter or margarine, and sugar together until fluffy. To the bowl of soaked poppyseeds add buttermilk, vanilla and lemon extracts, and baking soda. Sift the flour a second time with baking powder into a medium bowl. Add flour mixture, a little at a time, alternately with the buttermilk mixture to the creamed butter and sugar. Fold in the stiffly beaten egg whites and pour into prepared tube pan.

Bake until well risen, light golden in color, and firm to the touch, about 1 hour and 15 minutes. Cool 5 minutes in the pan, then loosen cake from sides of pan and from the center cone with a knife and turn out onto a serving plate (the cake should be bottom side up). Cool while preparing Tangy Lemon-Orange Glaze. While the cake is still warm, spread glaze over the top and let it stream down over the sides.

♥

Tangy Lemon-Orange Glaze

MAKES ENOUGH FOR ONE 10-INCH TUBE CAKE

1½ cups powdered sugar   ½ cup orange juice, strained
1 teaspoon lemon extract

Combine all ingredients in a small bowl. Beat until glossy.

ART

SLY elves steal in and paint the flowers
With gorgeous hues in still night hours,
Their brushes wondrous fine;
The dew a crystal drop imparts
To linger prisoned in the hearts
Like magic wine.

The tints of mystic mountain haze,
The pastel tones of twilight rays
All reappear—
The Autumn's bronze and yellow-gold
Within some flower's heart unfold,
When Spring is here.

We pause and quaff the incense rare
That blossoms toss upon the air,
Drink deep the gift,
Ere earth again receives her own,
As petals fall and lose their tone,
And in the soft winds drift.

But oh, the wonder of such art!
The mystery within the heart
Of each sweet flower!
The elfin artist paints with care—
We see their skilled touch everywhere
In blossoming woodland bower.

—Grace E. Hall

'BOUT THE TIME STRAWBERRIES MELT ON THE VINE

~~~~~~~~~

Aunt El, Mother's favorite aunty, called June the light and airy month, and would sing praises of warm days, gentle rains, abundant growth, gloriously colored flowers, and ripe strawberries melting on the vine. When pressed, she might admit that rolling thunderstorms frightened her, and that she did not take pleasure in the jagged streaks of lightning that lit up the summer sky. Even so, she never abandoned her favorite month. "June," she would tell anyone who would listen, "is that special time of year when the door of summer is wide open and all creatures, large and small, are invited to revel in the sun."

Pickin' Weather

As STRAWBERRY SEASON PEAKS and then begins to fade, those berries left ripening on the vines become soft and sweet. In our area gleaners go out and finish the harvest, gathering enough berries to make jam, end-of-the-season desserts, and gifts for people down on their luck, neighbors, and older folks.

Effie's Strawberry Mousse

MAKES 4 TO 6 SERVINGS

EFFIE KEPT A LARGE strawberry patch, planted, tended, and picked by her own hand. Through the years she sold berries to local stores, to folks traveling through, and to a roadside produce stand which sat on the corner of a nearby farm. True to her nature, she also gave basketsful away.

> *1 teaspoon unsweetened gelatin*
> *2 cups (1 pint) heavy cream, chilled*
> *About 3 to 5 tablespoons powdered sugar, more as desired*
>
> *½ teaspoon vanilla extract*
> *1 cup strawberry pulp, mashed and drained*

In a small bowl, dissolve gelatin in *1 tablespoon hot water;* set aside to cool. When gelatin has the consistency of an egg white, whip the cream in a large straight-sided bowl until it forms soft peaks. In another bowl, add sugar and vanilla extract to the strawberry pulp. Fold the whipped cream and strawberry pulp together. Pack with a spoon into refrigerator trays, cover with foil or waxed paper, and freeze until semi-firm, 1 or more hours. Spoon out of trays into dessert dishes and serve immediately.

♥

Young Martha's Strawberry Topping for Ice Cream

MAKES ABOUT 1½ CUPS

AUNT CLARY'S DAUGHTER MARTHA makes this topping for those who crave a little something extra on their ice cream.

¼ cup strawberry jam	1 cup fresh strawberries, lightly
¼ cup light corn syrup	rinsed, drained, and crushed

Dip a measuring cup in cold water, then measure strawberry jam and turn into a small saucepan; dip the cup again, measure the corn syrup, and add it to the jam. Bring to a boil over medium heat. Remove from heat and cool. Just before serving, add fresh berries and let the topping sit 10 to 15 minutes to blend. Spoon over servings of ice cream (or over a plain cake).

♥

Aunt El's Strawberry Pie

MAKES ONE 9-INCH PIE (6 SERVINGS)

WHEN WE WERE YOUNG and just learning how to make double-crusted fruit pies, Aunt El used to tell us that of all the berry pies—blackberry, gooseberry, huckleberry, and any other she could think of—strawberry pie is the juiciest and is most apt to spill over while baking. As a precaution she would put an old cookie sheet on the rack just below the strawberry pie to catch drips, give the crust around the edge of the pie a special turn to seal it (see instructions below), and cut generous vents in the top crust.

Double-Crust Plain Pastry (recipe follows)	into a sieve, lightly rinsed under a gentle stream of cold tap water,
⅔ cup sugar	and drained
4 tablespoons cornstarch	1 tablespoon butter or margarine,
⅛ teaspoon salt	softened at room temperature
3 cups fresh strawberries, turned	

Prepare pastry before assembling pie. Chill until needed.

Preheat oven to 450°F. Set out a 9-inch pie pan.

In a small bowl, combine sugar, cornstarch, and salt; add to berries and fold together. Remove pastry from refrigerator; divide into two portions. On a lightly floured flat surface roll out half the pastry ⅛ inch thick. Line pie pan. Trim, leaving ½-inch overhang. Turn berry mixture into the lined pie pan. Dot with butter. Moisten the edge of the bottom crust. Roll out remaining pastry ⅛ inch thick. Dust with flour, fold in quarters, and arrange over berries. With kitchen shears, trim top crust so that it lies evenly around the edge of the pan, then moisten the edge. Turn the bottom crust overhang back over the moistened edge of the top crust so that it too is even with the edge of the pan. Press together with the tines of a fork.

Bake at 450°F for 10 minutes. Reduce temperature to 350°F and bake until crust is crisp and golden brown and the berries are bubbly, about 30 minutes longer.

Set on a wire rack to cool. Serve as is or with a scoop of vanilla ice cream.

♥

Double-Crust Plain Pastry

MAKES ENOUGH FOR ONE DOUBLE-CRUST 9-INCH PIE

2 cups all-purpose flour, sifted
¾ teaspoon salt

⅔ cup butter or margarine, chilled

Into a large bowl sift flour and salt together. Using a pastry cutter or two table knives, cut the butter into the flour until the texture is granular, with pieces about the size of small peas. Slowly add 4 to 6 tablespoons cold water, a small amount at a time, until the mixture holds together and can be shaped into a ball. (Add a little more cold water if it seems too dry.) Cover and chill.

Beneath the Hollyhocks

On a dewy summer morn, Old Missus Upjohn saw
from her window sprites slipping into her flower
garden to nestle beneath the great spreading
leaves of her hollyhocks.
All throughout the cool morning, the tall
spires stood guard.
At the lightest breeze, their deep-pink,
double-flowered blossoms nodded
approval.
By mid-day, the sun cast its toasting golden
rays deep into the leafy bower, until like babes,
rubbing the sleep from their deep brown eyes,
the sprites crawled out of their nest.
On spying her, they scampered through the petunias,
past the cosmos,
and the deep blue Canterbury bells.
They leapt and bounded, into the nearby woods,
deep into a moist, shaded bed of wild ferns.
Never to be seen again!

—Jane Watson Hopping

Old Missus Upjohn's Herb Teas, Honey, and Buzzin' Bees

THE Pedigree of Honey
Does not concern the Bee—
A Clover, any time, to him,
Is Aristocracy—

—Emily Dickinson

❧

OLD MISSUS UPJOHN, WHO was older than Grandpa, was not blood kin, but was certainly our aunt in spirit. She came from southern Missouri (Missoura, she called it). Many of her ways were old-fashioned, and even in Mother's childhood she seemed to come from a different age. She planted by the moon and forecast weather by observing signs: When clouds moved rapidly or rabbits were seen in unprotected places, good weather was on its way; when pigs ran about with sticks in their mouths and acted up, a storm was coming in.

Though a lovely, gentle woman, she could get "riled up" about doctors. Born shortly after the Civil War and deeply affected by the human tragedy of that great conflagration, she thought medical men of the day were butchers who could not be trusted. Her old face would become flushed as she told about natural healers, midwives, and herb doctors who healed their patients with potions, poultices, teas, and medicated baths. Such healers, she would say, perhaps could not help some of those who came to them, but neither did they harm anyone.

For years, she treated herself with bloodroot, golden seal, May apple, and other plants. All along the back of her house was an extensive herb garden which she tended carefully, and her yard was filled with blossoms all summer long, since it not only provided flavoring for her cooking, but teas and infusions to ease an aching stomach, nerves, indigestion, or sleeplessness.

When Mother visited as a girl, Missus Upjohn always made a cup of tea for her guests. She warmed the teapot—always a china pot, never a metal one—by filling it with boiling water. She heated fresh water to a boil, emptied the teapot, and measured into it one teaspoon of dried herb for each cup of tea and an extra one for the pot, or one tablespoon if she was using herbs picked fresh from her garden. She then poured the boiling water into the pot, one cup for each person, and covered the pot with a lid and a cozy while the tea steeped for about three minutes. Then the guests sat at her heavy oak table, sipping the pungent tea and nibbling on old-fashioned tea biscuits.

♥

Balm Melissa, Bee Balm, or Lemon Balm

DELICATE LEMON-FLAVORED BALM MAKES a nice light drink, hot or cold, for spring and summer.

Add 2 tablespoons lightly rinsed fresh balm leaves to mint tea or oriental tea. Or try this mixture: 1 part mint tea, 2 parts balm, 1 part lemon verbena, and 1 part lavender flowers. Use either fresh or dried ingredients. Use honey for sweetener.

♥

Basil Tea

THIS HERB-GARDEN TEA HAS a delightful flavor and aroma, especially when made with fresh basil, which should be picked early in the morning. Missus Upjohn thought a mixture of basil and oriental tea was the best, a good drink for a midafternoon pick-me-up.

♥

Geranium (Pelargonium) Tea

THERE ARE MANY VARIETIES of geraniums with flavored leaves: rose, apple, nutmeg, lemon, and others. Mother's favorite was tea made with fresh leaves in summer. She also dried a generous amount for winter teas. Such leaves can be used alone or with other flowers or herbs. She thought the dried, finely ground leaves were a nice addition to any of her other comfort teas.

♥

Goldenrod or Blue Mountain Tea

THIS HERB TEA OF the Allegheny slopes and the golden anise-flavored tea of the Pennsylvania Dutch are both made out of the leaves of goldenrod, which are gathered in summer before they become strong and coarse. Tea made of the dried crushed leaves, when steeped, is richly colored and delicious when sweetened with brown sugar. Our great-grandmother thought it rivaled oriental teas. She used it alone and mixed it with other sweet herbs.

♥

Old Missus Upjohn's Sour Cream Cookies

MAKES ABOUT 3½ DOZEN COOKIES

COOKIES OR TEA CAKES, as many older women like Missus Upjohn called them, were nearly always served to drop-in or expected guests with meticulously brewed tea in our home and in the homes of our English and Irish neighbors.

2 cups all-purpose flour, sifted
1 teaspoon baking powder
½ teaspoon salt
¼ teaspoon baking soda
1 teaspoon ground cinnamon
½ teaspoon ground nutmeg
½ cup butter or margarine,
  softened at room temperature

1 cup sugar
1 egg, well beaten
1 teaspoon lemon extract
½ cup sour cream (or ½ cup sweet
  cream with 1 tablespoon
  vinegar or lemon juice added)

Preheat oven to 375°F. Set out and thoroughly grease a large baking sheet.

In a medium bowl, sift flour a second time with baking powder, salt, baking soda, cinnamon, and nutmeg. In a large bowl cream butter or margarine until waxy, then gradually add sugar and continue creaming until light. Add egg and lemon extract to the butter mixture; blend. Stir in the flour, a small amount at a time, alternately with the sour cream until well blended. Drop batter by teaspoonfuls about 2 to 3 inches apart onto the prepared baking sheet.

Bake until cookies are well risen, lightly browned, and firm to the touch, about 15 to 20 minutes. Using a spatula, immediately transfer cookies to brown paper or a wire rack to cool. When all cookies are cooled, serve or store in an airtight container.

JUNE'S
THE MONTH
WHEN THE
BOBOLINK SINGS

~~~~~~~~~

IN EARLY JUNE WILD birds flit about the countryside singing their territorial lays. In some parts of the country bluebirds can be heard in the thickets long after their nesting in hollow trees is over, singing their gentle, mellow songs. To the east, gloriously golden and black Baltimore orioles sing clear whistled melodies. Mother recalls seeing in her childhood a modest wood thrush, feeding on caterpillars among the leaves of a tree, and that she hid in the bushes so as not to interrupt its singing. Even today she vows that the wood thrush must be one of the most gifted songbirds of them all.

At our house, a brilliant blue jay has staked out the front porch and claims it as his very own territory. When I sit there to rest, he swoops down nearby, or settles in a neighboring tree to raucously call out for me to leave, and is only mollified by crusts of bread.

If our cats dash out to steal the bread, the blue jay dive-bombs them, sometimes tweaking the hair on their heads, at which they flee to safety under the corner of the porch.

In the pastures, the meadow lark, lilting, sings, "Please give me a bushel of wheat, please give me a bushel of wheat, please give me a bushel of wheat."

JUNE

JUNE'S the month when the Bobolink
Sings all through the daytime,
Down here by the river side
Where we spend out playtime.

Where's his house?—I mean, his nest—
Oh, here it is, I've found it!
In a garden of green grass,—
Daisy trees around it.

—May Aiken

A Father's Day Outing

OUR FAMILY GATHERINGS WERE usually held at one home or another, but great outings were held at the river or in the park. One year, the Father's Day Outing became enormous even by our standards. Neighbors and friends who had been invited to the potluck dinner began to remind us that this family and that had not yet been invited. Ada called to tell us that the Baker families had not been asked to come, and Effie dropped by to mention that the whole Hoskins family had been neglected. Mother put out the word to check on those left out, to invite them and ask that they bring a covered dish, a salad, or dessert and be at the park about midmorning on Father's Day. There were also some secret instructions given, something to do with surprises.

Uncle Ben thought the men ought to go down early to set up tables and benches and to reserve a large shaded area near the spot where games of horseshoes were played. The rest of us arrived about ten-thirty. Mothers got out balls and bats and spread blankets in the shade for small children to play or rest on. As more and more people kept coming, the conversation doubled, then trebled, and women's pretty laughter and children's shouts punctuated the gossiping and sharing of information.

The children were abuzz with excitement; they had all brought Father's Day cards and presents with them (which were supposed to be kept secret). And they were all set to read a Father's Day verse, or as a group to lead the singing before we ate.

At noon the festive dinner began with some of the children reading their verses and with all the children leading the rest of us in singing:

THE more we get together,
Together, together,
The more we get together,
The happier we are.

Then all the children brought Father's Day gifts out of hiding and watched with glittering eyes as their fathers opened the gifts, looked surprised, and called out for a hug or a pat as the occasion demanded.

Then we ate! The men talked baseball and farm prices, hard times and good times. You could hardly hear above the laughter, and bits of conversation about plans for a quilting bee, about young women preparing to get married or give birth, about children who had been sick and babies who were growing like weeds. You could hear mothers everywhere telling the children to sit still and eat their dinner, and you could see the children wriggling on the benches or kicking at friends under the table. Eventually, the women sent them off to play, with some serious talk about not wandering off too far.

In the afternoon, the women walked with all the children following after like a gaggle of geese down to the duck pond, where the children threw bread to the graceful mallards, white Pekin, and Indian Runner ducks, along with a few Toulouse, Embden, and African geese.

Everyone—men, women, girls, and boys—played baseball and other team games. Small children flitted like butterflies from one game to another: Run Sheep Run, Kick the Can, tag, jump rope, London Bridge, and others.

By four o'clock, the crowd began to thin, amid much laughing and chattering. Babies and toddlers were carried off sound asleep in their mothers' or fathers' arms. Older children, hair tangled, faces flushed from boisterous play, tagged along after their families, looking back, calling out, hating to end what had been such a joyful occasion.

Mothers and fathers, softly, comfortingly, told them that there would be another time, another day. . . .

♥

Fried Spring Chicken

MAKES ABOUT 8 PIECES

WHEN I WAS A child, Aunt Mabel, who raised frying chickens, always brought a large platter of chicken to family picnics. She was the first in the family to switch from pure lard to shortening, then to oil for frying chicken. She was also the first to buy butcher paper (in those days neither side was coated) for absorbing the excess fat off of her fried chicken.

1½ teaspoons salt
¼ teaspoon freshly ground black pepper
½ cup all-purpose flour, more as needed
A 3- to 4-pound young frying chicken, cut into serving-size pieces

About ¼ cup vegetable oil, more or less as needed

Set out a frying pan large enough to fry all the chicken pieces at once, or set out two smaller pans.

In a large paper bag combine salt, pepper, and flour, and shake pieces of chicken, a few at a time, in the bag until each piece is well coated.

In the heavy skillet (or skillets) heat about 3 tablespoons of oil until it begins to smoke, then turn down the heat. Arrange pieces of chicken in the skillet, keeping in mind that the thinner pieces will cook more quickly than the thick ones. Fry over moderate heat until meat is golden brown on the bottom and blood has come to the surface on top; turn pieces. Cook until well browned and firm to the touch, 35 minutes or more. Remove the cooked pieces of chicken one at a time, small pieces first as they become well done, then meatier pieces. Drain on absorbent paper. Serve hot or cold.

♥

Mother's Potato Salad

MAKES ABOUT 25 HALF-CUP SERVINGS

FOR PICNICS AND FAMILY gatherings, Mother made this large salad, which served from fifteen to twenty-five people, depending on how many came.

About 4 pounds raw, scrubbed, unpeeled potatoes to make about 2¾ quarts cooked, diced potatoes

1⅓ teaspoons salt

¼ teaspoon freshly ground black pepper

2½ cups celery, finely chopped

1 cup dill pickles, chopped (sweet pickles can be used if preferred)

2 cups hard-boiled eggs, chopped (about 6 or 8 eggs)

1 medium sweet onion, chopped (Bermuda or another sandwich onion; green onions, both white and green parts, can be substituted)

1½ cups mayonnaise

½ cup pickle juice for moistening salad

¼ cup prepared mustard (a coarse-ground mustard preferred)

1½ cups pitted olives, whole or sliced

In a large saucepan, cook the potatoes: Cover with warm water, put a lid on the pan and boil until fork-tender, about 30 minutes, depending on the variety of potato. Baking potatoes sometimes turn mushy; waxy red or white potatoes hold their shape much better.

When potatoes are done, immediately remove them from the heat; pour off hot water and cover with cold tap water. Chill them a bit, but don't soak them.

When unpeeled potatoes are barely cool enough to handle, remove the skins (if they seem to stick, rinse quickly in cold water, then resume peeling); dice and measure into a very large bowl. Add salt, pepper, celery, pickles, eggs, and onion. Blend in mayonnaise, pickle juice, and mustard (salad should be a bit moist, as it firms up when chilled).

Fold in the whole or sliced olives, or use as a garnish. Chill.

NOTE: When taking potato salad to a picnic supper, keep chilled until served, and as soon as the meal is over return salad to the ice chest, or throw away leftovers.

♥

Lemon Batter Rolls

MAKES 36 ROLLS

THESE FEATHER-LIGHT ROLLS HAVE always been a favorite picnic roll in our family. For get-togethers both Effie and Ada bake a batch, which makes a large basketful. Even so, there are few left over.

1 tablespoon granulated yeast
2½ cups lukewarm milk (only raw
  milk need be scalded)
½ cup butter or margarine,
  softened
¼ cup sugar

2 teaspoons salt
1 egg, lightly beaten
Grated rind of 1 lemon
2 tablespoons lemon juice
5 cups all-purpose flour, sifted

In a small bowl combine yeast and warm milk. Set aside until yeast is foamy.

In a large bowl cream butter, sugar, and salt until light. Add egg, lemon rind, and juice; thoroughly blend into the butter-sugar mixture. Stir in the combined yeast and milk. Add flour and beat with a spoon until smooth. Cover with a clean kitchen towel and let rise until doubled in bulk, about 1 hour.

Preheat oven to 425°F. Set out and thoroughly grease three muffin tins. When batter is well risen, carefully turn it over so as not to lose the volume. Place a spoonful of dough in each muffin cup (the cup should be about two-thirds full). Set to rise again for about 20 to 25 minutes.

When rolls are very light, gently set in oven and bake until well puffed, golden tan on top, and browned on the bottom, about 20 to 25 minutes.

NOTE: If all three tins do not fit in the oven, set one pan aside before it is fully risen in a place just cool enough not to chill the dough, but to slow the action of the yeast. By the time the first two pans have baked, the third pan should be well risen.

As each batch is done, remove from the oven and turn rolls out onto a wire rack or brown paper. Serve piping hot with butter, or at room temperature, plain or buttered.

♥

Sweet-Cherry Crunch

MAKES 6 TO 8 SERVINGS

AT THIS TIME OF year our young cherry trees are producing enough great, black sweet cherries for eating out of hand, and for making a dessert like this one.

½ cup sugar
3 tablespoons all-purpose flour

4 cups black sweet cherries, pitted

OATMEAL TOPPING
½ cup sugar
½ cup quick-cooking rolled oats
½ cup butter or margarine, chilled
 but not too firm

⅓ cup all-purpose flour

Preheat oven to 350°F. Set out a casserole dish that measures 9 by 9 by 2½ to 3 inches.

In a small bowl, combine the sugar and flour; blend well. Turn pitted cherries into a large bowl and add sugar-flour mixture, tossing until cherries are coated. Turn the prepared cherries into the casserole dish.

In a medium bowl, stir the topping ingredients together until the mixture is crumbly. Sprinkle topping over the cherry mixture.

Bake until cherries are tender, juices are thick and bubbling, and topping is lightly browned and crusty, about 45 minutes. Cool at room temperature; eat while still quite warm or when thoroughly cooled.

♥

Easy-to-Make Picnic Punch

MAKES ABOUT 4 QUARTS

EFFIE ALWAYS BROUGHT THIS summertime punch to our picnics in a glass gallon jar, chilled with ice, wrapped in a heavy bath towel. Needless to say, on a hot afternoon it disappeared in a twinkling.

2 cups tea
4 cups unsweetened pineapple juice
4 cups unsweetened orange juice
1 cup lemon juice

4 cups grapefruit juice
1 bottle (15 ounces) maraschino cherries, sliced thin (reserve juice)

In a large container combine tea with pineapple, orange, lemon, and grapefruit juices. Add sliced cherries and reserved juice.

NOTE: Effie did not add sugar to this punch, but it can be added as desired. Some of the women in the family also thinned the punch with ice water.

Chill thoroughly and pour into a large thermos jug just before leaving for the picnic grounds.

à

SUMMER IS HERE, HOORAY!

SUMMER is here, hooray!
What shall we do today?
Fishing, swimming in the brook?
Oh, what fun it will be!
Now, let's go for a rest
Under my favorite tree.

—Brian Mulhollen (age 8)
Jacksonville, Oregon

A Picnic in the Rain

WHEN THE CHILDREN WERE smaller, we loved to go up to Fish Lake to picnic under a massive shelter which had been built in 1936 of huge barked logs, some of them two feet in diameter. The sturdy open-air shelter still stands along the lakeside. Inside are a wide and deep old fireplace, two metal wood-burning cookstoves, a brace of stout picnic tables, and a lively population of bushy-tailed chipmunks.

From the open side of the building, we loved to look out over the lake. In early June, the water has a rich, pine-green hue along the shore, nearly matching the color of the giant conifers that stand sentinel. Out on the water, far from shore, light breezes blow, sending miniature waves scurrying across the lake's frosted silver-green surface.

One year we were picnicking there when a storm came in. Rain sheeted down over distant mountains which were still lightly streaked with snow; at first the rain misted over the lake and sprinkled the dust around the shelter. Then the darker storm-clouds began to move our way, which occasioned some grumbling among the fishermen and some of the children. Women dashed about looking for sweaters and coats. Most of us, however, loved the rain and blowing wind, the sound of which no longer sighed in the huge trees, but roared through the swaying branches, sounding for all the world like a distant waterfall.

To amuse the children, Uncle Ben began to tell jokes, ask riddles, tell a few wild stories, and even recite a bit of poetry he had learned from his older sister Mabel.

From Wynken, Blynken, and Nod

WYNKEN, Blynken, and Nod one night
 Sailed off in a wooden shoe,—
Sailed on a river of crystal light
 Into a sea of dew.
"Where are you going, and what do you wish?"
 The old moon asked the three,
"We have come to fish for the herring fish
 That live in this beautiful sea;
 Nets of silver and gold have we!"
  Said Wynken, Blynken, and Nod.

All night long their nets they threw
 To the stars in the twinkling foam,—
Then down from the skies came the wooden shoe,
 Bringing the fishermen home:
'Twas all so pretty a sail, it seemed
 As if it could not be;
And some folk thought 'twas a dream they'd dreamed
 Of sailing that beautiful sea;
 But I shall name you the fishermen three:
  Wynken, Blynken, and Nod.

Wynken and Blynken are two little eyes,
 And Nod is a little head,
And the wooden shoe that sailed the skies
 Is a wee one's trundle-bed;
So shut your eyes while Mother sings
 Of wonderful sights that be,
And you shall see the beautiful things
 As you rock in the misty sea
Where the old shoe rocked the fishermen three:—
  Wynken, Blynken, and Nod.

—Eugene Field

♥

Pan-Fried Mountain Trout

MAKES 4 SERVINGS

IN THE EARLY DAYS people had to hike in to catch a few trout out of Fish Lake, but as the years passed, better and better roads were built through the woods. Some old-timers here can remember those years before the roads. My children are grateful that in their generation they can still enjoy the pristine quiet and beauty of the lake.

4 medium (less than a pound
   apiece) trout
1 teaspoon salt
⅛ teaspoon freshly ground black
   pepper
1 egg, lightly beaten

⅔ cup all-purpose flour
⅓ cup yellow cornmeal
¼ cup margarine or vegetable
   shortening

Set out a large, heavy frying pan.

Wash trout and drain. Season both sides of each fish with salt and pepper. In a pie pan or deep platter, thoroughly blend egg and 1 tablespoon water. In a second pie pan or platter, stir flour and cornmeal together, blending well. Dip the fish, one at a time, first into the egg wash, then into the flour-cornmeal mixture, until each is well coated.

In the skillet, heat margarine or shortening (it should be ⅛ inch deep in the pan). Lower fish carefully into the fat and brown them first on one side and then the other. Cook until the fish flakes, about 10 minutes. Immediately remove from skillet and drain on absorbent paper. Serve piping hot.

♥

English Pea Salad

MAKES ABOUT 4 SERVINGS

UNCLE BUD USED TO grow a big spring garden. He planted peas just as soon as the ground could be worked, often in March or April. By late May or early June, green onions, beets, and of course garden peas were ready for harvest. His friend Elsie loved to drop by and help pick peas. Uncle Bud would give her a big bagful to take home with her. She would shell them, can a few, and make this delicious salad.

2 cups fresh peas, boiled to tender-
    doneness, drained, and set
    aside to cool
2 tart early summer apples (Red
    June preferred), peeled, cored,
    and chopped
¼ cup pimiento (2-ounce jar),
    finely sliced
¼ cup celery, finely chopped (light-
    colored stalks preferred)

1 small sweet pickle, finely chopped
⅓ cup nutmeats (walnuts
    preferred), finely chopped
½ cup mayonnaise
2 tablespoons lemon juice, strained
½ teaspoon sugar
½ teaspoon salt

Into a large bowl put peas, apples, pimiento, celery, pickle, and nutmeats; do not stir. Add mayonnaise, lemon juice, sugar, and salt. With two forks, toss gently together until ingredients are mixed and coated with dressing. Serve on a bed of shredded lettuce.

♥

Potato Butter Horn Rolls

MAKES ABOUT 36 ROLLS

BY LATE SPRING ALL the farm women in our families were making every recipe they had for stored potatoes that were beginning to sprout. Some made scalloped potato dishes, adding bits of cheese, vegetables, leftover meats, and such. Some, spoiled a bit by the abundance of early summer grabbled potatoes and earthy, delightfully flavored, just-harvested fall potatoes, complained a bit about the flavor of rolls made with the winter-stored potatoes. The menfolk just laughed and teased them—and ate two or three rolls each, topped with golden-colored, freshly made spring butter.

At our house, Daddy and Grandpa and we womenfolk, large and small, loved the Potato Butter Horn Rolls we made for Sunday dinner.

2 tablespoons sugar	*2 eggs, well beaten*
1 tablespoon salt	*1 tablespoon granulated yeast*
4 tablespoons butter or margarine,	*1¾ cups lukewarm milk, plus*
melted	*¼ cup for softening yeast*
2 cups hot mashed potatoes	*6 cups all-purpose flour*

In a large bowl, combine sugar, salt, and butter or margarine with hot mashed potatoes. Set aside to cool; add eggs. Soften the yeast in the ¼ cup warm milk, add remaining milk to the potato mixture, and stir until thoroughly blended.

Add flour a little at a time, beating well after each addition. Turn dough out onto a lightly floured surface. Knead until dough is soft, smooth, and elastic (it should be just firm enough to handle). Gently place ball of dough in a large, well-greased bowl, turn dough greased side up, and set in a warm place to rise until doubled in bulk, about 45 minutes.

Preheat oven to 450°F. Thoroughly grease a large baking sheet. Set aside.

When dough is well risen, turn out onto a lightly floured surface. Roll into a round sheet, ½ inch thick. Cut as you would a pie into wedges 3 inches wide at the outer edge. Beginning at the outer edge, roll each section toward the center. Form into crescents. Place on prepared baking sheet and cover with a warm, damp cloth. Let rise until puffy and trebled in bulk. Handling carefully, place rolls on baking sheet.

Bake until rolls are fully puffed, golden brown, and firm to the touch, about 12 minutes. Serve piping hot. These rolls keep well when wrapped in a large dishtowel (or when put into a plastic bag). Freeze extra rolls if you wish.

♥

Sour Cream Red June Apple Pie with Butter-Cinnamon Topping

MAKES 6 SERVINGS

MOTHER HAS ALWAYS LIKED to bake pies, and she would usually take two or three to a large family gathering. Uncle Ben thought the best pies she had ever made were those in which she used the Red June apples off the Old Hubbard Place. These early apples were always ready before the rest, and since none of us had had fresh apple pie for months, they were a treat, mighty tasty!

*Single-Crust Flaky Pastry
    (recipe follows)*
*Butter-Cinnamon Topping
    (recipe follows)*
*2 cups tart, early summer apples
    (Red June preferred), finely
    chopped*

¾ cup sugar
2 tablespoons flour
1 cup sour cream
1 egg, well beaten
½ teaspoon vanilla extract
⅛ teaspoon salt

Before assembling pie, make pastry and line a 9-inch pie pan, and combine and set aside ingredients for topping.

Preheat oven to 450°F.

Set chopped apples aside. In a large bowl, combine sugar and flour. Add sour cream, egg, vanilla, and salt; beat until smooth. Add the apples and mix thoroughly. Pour apple filling into prepared pan.

Bake in 450°F oven for 15 minutes, reduce the heat to 325°F, and bake 20 minutes more. Remove from the oven, sprinkle prepared topping over the pie, and bake 20 minutes more. Set on a wire rack to cool.

♥

Single-Crust Flaky Pastry

MAKES ENOUGH FOR ONE 9-INCH SINGLE-CRUST PIE

*1 cup all-purpose flour, plus flour
    for rolling out dough*

½ teaspoon salt
½ cup cold butter

Into a large bowl sift the flour and salt together. Cut the butter in, using a pastry blender or two dinner knives, or rub butter into the flour with your fingertips until all pieces of dough are the size of small peas. Gradually sprinkle on just enough cold water (2 to 4 tablespoons) to hold the pastry together, mixing lightly and quickly with a fork after each addition. (This makes a flakier pie crust.) Turn dough onto a floured surface and form into a ball. Wrap in aluminum foil or waxed paper and chill until needed.

♥

Butter-Cinnamon Topping

MAKES ENOUGH TO TOP ONE 9-INCH PIE

⅓ cup sugar
1 teaspoon ground cinnamon
⅓ cup flour

¼ cup butter or margarine,
  softened at room temperature

In a small bowl, blend all ingredients thoroughly.

🐦

MEMORY

My mind lets go a thousand things,
Like dates of wars and deaths of kings,
And yet recalls the very hour—
'Twas noon by yonder village tower,
And on the last blue noon in May—
The wind came briskly up this way,
Crisping the brook beside the road;
Then, pausing here, set down its load
Of pine-scents, and shook listlessly
Two petals from that wild-rose tree.

—Thomas Bailey Aldrich

Aunt Clary's Ninety-eighth Birthday Party

IN 1930 ALL THE family celebrated Aunty's ninety-eighth birthday. Her dearest friends —Missus Upjohn, Mama Lowery, and Aunt Alice—were the guests of honor. Ada and Aunt Clary's daughters agreed that the party should be a simple one. So they sent invitations to family and friends alike, asking them to drop by Effie's house, where the party would be held, to share a cup of tea and a treat and to wish Aunty a happy birthday. And they asked everyone to stay only a short while so as not to overtax Aunt Clary and her guests of honor.

Aunty wore the new flowered-silk dress that Effie had made for her, and the new pair of white shoes that Martha, her daughter, had bought her for the occasion. All her grandchildren and great-grandchildren came or were brought to the party early; some had bouquets of flowers, others carried new babies. Theirs was a pilgrimage of love, as though Aunt Clary's tender words and praise for each child were a blessing that would stay with them for the rest of their lives.

Older friends and family members came later to quietly sit and talk, to reminisce a bit, and after tea to give all the old ladies a kiss and a hug and to wish them well. For days after the party, family and friends spoke of how radiant Aunt Clary had looked, how sharp-witted she was for her age, how the beauty of her youth had shown through. Everyone thought her hair was like a halo, so lovely with the diamond-chip combs that Uncle Bud had given her tucked in to hold the silver strands in place.

♥

Scottish Fancies

MAKES 26 TO 28 SMALL FANCIES

THESE LITTLE TEATIME TREATS were one of Aunt Clary's favorites. She had marked them so in *The Boston Cooking-School Cook Book,* which was written by a woman she admired greatly—Fannie Merritt Farmer.

Vegetable shortening (no substitutes) for greasing baking sheet
1 egg, beaten until stiff
½ cup sugar
⅔ tablespoon butter or margarine, melted

1 cup quick-cooking or regular rolled oats
⅓ teaspoon salt
¼ teaspoon vanilla extract

Preheat oven to 350°F. Thoroughly grease with vegetable shortening a large baking sheet, line with brown paper (unprinted brown bag will do), and generously grease paper. Set aside.

In a medium bowl, gradually add stiffly beaten egg to sugar and combine. Stir in melted butter or margarine, rolled oats, salt, and vanilla. Drop mixture by teaspoons onto prepared baking sheet, 1 inch apart. Using a spatula which has been dipped in cold water, spread dough into circles. Place baking sheet in the center of the oven.

Bake until a delicate brown, about 10 minutes. Remove from oven and cool on pan overnight to mellow. Remove cookies gently as they tend to crumble (broken cookies make a delicious topping for ice cream).

♥

Wellesley Tea

MAKES 4 GLASSES OF TEA

AUNT ALICE, WHO WAS Aunt Clary's dear friend, was an English woman of quality who always served orange pekoe tea at parties. In her still-accented voice she would carefully explain that this first-quality tea was made from very young leaves, which gave the beverage its delicate flavor, and was enhanced by the orange leaves which scented it.

4 teaspoons orange pekoe tea
12 mint leaves, crushed

Crushed ice

Scald an earthenware or china teapot.

Put in tea and pour 2 cups boiling water over it. Let stand on the range or in some other warm spot to steep for 5 minutes. Then strain into glasses which have been filled one-third full of ice and topped with 3 crushed mint leaves each. Sweeten to taste.

NOTE: For an excellent flavor, chill infusion quickly.

♥

Fannie Merritt Farmer's Gossamer Gingerbread

MAKES ABOUT 4 DOZEN PIECES

AUNTY WAS VERY FOND of her Fannie Farmer cookbook, a first edition given to her in 1896 by her husband. She loved to serve this gingerbread with tea.

⅓ cup butter or margarine,
    softened at room temperature
1 cup sugar, plus additional sugar
    for sprinkling over top of
    gingerbread
1 egg, well beaten

½ cup milk
2 cups all-purpose flour, sifted,
    with 2 tablespoons removed
    and discarded
3 teaspoons baking powder
1 teaspoon ground ginger

Preheat oven to 350°F. Thoroughly grease an 18-by-12-by-1-inch baking sheet. Set aside.

In a large bowl, cream butter or margarine and gradually add sugar, egg, and milk, stirring after each addition. Sift the flour a second time with the baking powder and ginger and stir into the butter mixture. Using a spatula, spread the dough as thinly as possible on the prepared baking sheet.

Bake until well risen and lightly browned, about 15 minutes. Sprinkle with sugar, cool to lukewarm, and cut into small squares or diamonds before removing from pan.

Heaven and Homemade Bread

AUNT CLARY WAS A loving soul. For decades she wrote letters to her girlhood chums, and got warm, gossipy letters in return. She sent valentines and birthday cards, and when she could afford it bright silver dollars to the children in the family. She loved to reminisce about her dear departed husband, John, and the good times, parties and weddings they had shared. Like a young girl, she recalled dancing with him by the lake under a summer moon.

And she never forgot her husband's boyhood friend, Floyd, who lived just down the road a piece. Each week, she made fresh bread for herself and Floyd, and jellies and jams in season. She scolded him when he didn't come over to have his hair trimmed often enough, and she sat with him and listened when he needed company.

Now and again, he would tell her that his friend John had sure got himself a fine woman. He would bring her fruit off his trees, and basketsful of wild blackberries from along the creek, and corn and sweet potatoes from his garden. And he gave her a little poem about Heaven and homemade bread.

THE SAME BLEST THING

AFTER Floyd's wife and Clary's man were dead,
Clary's late husband's best friend, Floyd, said,
"Clary you've kept my life so warm
with the taste of your homemade bread.
I learned to swing a hammer.
I learned to hammer things.
I learned to saw a two-by-four,
but I never learned to sing.
But if I ever learned," Floyd said,
"I'd sing of Heaven and your homemade bread.
That's the song I'd sing.
It'd be an easy tune
'cause they're both the same Blest Thing."

—Alvin Reiss

♥

Anadama Bread

MAKES 2 LOAVES

AUNT CLARY CALLED THIS treat Mama Lowery's Molasses Corn Bread for years, until someone told her the correct name for this old American bread is Anadama Bread.

½ cup water-ground cornmeal
2 tablespoons butter or margarine
½ cup molasses
1 tablespoon salt

2 tablespoons granulated yeast
About 7 or 8 cups all-purpose
flour, sifted

Thoroughly grease a large bowl and two 10-by-5-by-3-inch loaf pans. Set aside.

In a large bowl, stir cornmeal into 2 cups boiling water. Add butter or margarine, molasses, and salt and cool to lukewarm. Meanwhile, sprinkle yeast over ½ cup warm water (105° to 115°F), stir a time or two, and set aside until yeast is thoroughly dissolved and a light foam has risen to the surface, about 5 minutes.

When cornmeal mixture is lukewarm, blend in yeast mixture. Add enough flour to make a stiff dough, *about 7 cups,* then turn dough onto a lightly floured flat surface and knead until smooth and elastic.

NOTE: If dough is not stiff enough to make a firm ball, knead in the *additional cup* flour.

Place dough in prepared bowl, move gently about until underside is greased, then turn greased side up. Cover with a clean kitchen towel and let rise in a warm place (about 80°F) until doubled in bulk. Punch down, turn underside up, cover again with a towel, and let rise again for 45 minutes.

Knead a second time for about 3 minutes (don't knead too thoroughly), then divide dough in half. Shape into loaves (pat into a rectangle, fold long side over, and pinch edges together; tuck ends under) and place in prepared pans. Set loaves in a warm place and let rise until doubled in bulk, about 45 minutes.

Preheat oven to 425°F. Set loaves in center of oven and bake until well puffed, about 15 minutes. Reduce heat to 375°F and continue baking until loaves are browned and sound hollow when tapped, about 45 minutes more.

Turn out loaves onto a wire rack, brush tops and sides with butter or margarine, and cool.

❧

From A Summer Sunrise
(After Lee O. Harris)

THE master-hand whose pencils trace
　This wondrous landscape of the morn,
Is but the sun, whose glowing face
Reflects the rapture and the grace
　Of inspiration Heaven-born.

And, spangled with the shine and shade,
　I see the rivers raveled out
In strands of silver, slowly fade
In threads of light along the glade
　Where truant roses hide and pout.

Yet over all the waking earth
　The tears of night are brushed away,
And eyes are lit with love and mirth,
And benisons of richest worth
　Go up to bless the new-born day.

—James Whitcomb Riley

THE PEARLS
OF DEW
AND ROSES
OF JUNE

~~~~~~~~~~~

ON EARLY SUMMER MORNINGS when tiny, glistening drops of water clung to her flowers and garden plants, Old Missus Upjohn would be up and about. She would take a handmade basket with her, one that was flat. Then carefully she would gather dewy rose petals and take them directly to the springhouse, hoping they would last long enough for a neighbor or friend to stop by and share their beauty.

Usually by midmorning a child on the way to school; boys looking for a stray horse, lamb, or calf, or on their way fishing; or a young woman with her small children would stop by to share a little family or neighborhood news and would look at the brilliant rose petals and smell them. When the dew was gone and the petals were beginning to wilt, Missus Upjohn would dry them for sachet bags.

A Vintage Fashion Show

IN RURAL AREAS THERE has always been a shortage of funds for new books, art supplies, and repair on school buildings. To meet such needs women in the community constantly search for creative ways in which to earn a few dollars.

One delightful idea began with Effie, who, with the help of the banker's wife, the preacher's wife, and several ladies from the church and grange, planned a Vintage Fashion Show to which all the women in the community, and those from neighboring towns, would be invited. Guests were encouraged to come early to tea, and were told that there would be a small charge for tickets.

The organizers of the fashion show began to go through family trunks, looking for suitable dresses and accessories. Effie found her grandmother's wedding dress; her friend Ella, the banker's wife, borrowed a dress that her German mother-in-law had brought from the old country. Ida Louise carefully mended and hand-washed a black lace dress that had belonged to one of her great-grandmothers in Civil War days. Other women, young and old, came forth with an array of dresses, hats, gloves, and high-buttoned shoes, until even the men had to admit that the gala event would be some kind of show.

Some of the menfolk, like Uncle Bud, wanted to buy tickets to the fashion show. They told the women that the fund-raising effort was for the benefit of the community's children and school, and that even though they did not want to come over for tea, they wanted to participate. Some farmers, mill workers, men and boys who worked in the mercantile, the barber, blacksmith, banker, lawyer, and doctor, and many others, were lined up to get tickets.

On the day of the fashion show, excitement crackled through the air like summer lightning. Every woman had stripped her flower garden for posies and roses, lilies and snapdragons, ivy and other greenery. The old schoolhouse looked like a bower deep in the woods, clean and green, softly beautiful with ferns and flowers. Women began to gather in the streets near the school. All had on their Sunday best; some had tucked flowers into their hatbands.

Eventually, the doors of the school were opened, tickets were collected, and the guests were invited in to take tea—much to their delight, for women of that day did not have much opportunity to attend such an elegant affair. From one side of the tea room to the other, women sat at lace-covered tables, pouring tea out of beautiful teapots. Effie and all her friends had brought their best china. Women off hardscrabble farms who had paid for their tickets with butter-and-egg money held the gold-rimmed china teacups and saucers gently in work-worn hands, almost as if they were afraid that they

JANE WATSON HOPPING

might break one. Rainbow Cakes and Effie's Boston Brown Bread Tea Sandwiches with assorted fillings were passed on silver trays which had been lent by the banker's wife.

When the fashion show began, the guests gravitated to spots where they could get a good view of the vintage dresses and accessories. The room was abuzz with pleasure and excitement.

It was late afternoon, almost three-thirty, when the ladies finally left the school, only to linger in the streets talking to each other and their men, recalling this or that lovely dress, the tea party, the cups with gold rims, and the funds raised for books, pens and pencils, colored paper, and songbooks.

When the money was counted, it was such a vast amount that Effie and the other women agreed that everyone in town, all the farm folk from the countryside, and every guest from out of town must have bought tickets. They then asked the pastor's wife to thank God on their behalf for the success of the fashion show, and for the enrichment it would bring to the lives of all the children.

※

From A Discouraging Model

JUST the airiest, fairiest slip of a thing,
  With a Gainsborough hat, like a butterfly wing,
Tilted up at one side with the jauntiest air,
And a knot of red roses sewn in under there
  Where the shadows are lost in her hair.

And that lace at her throat—and the fluttering hands
Snowing there, with a grace that no art understands
The flakes of their touches—first fluttering at
The bow—then the roses—the hair—and then that
  Little tilt of the Gainsborough hat.

—James Whitcomb Riley

♥

Rainbow Cakes

FOR SPECIAL OCCASIONS, EFFIE and her friends made sheet cakes, cut them into diamonds, squares, triangles, circles, and rectangles, then frosted them with lightly tinted butter frosting. Using large tweezers, they decorated the cakes with thinly sliced nutmeats, candied fruit, and bits of gumdrops. When they were all set out, the serving plates looked as if they had passed through a rainbow and taken on its colors.

♥

White or Pink Velvet Cakes

MAKES ABOUT 36 SMALL CAKES, DEPENDING ON SHAPES

2 cups cake flour
1¼ cups sugar
1 tablespoon baking powder
1 teaspoon salt
½ cup white shortening or light-colored butter, softened at room temperature

1 cup milk
4 egg whites
1 teaspoon vanilla
2 or more drops red food coloring for tinting the cake pink (don't use too much coloring)

Preheat oven to 375°F. Thoroughly grease and flour a 9-by-12-inch sheet cake pan. Set aside.

In a medium bowl sift cake flour once with sugar, baking powder, and salt. Add softened shortening or butter and ½ *cup* of the milk; beat until creamy. Add *remaining* milk, egg whites, vanilla, and food coloring and beat until light.

Pour into prepared pan. Bake until batter is well risen, firm to the touch, and lightly browned, 30 to 35 minutes.

NOTE: The cake's surface should spring back when touched lightly.

Cool cake for 8 to 10 minutes before turning out of the pan onto a large piece of waxed paper. When completely cool, turn right side up. Using a long, sharp knife, and using firm, sure strokes, cut cake into squares, triangles, diamonds, or other shapes. Frost with Tinted Butter Frosting (recipe follows) and decorate as you wish, perhaps piping a small flower on the top of each cake.

♥

Light-Yellow Cake

MAKES ABOUT 36 SMALL CAKES, DEPENDING ON SHAPES

1²⁄₃ cups cake flour, sifted
1¹⁄₂ teaspoons baking powder
¹⁄₃ cup butter, softened
1 cup sugar

2 eggs, well beaten
1 teaspoon lemon or vanilla extract
¹⁄₂ cup milk

Preheat oven to 375°F. Thoroughly grease and lightly flour a 9-by-12-inch sheet cake pan. Set aside until needed.

Into a medium bowl sift flour a second time with baking powder and set aside. In a large bowl, cream butter thoroughly, add sugar gradually, and cream together until light. Add eggs and blend well. To the butter and egg mixture add flour alternately with milk and extract, a small amount at a time, beating after each addition until batter is smooth. Pour into the prepared pan and place in the center of the oven.

Bake until well risen, firm to the touch, and golden brown, about 20 to 25 minutes. Cool for 10 minutes in the pan, then turn out onto a piece of waxed paper to cool thoroughly. Carefully turn over cake and pull waxed paper off top. Using a long, sharp knife, cut with firm, clean strokes into strips. Then cut strips into squares, diamonds, or other desired shapes. Fancy cutters also can be used. Frost with Tinted Butter Frosting (recipe follows).

♥

Tinted Butter Frosting

MAKES ENOUGH TO THINLY FROST 3 DOZEN OR MORE RAINBOW CAKES

3 cups powdered sugar
¹⁄₃ cup melted butter
A few grains salt

1 tablespoon milk
2²⁄₃ tablespoons lemon juice
Food coloring

Sift sugar and combine with melted butter, salt, milk, and lemon juice. Beat until creamy. Divide into four portions. Leave one white and tint the remaining three portions yellow, light orange, and pink.

♥

Orange Rainbow Tea Cakes

MAKES 20 SMALL OR 12 MEDIUM CAKES

2 cups cake flour, sifted	1 cup sugar
2 teaspoons baking powder	1 egg, unbeaten
¼ teaspoon salt	¼ cup milk
1 tablespoon grated orange rind	½ cup orange juice
2 tablespoons butter or margarine, softened at room temperature	

Preheat oven to 375°F. Thoroughly grease a 20-cup muffin tin (a 12-cup will do if it is not filled too full). Set aside.

Into a medium bowl sift the flour a second time with the baking powder and salt; set aside. In a large bowl, add orange rind to butter or margarine and cream thoroughly. Add sugar gradually and continue to cream until light. Add egg and beat until mixture has a soft, smooth texture. To the egg and sugar mixture add flour mixture alternately with milk and orange juice, a small amount at a time, beating well with each addition. When batter is smooth, pour into prepared muffin tins, filling small tins two-thirds full, larger ones half full.

Bake until well risen, spongy to the touch, and golden brown, about 20 minutes. Frost with Tinted Butter Frosting (recipe follows).

♥

Effie's Boston Brown Bread Tea Sandwiches with Assorted Fillings

MAKES 2 LOAVES

IN A SMALL TOWN like the one in which Effie lived, most charitable events were sponsored by the Christian Women's Society, which included women from Baptist and Methodist churches and other denominations in the area, including Father McBride's Catholic church. It was the women's opinion that they were all workers for the Lord and that it was their duty to improve the quality of life in their area wherever and whenever they could.

Fund-raising events were sometimes the work of one church or another; sometimes it was the grange ladies who served delicious breakfasts to raise money for scholarships to send the brightest youngsters in the area off to college; sometimes the various groups pulled hard together to earn money to care for the old and destitute among them.

1 cup whole-wheat flour
1 cup rye flour
1 cup yellow cornmeal
1½ teaspoons baking soda

1½ teaspoons salt
2 cups buttermilk or sour milk
¾ cup light molasses (or sorghum)

Grease and flour two 1-quart pudding molds or two 1-pound coffee cans. Set out a steaming kettle (a boiling-water-bath canning kettle will do nicely).

In a large bowl combine the whole-wheat flour, rye flour, cornmeal, baking soda, and salt. In a small bowl mix the buttermilk or sour milk and molasses. Make a hollow in the center of the flour mixture and pour in the buttermilk-molasses mixture. Stir together until well blended (don't beat).

Fill prepared molds or coffee cans two-thirds full. Cover, fastening the lid on so that it is watertight.

NOTE: When using coffee cans, press original lids on or cover tightly with aluminum foil.

Place the rack in the steaming kettle and pour in 1 inch of boiling water. Set covered molds on the rack and cover the pan with a tight-fitting lid. Carefully add enough boiling water to come halfway up around the mold. Keep the water boiling, adding more to keep the water at the proper level. Steam for 1½ hours or until a broomstraw comes clean when inserted in the center of the loaf.

Remove the pans from the kettle and unmold the bread. The surface of the bread can be dried slightly in the oven at 300°F for 5 to 10 minutes and then sliced thickly and eaten warm, or it can be cooled and eaten sliced quite thin.

♥

Chicken Filling

MAKES ABOUT 1½ CUPS

1 cup cooked chicken breast,
minced very fine

¼ cup mayonnaise
1 tablespoon lemon juice

In a small bowl blend ingredients. Chill. Just before assembling, spread thin halves of bread with mayonnaise. Fill with prepared chicken; refrigerate not more than 20 minutes. Serve while still cold.

♥

Cream Cheese and Marmalade Filling

MAKES ENOUGH FOR 2 LOAVES OF BREAD

*One package (8 ounces) cream
  cheese*

½ cup light cream
½ cup orange marmalade

In a small bowl, cream the cheese until light; add cream until mixture is of a spreading consistency. Slice Boston Brown Bread in thin slices and then cut slices in equal halves. Spread cream cheese on one half of the slices and marmalade on the other half. Press firmly together. Layer on a platter with waxed paper between each layer until ready to serve, then arrange on a decorative tray.

♥

Peanut Butter Date and Honey Filling

MAKES 1 CUP OR SLIGHTLY MORE

*½ cup peanut butter (chunky
  preferred)*
½ cup dates, finely chopped

1 tablespoon light clover honey
2 tablespoons orange juice

In a small bowl, blend ingredients until mixture has a spreadable consistency.
  NOTE: If mixture seems a little stiff, add more orange juice, a little at a time.
  Spread thinly on each slice of bread. Press together and layer on a platter with waxed paper between each layer.

'Mid Streaming Rays of Golden Sunshine

NOT SO LONG AGO, I saw a well-groomed old man sitting alone on a park bench, clasping his cane in both hands. A flock of pigeons flew by, dipping gracefully over the church steeple and swooping past the grey buildings to land at his feet. He watched them with a studied lack of interest.

Then a small girl, about four years of age, whose hair reflected all the glory of the sun's rays, came up with her mother to stand nearby. They began to throw pieces of bread to the pigeons, which leapt in half-flight from crumb to crumb. In her excitement, the child danced joyfully among the birds, setting them off into flight only to see them return again and again for the free meal.

The old man began to watch her at play; then, when she handed him a few crumbs of bread, he too fed the birds. She said to him, "Look at the color on them, white and grey and shiny greens, and browns—see this one, look over there!" As she ran back and forth, first to her mother, then to the old man, the light that streamed over her, the flying sunlit hair, the joyful sound of her voice warmed the spot and made it live.

In time, her mother took her by the hand, brushed her hair and led her down the street to a nearby car. Even to me, an observer, it seemed that when they left, the park felt vacant, colder, less alive. Feeling it too, perhaps, the old man got up and walked on down the sidewalk. I thought I could see a certain vigor in his step, and could not help wondering if he carried the child's delight in his bosom, warmed by having shared in the innocence of her play, reminded of another time and of fair-haired loved ones of his own.

❧

JACKSONVILLE: PIGEONS

A DOZEN they perch
in twos and threes;
their east eyes hold the sun.

Then away as one,
sudden and sure,
like the chord of a Segovia guitar

the flock of them
swooping, rising, a liquid scimitar
curves around the meadow tree

and back to the roof
to perch
in groups of two and three.

—Alvin Reiss

♥

Chicken Salad with
Homemade Curried French Dressing

JUST ENOUGH FOR A MAN AND A MAID

WHEN I WAS GROWING UP, families often spent Sunday afternoon in the park. Small children played on swings and slides and took walks with their mothers. Young girls visited in clusters with friends in sight of their fathers, who also chaperoned older daughters while brothers and cousins played baseball or pitched horseshoes.

In time, the women of the family would set out a finely wrought wicker basket—or two—filled with delicacies designed to tempt the men's appetites. One such dish was this Chicken Salad dressed with a Homemade Curried French Dressing.

1½ cups cooked, diced chicken
1 cup celery, chopped
2 tablespoons apple chutney
¼ teaspoon salt
⅓ to ½ cup Homemade Curried French Dressing (recipe follows)

Salad greens: leaf or head lettuce or parsley as available in midsummer
Fruit: fresh plums, peaches, or pears in season

In a medium bowl, combine chicken, celery, chutney, and salt. Blend in Homemade Curried French Dressing. Chill for several hours. Meanwhile, wash the greens and wrap them in waxed paper (or put them in a crisper) to keep them fresh. Leave fruit whole to be eaten out of hand.

Just before leaving for the park, pack salad and other picnic fare in a basket and cover with a dishtowel.

Once you arrive and find a spot of shade, lay a blanket on the grass. Serve the picnic lunch immediately while the salad is still cold, with fruit, Deluxe Bran Muffins (page 69), and Summertime Iced Cider Punch (page 70). *For family fare double the recipe.*

♥

Homemade Curried French Dressing

MAKES ¾ CUP

2/3 cup salad or olive oil
3 tablespoons vinegar
1/4 teaspoon salt

Dash of white pepper
1 teaspoon curry powder

Using a wire whisk, beat ingredients until well blended. Chill. Shake well just before adding to the salad.

♥

Deluxe Bran Muffins

MAKES 12 MEDIUM MUFFINS

YOUNG GIRLS OF THE late twenties and early thirties thought these muffins were very fancy. They made them for potluck suppers, picnics in the park, and box-lunch socials.

1 cup whole-wheat flour
3/4 cup bran
1 tablespoon baking powder
3/4 teaspoon salt
1/4 cup molasses

1 egg, well beaten
2/3 cup milk
4 tablespoons butter or margarine,
    melted

Preheat oven to 425°F. Set out and thoroughly grease a 12-cup muffin pan.

In a medium bowl combine whole-wheat flour, bran, baking powder, and salt. Stir to blend. In a small bowl combine molasses, egg, milk, and melted butter. Make a well in the flour mixture, pour the liquid mixture into it and, using two forks, stir only as much as is needed to moisten and blend the batter. Spoon batter into prepared muffin cups, filling them about two-thirds full.

Bake until well risen, browned, and firm to the touch, about 25 minutes. Turn out onto brown paper or a wire rack. Serve piping hot, plain or with butter.

NOTE: These muffins keep well in an airtight container and can be reheated.

♥

Summertime Iced Cider Punch

MAKES SLIGHTLY MORE THAN 2½ QUARTS

GIRLS IN OUR FAMILY thought this fruited punch was just right to serve on warm summer evenings. On the farm it was set in the springhouse to cool; city women bought an extra chunk of ice from the ice man.

1 quart cider
1 quart ginger ale
2 cups orange juice, strained

½ cup lemon juice, strained
Sugar to taste

In a large bowl, combine cider, ginger ale, orange juice, and lemon juice. Sweeten to taste. Chill before serving or pour over ice.

Baby Sister

A MERRY
FAIRY
DREAM

~~~~~~~~~

WHEN AUNT CLARY'S DAUGHTER Martha was a little girl, she loved fairy stories, and she loved to tell about the time she saw a fairy ring in the grass that was six feet across (she measured it with her father's carpenter's tape). She read classic tales like "Hansel and Gretel," "The Goose Girl," "Cinderella," and "Rumpelstiltskin," all of which, at one time, had been oral stories, told about the countryside on cold winter nights, or told in the shade of a tree in summer.

Martha loved to tell about the Grimm brothers, Jacob and Wilhelm, who sat in gardens and on walls listening and writing while grandmothers related ancient fairy tales. And she loved the work of Hans Christian Andersen, who wrote "The Tinder-Box," "The Red Shoes," "The Snow Queen," and "Only A Fiddler."

"The Pixy People" by James Whitcomb Riley reminds us all of that thin, wiry child who used to sit in the fork of a tree and read for hours. Now young Martha is a woman, a mother, and one can find her settled instead in the shade under a tree reading or telling stories to the little ones.

From THE PIXY PEOPLE

THROUGH the breezy mazes
   Of the lazy June,
Drowsy with the hazes
   Of the dreamy noon,
Little Pixy people
   Winged above the walk,
Pouring from the steeple
   Of a mullein-stalk.

One—a gallant fellow—
   Evidently King,—
Wore a plume of yellow
   In a jeweled ring
On a pansy bonnet,
   Gold and white and blue,
With the dew still on it,
   And the fragrance, too.

One—a dainty lady,—
   Evidently Queen,—
Wore a gown of shady
   Moonshine and green,
With a lace of gleaming
   Starlight that sent
All the dewdrops dreaming
   Everywhere she went.

One wore a waistcoat
   Of rose-leaves, out and in,
And one wore a faced-coat
   Of tiger-lily-skin;
And one wore a neat coat
   Of palest galingale;
And one a tiny street-coat,
   And one a swallow-tail.

And Ho! sang the King of them,
   And Hey! sang the Queen;
And round and round the ring of them
   Went dancing o'er the green;
And Hey! sang the Queen of them,
   And Ho! sang the King—
And all that I had seen of them
   Wasn't anything!

—James Whitcomb Riley

A Kiss As Sweet As Heated Honey Is

WHEN UNCLE BUD FIRST saw Aunt Sue, she was only twelve years old, a child with long brown braids hanging over her shoulders, riding like a wild Indian on a pinto mare. He was just twenty, a big kid out looking for work, going from one ranch to another. He loves to tell how when he first saw her, he knew he would work for her father, for as long as it took, until she grew up and until her family learned to like and trust him. Then, if she would have him, he would marry her.

When the men left, Aunty would smile and tell the women how, the moment she saw Bud standing there, tall and powerful, his eyes drinking her in, she knew with the womanly wisdom of a twelve-year-old that when the time came, she would marry him. And she would softly confide, "Bud waited for me until I was eighteen years old, then we married. We've been together now for nearly fifty years."

♥

Bride's Orange-Blossom Cake

MAKES ONE 9-INCH, 3-LAYER CAKE

THIS OLD-FASHIONED three-layer cake all decked out in Fluffy Orange Frosting is a beaut!

*1 cup butter or margarine, softened
    at room temperature*
2 cups sugar, sifted
3⅓ cups flour, sifted
4 teaspoons baking powder
½ teaspoon salt
1 cup milk

1 teaspoon vanilla extract
½ teaspoon orange flavoring
6 egg whites, beaten until stiff
1 cup orange marmalade
*Fluffy Orange Frosting (recipe
    follows)*

Preheat oven to 375°F. Thoroughly grease three 9-inch layer cake pans. Set aside.

In a large bowl, cream butter or margarine until light, add sugar, and cream the two together until smooth. Sift flour a second time with baking powder and salt. To the creamed butter and sugar, add flour mixture alternately with milk. Add vanilla and orange flavoring. Finally, fold in the stiffly beaten egg whites. Divide equally between prepared pans.

Bake until batter is well risen and lightly browned and the layers feel firm to the touch, about 20 to 25 minutes. Set on a wire rack to cool for about 5 minutes, then carefully loosen edges with a spatula and turn layers out onto the wire rack; cool for at least 20 minutes before turning upright.

When layers are thoroughly cool, assemble the cake: Put the bottom layer, top side up, on a serving plate and spread lightly with orange marmalade; put the second layer upside-down on top of the first and spread it with marmalade; then put the third layer on the cake top side up. Spread generously with Fluffy Orange Frosting, top and sides. Using the back of a teaspoon, swirl frosting into a high-low pattern. If you wish, decorate with sugar rosebuds or with tiny yellow or golden buds from the rose garden, freshly picked, rinsed, and air-dried.

♥

Fluffy Orange Frosting

MAKES ENOUGH FOR ONE 9-INCH, 3-LAYER CAKE

¾ cup sugar
½ teaspoon cream of tartar
⅛ teaspoon salt (or slightly less)
2 egg whites

¼ cup cold water
1 teaspoon orange flavoring
½ teaspoon vanilla extract

Set out a large saucepan and fill with about 3 inches of water. Heat until water begins to simmer. Turn heat off.

Then in a 2-quart, straight-sided heat-proof bowl, combine the sugar, cream of tartar, salt, egg whites, and cold water. Reheat water in pan until it is again simmering, but not boiling. Set bowl in hot water. Beat with rotary beater until frosting stands in peaks, about 5 to 7 minutes. Remove from water, add orange flavoring and vanilla, and beat a few minutes longer to blend and to firm up the frosting.

❧

From JUDITH
(Uncle Bud's favorite poem)

O HER eyes were amber fine—
*   Dark and deep as wells of wine,*
While her smile is like the noon
Splendor of a day in June.
If she sorrow—lo! her face
It is like a flowery space
In bright meadows, overlaid
With light clouds and lulled with shade.

—James Whitcomb Riley

♥

Groom's Cake with Creamy Chocolate Butter Frosting

MAKES ONE 9-INCH, 2-LAYER CAKE

IN OUR FAMILY YOUNG men tend to prefer chocolate cake, so at wedding receptions we often see a lovely white bride's cake with delicate roses on it and a rich chocolate groom's cake with swirls of Creamy Chocolate Butter Frosting.

2 cups cake flour, sifted
2¾ teaspoons baking powder
¼ teaspoon salt
⅔ cup butter or margarine,
   softened at room temperature
1½ cups sugar
3 eggs, well beaten

3 squares unsweetened chocolate,
   melted and cooled
1 teaspoon vanilla extract
¾ cup milk
Creamy Chocolate Butter Frosting
   (recipe follows)

Preheat oven to 350°F. Set out and thoroughly grease two 9-inch round layer cake pans.

In a medium bowl, sift flour a second and third time with baking powder and salt; set aside. In a large bowl, cream butter or margarine until waxy; add sugar gradually and cream together until light. Add eggs and beat well. Thoroughly blend in chocolate and extract. To the butter mixture add the flour mixture alternately with milk, a small amount at a time, beating after each addition. Divide batter evenly between the prepared pans.

Set pans in the center of the oven. Bake until well risen, a little browned, and firm to the touch, about 35 minutes. (To test, insert a toothpick into the center of one layer; if it comes out clean, the cake is done.)

Let sit in pans for 10 minutes, then turn out onto a wire rack to cool. When the cake is firm enough to handle, turn right side up. Cool completely before frosting with Creamy Chocolate Butter Frosting.

JANE WATSON HOPPING

♥

Creamy Chocolate Butter Frosting

MAKES ENOUGH TO LIGHTLY FILL AND FROST A 9-INCH, 2-LAYER CAKE

*⅓ cup butter or margarine,
    softened at room temperature*
*2 squares unsweetened chocolate,
    melted and cooled*

2 cups powdered sugar
1½ teaspoons vanilla extract
About 2 tablespoons milk

In a medium bowl thoroughly mix butter or margarine and cooled chocolate. Blend in powdered sugar, vanilla and *1 tablespoon* of the milk. If too thick for spreading, add a *second tablespoon,* and a little more as needed.

♥

A Housewarming Cake

AFTER THE WEDDING IS over and the bride and groom have settled into their new home, friends of the family plan a housewarming party. The women decide who will bring cakes and cookies, juices for the punch, extra coffee, tea, sugar, and cream—just in case the bride doesn't have enough for company.

In advance of the party, aunts and neighbors drop in to visit with the new bride and, after admiring all the wedding gifts and making a fuss about her new home, share among themselves a "needs" list they have in mind. A day or two before the party, the bride's mother usually tells her daughter to have everything spruced up by Saturday, and since all brides in farm country know about housewarmings, she knows what to expect.

The housewarming is always a success; the young married woman is delighted to receive gifts that fill out her housekeeping needs. The men usually go outside, smoke strong-smelling cigars, and give the groom some good advice. When the party is over, folks go home quite satisfied with themselves, happy to think they've given the young folk not only a financial boost, but encouragement and approval.

♥

Orange Chiffon Cake with Creamy Orange Butter Icing

MAKES ONE 10-INCH TUBE CAKE

MOTHER'S DEAR FRIEND EFFIE was the first one in our family and social circle to make a chiffon cake. Soon she was making chocolate and lemon chiffon cakes, as well as this delicious orange one! Once she got started, it seemed that the men and womenfolk were always asking her to try this kind of chiffon cake or that. Uncle Bud thought she should make a maple cake, and Grandpa thought a spicy chiffon cake would top them all.

2¼ cups all-purpose flour, sifted
1½ cups sugar
3 teaspoons baking powder
1 teaspoon salt
½ cup salad oil
7 eggs, separated, yolk beaten just enough to blend

2 tablespoons grated orange peel
1 teaspoon cream of tartar
Creamy Orange Butter Icing
(recipe follows)

Preheat oven to 325°F. Set out an ungreased 10-inch tube pan.

In a large bowl sift flour a second time with sugar, baking powder, and salt. Make a well in the flour mixture and add oil, *egg yolks,* ¾ cup cold water, and grated orange peel and stir until well blended.

In a large bowl combine egg whites and cream of tartar. Beat with a rotary or electric beater into very stiff peaks. A little at a time, pour cake batter over beaten whites. Fold gently in until blended (don't stir vigorously or beat this batter). Pour into tube pan. Set in the center of the oven.

Bake until the cake is well risen and lightly browned and the top springs back when touched lightly with fingertips, 1 hour and 15 to 20 minutes. When done, invert tube pan on a funnel and let cake hang upside down until completely cooled. Turn top side up and, using a thin spatula or knife blade, gently loosen cake from the sides of the pan and the center tube. Carefully remove from the pan and transfer to a cake plate. Serve plain, or ice with Creamy Orange Butter Icing.

♥

Creamy Orange Butter Icing

MAKES ENOUGH TO ICE ONE 10-INCH TUBE CAKE

⅓ cup butter or margarine,
   softened at room temperature
3 cups powdered sugar

1½ teaspoons grated orange peel
About 3 tablespoons lemon juice,
   strained

In a medium bowl, blend ingredients until icing is of a spreading consistency.

God Bless Her Gentle Heart

Drinking All That Life Holds, Love

EARLY IN THIS CENTURY, in rural America, relationships between men and women were forged not only of love and passion, but also of necessity. The labors, skills, and nurturing of a good wife, or devoted mother, could mean the difference between the success or failure of a farming venture.

It was not always easy for a man to find a mate, a woman who wanted to make a home and raise children in the Wild West or out on the windswept prairie. And the farther west one lived, the higher the proportion of men to women, which meant that many a farmer or rancher remained a lifelong bachelor who not only cooked for himself but washed his clothes and kept his surroundings clean and in good repair. If he was a widower, he had the awesome responsibility of raising his children alone. Some men made long journeys to the Midwest and East to search for women who wanted to marry, and they counted themselves blessed if they won a gentle, hardworking woman's heart.

A LITTLE WAY WITH ME

COME walk a little way with me,
The sunlight lingers on the hill;
The winds are murmuring cheerily,
The pool is dark and still,

My hand in yours—oh, let us stroll,
With hearts at rest, a little while;
The daisies bloom on yonder knoll,
The skies are fair—and smile.

Come, walk a little way with me:
The path has drear and somber grown;
The winds are whispering plaintively,
I fear to go alone.

Oh, walk a little way with me—
The lonely night draws on apace;
But still the sunshine I shall see
Forever—in your face.

—Grace E. Hall

♥

An Old-Fashioned Fruit Salad Platter with Honey-Lemon Mayonnaise

MAKES 6 TO 8 SERVINGS

GRANDPA, WHO WAS A widower, lived alone for many years in a cabin on our home place. In summer, just before mealtime, he would take his picking basket and gather all sorts of fruit—berries, melons, grapes, and anything else that was ripe—for Mother, who would then wash and, if necessary, pare them before laying the fruit out on a large platter for the upcoming meal.

Honey-Lemon Mayonnaise (recipe follows)
1 cantaloupe, peeled and cut into slices about 1½ inches thick
½ honeydew melon, peeled and cut into 1½-inch slices
6 or more wild plums (store-bought plums will do)
3 peaches, peeled, pitted, and quartered (treat with a wash of 2 tablespoons sugar, 1 tablespoon lemon juice, and 2 tablespoons water to keep them from darkening)

3 Bartlett pears, peeled, cored, and quartered (treat as you did peaches)
A bunch of fresh parsley rinsed in cold water and air-dried

Make Honey-Lemon Mayonnaise before preparing the fruit and melons. Chill. Set out six salad plates.

Around the edge of a large platter arrange the parsley. Then lay the melons, plums, peaches, and pears on the platter in a way that shows off their colors and shapes. Chill for just a few minutes, then serve. Pass the platter from hand to hand, and pass the Honey-Lemon Mayonnaise with it.

♥

Honey-Lemon Mayonnaise

MAKES ABOUT I CUP

1 cup mayonnaise
2 tablespoons lemon juice, strained

1 tablespoon honey (clover
    preferred)

In a small bowl blend ingredients until smooth. Chill.

♥

An Old-Fashioned Ham Loaf

MAKES 6 TO 8 SERVINGS

BEFORE UNCLE BUD WAS married he lived in a small cabin on the ranch where he worked. He was not only a good hand, but a good cook as well. He liked to talk about recipes with the women in the family. They made the ham loaf with ham left over from a big Sunday dinner; he made his with plain, smoked, uncooked ham.

2 cups milk
3 cups fine soft bread crumbs
2 eggs, beaten to a froth
½ teaspoon salt
½ teaspoon dry mustard

1½ pounds lean ground beef
¾ pound ground ham, uncooked
½ cup firmly packed light brown
    sugar
1 teaspoon freshly grated nutmeg

Preheat oven to 350°F. Set out and thoroughly grease a 10-by-5-by-3-inch loaf pan.

Pour milk into a medium bowl; add bread crumbs and let soak for 5 minutes. Add eggs, salt, mustard, ground beef, and ground ham. Stir milk and crumbs into the meat mixture and work with hands until well blended. Sprinkle brown sugar in the bottom of the prepared loaf pan. Sprinkle nutmeg over sugar. Turn meat mixture into the pan and pack firmly.

Bake until meat is done throughout, registering 170°F on a meat thermometer (about 1 hour and 15 minutes). Drain off juices before unmolding onto a medium platter. Serve hot or cold.

♥

Garden-Fresh Green Bean Medley

MAKES 10 TO 12 SERVINGS

FRUGAL TO A FAULT, many early-day bachelors raised a large garden which often included a winter's supply of potatoes, onions, parsnips, and beans, which they dried. More tender and seasonal vegetables were grown in such a wide assortment that it took considerable ingenuity on the cook's part to think of uses for the embarrassment of riches.

2 pounds fresh green beans, washed, strings and ends removed, and cut into 1-inch pieces (3 cups or more)

4–5 ears fresh corn

1 cup green lima beans, shelled (frozen beans can be substituted)

6 or more sliver-skin onions (small white boiling onions), or small onion, diced

½ cup celery, chopped

1 cup mushrooms, washed, trimmed, and sliced

2 tablespoons butter

In a medium covered saucepan cook green beans in 1 inch boiling salt water until tender-crisp, about 15 to 20 minutes. Drain and set aside. Cook husked corn with silks removed just until the milk is set (5 to 6 minutes) and cut kernels off cob. Meanwhile, put the lima beans on to boil in a saucepan containing 1 inch boiling salt water; cook until beans are just tender when tested with a fork, about 25 minutes. (For frozen beans, cook according to package directions.) While both kinds of beans are cooking, boil onions in 1 inch boiling salt water in a small saucepan for about 20 to 25 minutes. Drain and set aside. In a medium skillet, sauté celery and mushrooms in butter until celery is tender-crisp and mushrooms are heated through.

Fold all the vegetables together in a large casserole dish, cover, and set in a warming oven to reheat. Serve piping hot. (This dish can be made ahead of time and reheated just before serving.)

♥

Honey Rice Pudding

MAKES 6 TO 8 SERVINGS

THIS SIMPLE OLD-FASHIONED PUDDING has always been a favorite of the men in our family. The women made it often as a dessert or as a bedtime dish. Grandpa, who sometimes made it, spooned thick icy-cold cream over his.

1 cup rice	*6 eggs, well beaten*
6 cups skim milk	*½ cup golden raisins*
¼ cup butter or margarine,	*Ground cinnamon to taste (about 2*
softened at room temperature	*teaspoons)*
¾ cup honey, at room temperature	*½ teaspoon salt*
¼ cup sugar	

Preheat oven to 350°F. Lightly grease a 13-by-9-by-2-inch baking dish. Set aside.

Wash rice and steam it in milk over low heat until grains are tender and have taken up most of the moisture; allow it to cool. Meanwhile, in a large bowl cream butter or margarine, honey, and sugar together until light. Add eggs, raisins, cinnamon, salt, and cooked rice. Pour into buttered baking dish and bake until custard is thick and the top of the pudding is lightly browned, about 1 hour.

NOTE: Test pudding by sticking a table knife into the center; if it comes out clean, the pudding is done.

Serve warm or cold. Refrigerate leftovers.

HE'S THE GOODEST MAN EVER YOU SAW

~~~~~~~~~~

IN THE OLD DAYS it wasn't uncommon for a young, single man to walk in off the roads and byways to ask for food in exchange for work. If he was personable and seemed a decent sort, a farm family would encourage him to stay, offering him room and board. And in time they often became fond of each other.

Eventually the man moved on, succumbing either to wanderlust or to a desire to return to his own family and home, leaving behind, and taking with him, fond memories.

The Raggedy Man

A Summer Apple Festival

LATE IN JUNE, WELL after school is out but before the weather turns uncomfortably hot, old-time people in apple-growing districts would celebrate the early summer apple harvest with a parade, an apple fair, and a small carnival of sorts.

Ida Louise, Effie's friend and ours, loves to tell stories about the day she marched in a summer apple festival parade:

ᖚ

On the day of the festival, townfolk and those of us on the farm got up early to get ready for the parade and carnival, and to do chores. We girls sorted out the largest and best-looking apples we could find for a display on a table at the apple fair. Papa and the boys loaded boxes of apples, which would be sold or traded, on the orchard wagon.

Those of us children who would march in the parade got into our costumes (Mother, like other women, had been sewing for weeks). Finally, when all was ready, my brother Andrew drove Mama and us girls to town in the buggy; Papa drove the team that pulled the wagon, and our brother Clyde, who was twelve and as independent as scat, rode his horse.

When we got to town, we gathered with neighbors and friends at the north end of Main Street. Everyone looked festive and the chattering and laughing was nonstop. Soon we would march down six blocks, to the other end of town, then change our clothes and gather again at the fairgrounds for the apple fair in the afternoon, and the carnival in the evening.

The parade began at nine o'clock sharp, with the school band in their fine new uniforms marching in place and crisply playing "I Want a Girl Just Like the Girl That Married Dear Old Dad." Then, all in step, they started down the street, still playing to the cheers of the crowd. By the time they were about halfway through the song, they reached the corner of Main and First streets, so they slowed down, and still playing, stopped at the corner, marched in place for a minute or two and then proceeded on down the street. Behind them were two twelve-year-olds—one was my brother Clyde and the other his best buddy—who carried a banner which read "Pollinators of the Future," and behind them a swarm of four- to seven-year-old little fellows wearing black shoes and pants, stuffed shirts with gold and black stripes running horizontally around them, and gold crowns on their heads with two bobbling antennas fastened to them. As they passed, eager eyes picked out parents in the crowd of onlookers, and sent little finger waves and beaming smiles to them.

Next girls, about five to seven years of age, in pastel green and apple-blossom-pink-and-white dresses, walked along, smiling at people they knew, and carrying placards which read "The Apple of My Eye"! Three doting fathers, with a banjo, fiddle, and guitar, played "Don't Sit Under the Apple Tree with Anyone Else But Me" and watched with loving eyes the giggling apple blossoms pass by, throwing kisses and waving to mothers and fathers, grandparents, aunts and uncles, and cousins, charming the whole crowd with their innocent loveliness.

The parade stopped then, while the Women's Cultural Society sang "Would God I Were a Tender Apple Blossom," which got a good round of applause and a few whistles. Following them, the local barbershop quartet sang "In the Shade of the Old Apple Tree," which was such a success they were persuaded by all to sing "Sweet Genevieve," and they could have stopped the parade entirely if the Young Women's Christian Temperance Union choral group had not stepped forward to sing "America the Beautiful."

By the time the ladies had finished bringing a patriotic tear to the eye here and there, the parade was within one block of the end of town, so the band regrouped, and struck up the final selection, "In the Good Old Summertime," in lilting waltz time, and all of the young folks, girls dressed in pastel gowns with wide ribbons tied at the waist and with handmade silk blossoms pinned in their hair, men in light-colored pants with white shirts, strolled down the final block, out of town, and across the field toward the fairgrounds. I was among them with my first beau.

About the grounds, tables were set up in the shade for the afternoon apple fair. Women stood in booths, selling pieces of their pies, or apple cookies; some had cobblers, crunches, and turnovers. Iced tea and cold milk (which had early in the day been packed in boxes of ice) were the drinks of the day.

Farmers who had brought in lugs of apples had them stacked on the ground or had left them on the beds of their wagons. All the women who were not involved with serving a bite to eat and drink were busy looking the boxes of apples over, hunting for special varieties among them: Gravensteins and Yellow Transparent, which give apple-sauce or pie a distinctive flavor and hue; or a good canning variety which would hold its shape—such summer apples have always been hard to find, later apples are better canners; or those which lend a natural light tan color and good texture to spiced apple butter.

By midafternoon, the sun had shifted and shade was gone. Families that lived nearby gathered the children together and went home, planning to return at dusk. Those who lived far out in the countryside, as we did, gathered up their belongings and either went to stay through the afternoon with friends, or went down to the creek to rest until the temperature cooled before going to the carnival or making the long trek home.

JANE WATSON HOPPING

About dusk, everyone began to drift onto the fairgrounds. The carnival was in place, and there were rides and games. One could toss a ring for a celluloid Kewpie doll, or even win a real silver-plated ring. Barkers invited people to step inside tents to see unbelievable sights, or to have their fortunes told.

The sounds of excitement and joy were everywhere; children's eyes lit up the night, and conversations rippled like foam-crested ocean waves through the crowd. Boys were already at the top of the Ferris wheel, and girls were spending all their money on the carousel.

♥

Ada's Apple Crisp

MAKES 6 SERVINGS

FOR THIS DESSERT ADA used medium-ripe, firm apples, preferring Lodi or Red June over Gravenstein or Yellow Transparent. On really hot days, she would bake the crisp early in the morning, set it in the pantry until evening, then bring it out for supper. If the evening was cooler, she might warm it slightly before serving.

4 cups (about 4 medium) apples,
    pared, cored, and sliced
2/3 cup firmly packed light brown
    sugar
1/2 cup all-purpose flour

1/2 cup quick-cooking rolled oats
1 teaspoon ground cinnamon
3/4 teaspoon ground nutmeg
1/3 cup butter or margarine,
    softened at room temperature

Heat oven to 375°F. Thoroughly grease an 8-by-9-by-2-inch cake pan, or a casserole dish of the same size. Set aside.

Layer apples in the pan. In a medium bowl thoroughly blend the brown sugar, flour, oats, cinnamon, and nutmeg. With your fingertips work the butter or margarine into the dry ingredients (as you might if making pie crust). When well blended, sprinkle over apples.

Bake until apples are tender, juice is bubbling, and topping is golden brown, about 45 minutes. Serve warm and, if desired, topped with a spoonful or two of light cream.

SUMMER APPLE

*In the golden weather of June, apple
trees hang loaded with ripening fruit.
The miracle of harvest is about to begin;
fragrance fills the air.—
A crunching bite reveals white flesh,
tinged yellow-green or pink,
fine-grained, crisp, tender, juicy,*

*pleasantly tart depending on ripeness.
Apples, old-fashioned apples:—June Wealthy,
dark red and tough skinned, tart and sweet;
Stark's Earliest, red blushed on white waxy
skin; Yellow Transparent, a ghost apple in
pale greenish-white; Red June a favorite;
early pie and applesauce.*

—Jane Watson Hopping

♥

Aunt Mabel's Cider Applesauce

MAKES 6 TO 8 SERVINGS

THIS DOUBLE-FLAVORED APPLESAUCE has always been served in our family as a dessert.

*1 quart apple cider
8 cups apples, pared, cored, and
    sliced into eighths*

*½ cup light brown sugar
    (optional)
Powdered sugar, if desired*

In a medium saucepan boil cider to half its original volume. Set aside.

Turn the sliced apples into a large saucepan and cover with the boiled-down cider. Simmer over low heat until apples are tender and cider is nearly absorbed, 20 to 25 minutes. Sweeten to taste with light brown sugar, if you wish. Turn into a heatproof serving dish and set aside to cool. Just before serving, refrigerate for about 10 to 15 minutes (sauce should not be chilled). Serve in dessert dishes, dusted lightly with powdered sugar if desired.

♥

Easy-to-Make Raw Apple and Carrot Cookies

MAKES ABOUT 75 COOKIES

MARTHA, WHOSE HUSBAND WAS a fruit grower, made these cookies for various social events. She and her mother, Aunt Clary, often served them with cold milk and cider to crowds that gathered at the summer apple festival.

¾ cup butter, softened at room
    temperature
2 cups firmly packed light brown
    sugar
2 eggs
3 cups all-purpose flour, sifted
1½ teaspoons baking powder
1½ teaspoons cinnamon
1 teaspoon nutmeg
1 teaspoon cloves

1 teaspoon salt
3 tablespoons apple cider (apple
    juice or milk can be
    substituted)
1½ cups nuts, coarsely chopped
    (walnuts or pecans preferred)
1½ cups apples, unpared, cored,
    and finely chopped
1½ cups carrots, grated

Preheat oven to 375°F. Lightly grease two large baking sheets. Set aside.

In a large bowl cream butter until waxy. Add brown sugar and cream until both are light. Add eggs one at a time, beating well after each addition. Into a second large bowl sift flour a second time with baking powder, cinnamon, nutmeg, cloves, and salt. To the butter mixture add flour mixture, a small amount at a time, alternately with apple cider; stir well after each addition.

Fold nuts, chopped apples, and carrots into the batter. Spoon by teaspoonful onto prepared baking sheets, leaving 1 inch between cookies. Set pan in the center of the oven.

Bake until cookies are well risen, firm to the touch, and lightly browned, 10 to 14 minutes.

The Runaway Boy

WHEN UNCLE BUD WAS about four, he got angry at his father and decided to run away from home. So, as fast as his short, chubby legs would take him, he ran through the pasture, the fields and woods, down the road toward Old Missus Upjohn's place.

It wasn't long before his mother missed him and began to look for him. When she couldn't find him in the yard, down by the chicken coop, or playing with the lambs, she called his father and grandfather to help her look. Soon neighbors and family were looking everywhere, calling Bud. But he was nowhere to be found.

They were still looking when the sun went down. Then he wandered in, smudged and tired; he had come home by himself. His mother, exhausted now with worry and fear, would have spanked him and put him to bed without his supper. But his father picked him up and held him, talking about the dangers of running away. And he asked Uncle Bud where he had been and why he was gone so long. The story rapidly unfolded: Uncle Bud had been out by Old Missus Upjohn's place and in the nearby woods. He had played in the waterfall with a great big toad, and he had scared little fishes off a bed of gravel. When he got tired he picked some berries and lay down on a bed of ferns and went to sleep. When he woke up, he decided to go home. As he came to the pasture fence he saw a fox and threw a rock at it.

Finley Spring - Elk Lick, Pa.

"It made me scared when it was getting dark," Uncle Bud confided to his father, who hugged him and ordered up some supper for him. Then Uncle Bud's father sat by his bed with him and sang a few old mountain songs for him until he was sound asleep.

JANE WATSON HOPPING

When the Little Boy Ran Away

WHEN the little boy ran away from home,
   The birds in the treetops knew,
And they all sang "Stay!"
But he wandered away
   Under the skies of blue.
And the wind came whispering from the tree,
"Follow—follow me!"
And it sang him a song that was soft and sweet,
And scattered the roses before his feet
   That day—that day
   When the little boy ran away.

The violet whispered: "Your eyes are blue
   And lovely and bright to see;
And so are mine, and I'm kin to you,
   So dwell in the light with me!"
But the little boy laughed, while the wind in glee
Said, "Follow me—follow me!"
And the wind called the clouds from their home in the skies,
And said to the violet, "Shut your eyes!"
   That day—that day
   When the little boy ran away.

Then the winds played leapfrog over the hills
   And twisted each leaf and limb;
And all the rivers and all the rills
   Were foaming mad with him!
And it was dark as darkest night could be,
But still came the wind's voice, "Follow me!"
And over the mountain and up from the hollow
Came echoing voices with "Follow him, follow!"
   That awful day
   When the little boy ran away.

Then the little boy cried, "Let me go—let me go!"
    For a scared, scared boy was he!
But the thunder growled from the black cloud, "No!"
    And the wind roared, "Follow me!"
And an old gray Owl from a tree top flew,
Saying, "Who are you-oo? Who are you-oo?"
And the little boy sobbed, "I'm lost away,
And I want to go home where my parents stay!"
    Oh! the awful day
    When the little boy ran away.

Then the Moon looked out from the cloud and said,
    "Are you sorry you ran away?
If I light you home to your trundle-bed,
    Will you stay, little boy, will you stay?"
And the little boy promised—and cried and cried—
He would never leave his mother's side;
And the Moonlight led him over the plain,
And his mother welcomed him home again,
    But oh! what a day
    When the little boy ran away!

—Anonymous

♥

Willie's Favorite Fruit Pockets

MAKES ABOUT 16 POCKETS

THE FLAVOR OF THESE old-fashioned fruit pockets, so basic and yet so delicious, always reminds me of earlier days. The dough is almost a biscuit dough, but not quite; the filling is sweetened primarily with raisins, currants, and citron and is flavored with orange, lemon juice, and spices.

FILLING

¼ *cup dark raisins, chopped*

¼ *cup nuts, chopped (walnuts or pecans preferred)*

¼ *cup currants*

¼ *cup citron, chopped*

2 *tablespoons orange juice, strained*

1 *tablespoon lemon juice, strained*

2 *tablespoons sugar*

½ *teaspoon ground cinnamon*

¼ *teaspoon ground allspice*

¼ *teaspoon ground cloves*

A few grains of salt

In a medium bowl, stir together raisins, nuts, currants, and citron. Add orange and lemon juice, and sugar; thoroughly blend with fruit mixture. Stir in cinnamon, allspice, cloves, and salt. Set aside to meld while making the dough.

DOUGH

2 *cups cake flour, sifted*

2 *teaspoons baking powder*

¼ *teaspoon salt*

2 *tablespoons butter or margarine, softened at room temperature*

⅔ *cup milk*

1 *egg white, lightly beaten, for sealing pockets*

2 *tablespoons powdered sugar for dusting tops of pockets*

Preheat oven to 425°F. Grease a large baking sheet. Set aside.

Into a large bowl sift flour a second time with baking powder and salt. Using a pastry cutter or two table knives, cut the butter or margarine into the flour mixture. Add milk and stir to form a soft dough. Turn onto a lightly floured flat surface. Roll into a sheet ⅓ inch thick. Cut into ovals 4 inches long.

TO ASSEMBLE POCKETS

Place 1 tablespoon of filling on half of each oval. Brush edges of dough with egg white, fold over, and press firmly together. With fingertips, press lightly to flatten. Using a sharp, small-bladed knife, cut three short slits in the top of each pocket to let steam escape. Sprinkle with powdered sugar. Carefully transfer pockets to the prepared baking sheet, spacing them 2 inches apart.

Bake until risen, firm to the touch, and evenly browned, about 12 to 15 minutes.

♥

Uncle Bud's Favorite Dried Fig and Honey Cookies

MAKES ABOUT 3 DOZEN COOKIES

INSTEAD OF MAKING A cake for Uncle Bud's birthday party, Aunt Sue baked plattersful of these fancy drop cookies, which she held back until the evening was waning, then served with coffee while Uncle Bud opened his presents.

1 cup dried figs
½ cup butter or margarine,
   softened at room temperature
¾ cup sugar
½ cup honey at room temperature
2 eggs, well beaten
2 tablespoons milk

2¾ cups flour, sifted
1 teaspoon baking powder
½ teaspoon salt
½ cup sweetened coconut
3 tablespoons orange rind, minced
1 teaspoon lemon extract

Preheat oven to 435°F. Thoroughly grease a baking sheet. Set aside.

Wash figs, then turn them into a small saucepan, cover with water, and simmer for 10 minutes. Drain and cut into small pieces. In a large bowl, cream butter or margarine until waxy, gradually add sugar, and continue creaming until light. Add honey, eggs, and milk and mix thoroughly.

Into a medium bowl sift flour a second time with baking powder and salt. Add flour mixture to butter mixture a little at a time, stirring vigorously after each addition.

Thoroughly fold in figs, coconut, orange rind, and lemon extract. Drop by teaspoonful onto the prepared baking sheet. Set sheet in the center of the oven (to brown cookies evenly). Bake until cookies are well risen, firm to the touch, and a medium brown, 12 to 15 minutes.

NOTE: Check cookies frequently, as baked goods which contain honey brown faster than those made with sugar.

♥

Old-Fashioned Hermits

MAKES ABOUT 3 DOZEN COOKIES

WHEN AUNT SUE MAKES these cookies, Uncle Bud eats them by the handful, sips scalding hot coffee, and reminisces about going on long visits to his grandmother's house and coaxing her to make one batch of hermits after another for his bedtime snack.

⅓ cup butter or margarine,
*   softened at room temperature*
⅔ cup sugar
1 egg
2 tablespoons milk
1¾ cups all-purpose flour, sifted
1 teaspoon baking powder

1 teaspoon ground cinnamon
1 teaspoon freshly grated nutmeg
½ teaspoon cloves
½ teaspoon salt
½ cup bran (oat or wheat bran, as
*   desired)*
⅓ cup dark raisins, minced

Preheat oven to 425°F. Thoroughly grease a large baking sheet. Set aside.

In a large bowl, cream butter or margarine until waxy. Gradually add sugar, and cream until both are light. Add egg and milk and stir until thoroughly blended. Into a medium bowl sift flour a second time with baking powder, cinnamon, nutmeg, cloves, and salt. Add flour mixture, a little at a time, to the butter-sugar mixture and blend well. Fold in the bran and raisins. Cover and chill for 20 to 30 minutes.

When dough is firm enough to handle, turn out onto a lightly floured flat surface. Roll out a sheet of dough ¼ inch thick. Cut with floured cutter. Place on prepared sheet, and set sheet in the center of the oven.

Bake until cookies have risen slightly and are firm to the touch and medium brown, about 10 minutes.

Raymond

When God Sorts Out the Weather and Sends Rain

ALONG ABOUT MID-JUNE THE hay is ready to cut, but the weather gets persnickety! At least that's what my husband, Raymond, says.

Through the years, he has developed a simple philosophy about such things. He just praises the good Lord for irrigating the land, watering down the forests and the steep, rocky corners of the pasture where only wild grasses grow, soaking the young orchard, and dampening the garden.

Such days, he tells people, Jane and I open up the house so the smell of rain can get in, and we build a little fire in the woodstove so we won't get chilled. Then we just sit back and relax. Such a day for me is a workingman's holiday, pure and simple.

And neighbors and friends, who know we will not be working in the fields, often stop by to visit. Some bring slices of salmon for our supper, and leave the rest of their catch to be cured and smoked. We in turn send them home with tender young Golden Acre cabbages and a basket of ripe Bing-Van cherries.

Women in the family, knowing that I work in the fields with Raymond in the summer, sometimes bring a plate of cookies or some rolls.

♥

Salmon with Tartar Sauce

MAKES 6 SERVINGS

IN SUMMER, FISHERMEN IN our area bring in bright-fleshed fresh salmon. Some fry them, others bake or barbecue them; many bring them out to our shop and have them smoked. This recipe for poached fish is one of our favorites.

*2 pounds (6 generous steaks)
    salmon*
*1 medium sweet summer onion,
    sliced*
*1 lemon, sliced (blossom and stem
    ends removed)*
*3 generous sprigs parsley for
    poaching salmon, plus 6 for
    garnish*

1 bay leaf
1½ teaspoons salt
4 black peppercorns
6 strips red pepper for garnish
12 large black pitted olives
Tartar Sauce (recipe follows)

Rinse and dry salmon steaks. Set aside.

On the bottom of a large skillet, layer onion slices, lemon slices, three sprigs of parsley, the bay leaf, salt, and peppercorns. Add water to a depth of 1½ inches and bring to a boil. Arrange fish in a single layer in the skillet. Cover and simmer until fish flakes easily with a fork, 8 to 12 minutes, depending on thickness of steaks.

Transfer fish to a platter and garnish with parsley, red pepper strips, and black olives. Top with Tartar Sauce if you wish, or pass sauce at the table.

♥

Tartar Sauce

MAKES 6 SERVINGS

1 cup mayonnaise
1 tablespoon minced dill pickle
1 tablespoon minced parsley
1 tablespoon minced pimiento

*1 teaspoon grated sweet summer
    onion*
A few grains of white pepper

In a small bowl, thoroughly combine ingredients. Cover and chill until needed.

GOALS

It isn't so much what a man has done,
As what he has tried to do;
It isn't the victories that he has won,
But the storms he has weathered through
With courage and faith and a cheery smile,
That make him a person so well worthwhile.

The man who has fallen has had his dream,
And maybe he saw a star
So high and so bright that his mortal scheme
Fell short of the gleam afar;
But if he has climbed 'til his strength is spent,
Then give him full credit for his intent.

It isn't the goal that a man may win
That counts the most in the score:
But the blows that have proven the worth of him,
In a million tests and more;
For it isn't always the man who leads
Who possesses the strength that the world needs.

—Grace E. Hall

♥

Green and Gold Snap Beans

MAKES 6 TO 8 SERVINGS

AT OUR HOUSE WE MAKE several plantings of both green and golden beans, which extends the picking season. We eat them freshly picked, and freeze and can them. Sometimes we fry a couple of strips of bacon until browned and crisp, blot the extra fat off, crunch them up, and substitute them for the butter called for in this recipe.

1 pound green snap beans
1 pound golden wax beans
½ teaspoon salt
2 tablespoons grated onion
1 tablespoon minced chives

1 tablespoon minced parsley
Pinch of thyme
Dash of grated nutmeg
3 tablespoons melted butter

Wash and break off stem end and pointed end of beans (most beans grown today do not have strings). Snap or cut beans into 1½-inch pieces. Pour 1 cup water into a large saucepan; add salt and bring to a boil over medium heat. Add beans to boiling water, a few at a time. Cover. Bring pot to a boil and cook just until green beans are of a bright, clear-green color. Sprinkle over all minced onion, chives, parsley, thyme, and nutmeg, and continue cooking until beans are tender-crisp, 12 to 15 minutes. Remove from heat, but do not drain off pot liquor. Turn into serving bowl, drizzle butter over all, and serve piping hot.

♥

Golden Acre Cabbage Salad

MAKES 6 SERVINGS

GRANDPA, A SKILLED GARDENER, kept our family in fresh vegetables year-round by working with the seasons and with the seeds and plants that grew best during every time of year. He was quite partial to Golden Acre cabbage, which he grew in the early spring. These crisp, sweet, meal-size cabbages would be ready in early June, when little else was. Golden Acre, Grandpa would say, can stand the heat without splitting. (Cabbage is a cold-weather crop. Heat causes the heads to crack open [split], which makes them strong-flavored and tougher. Such cabbage can be boiled until tender.)

*4 cups cabbage, finely shredded
(about 1 small head, or
½ medium head)*
1 teaspoon salt
*¼ teaspoon freshly ground black
pepper*
½ teaspoon dry mustard
½ teaspoon celery seed
2 tablespoons sugar
*1 tablespoon fresh pimiento pepper,
chopped (store-bought bottled
pimiento can be used)*

1 tablespoon chives, finely minced
3 tablespoons salad oil
*About 2 sprigs of parsley for
garnish (optional)*
*10 or 12 black olives for garnish
(optional)*

Turn shredded cabbage into a large bowl with a cover.

Into a small bowl measure the salt, pepper, mustard, celery seed, sugar, pimiento, chives, and salad oil; blend well and pour over the shredded cabbage. Stir to coat. Cover and refrigerate for about 3 hours. Just before serving, drain cabbage. Turn out into a 1-quart salad bowl and garnish, if desired, with sprigs of parsley and black olives.

♥

Effie's Poppyseed Rolls

MAKES ABOUT 3 DOZEN ROLLS

EFFIE MADE THESE fancy little rolls for a grange supper; they were so popular she continued to make them, on request, for many socials. When she made basketsful for the church supper, the pastor praised her rolls from the pulpit!

2 tablespoons granulated yeast
1½ cups lukewarm milk (only raw
milk need be scalded first)
¼ cup sugar, and more for
sprinkling on unbaked rolls
1 tablespoon salt
3 eggs
¼ cup butter or margarine,
softened at room temperature,
plus 4 tablespoons, melted, for
brushing an unbaked rolls

7 to 7½ cups all-purpose flour,
plus a little more as needed for
kneading
A generous sprinkling of poppyseeds

Preheat oven to 425°F. Grease a large baking sheet; set aside.

In a large bowl dissolve yeast in ½ cup warm water (105° to 115°F), letting it stand until a foamy head forms. Add lukewarm milk, sugar, salt, eggs, softened butter, and *4 cups* of the flour. Beat until a thick, smooth batter is formed. Stir in enough of the *remaining* flour to make a soft dough that is easy to handle.

Turn dough out onto a lightly floured flat surface and knead until smooth and elastic, about 5 to 8 minutes. Place in a large, well-greased bowl; turn greased side up. Cover and let rise in a warm place until doubled in bulk, about 1½ hours. Dough has risen enough when an impression made with the finger remains in the dough.

Using fingers or fist, punch down the dough without working it too much. Shape bits of dough, without kneading, into 1-inch balls. Place on prepared baking sheet. Brush rolls with melted butter and sprinkle with poppyseeds and sugar. Set in a warm place and let rolls rise until trebled in bulk (the dough will be very light).

NOTE: Letting dough rise too much can make it fall. When well risen, set pan of rolls in the center of the oven.

Bake until puffed and light golden brown, 12 to 15 minutes. Serve rolls piping hot. Freeze those left over for another meal. Wrap in foil and reheat in the oven at 350°F.

♥

Marshmallow Bavarian Cream

MAKES 8 SERVINGS

IN THE EARLY THIRTIES women in our family learned to make numerous gelatin salads and desserts. Martha loved to put shaved almonds in this dish, but it's delicious when made with almost any variety of nut.

1 cup unsweetened crushed canned pineapple, drained and the juice reserved

1 package orange-flavored gelatin

1 cup marshmallow cream

1 cup almonds, shaved

1 cup heavy cream, whipped until stiff

Into a medium saucepan measure the drained pineapple juice. Add enough boiling water to make 2 cups of liquid. Heat to boiling. Empty dry gelatin into a large bowl; pour the boiling liquid over it and stir until thoroughly dissolved. Set aside to cool, first at room temperature to lukewarm, then in the refrigerator, until the mixture has the consistency of an egg white, about 30 to 40 minutes. Beat with a rotary or electric beater until fluffy. Fold in the marshmallow cream, pineapple, and almonds. Fold in the stiffly whipped cream. Spoon into eight individual molds and chill until firm, 1 to 1½ hours. Just before serving, turn out onto small dessert plates.

UP
AND DOWN
OLD
BRANDYWINE

IN ALMOST EVERY PART of the country, there are special streams, creeks, cricks, branches, and fast- or slow-running rivers that draw people to them, that enfold in their cool, green embrace those who need quiet rest and a chance to find themselves. I've always thought that there is a sanctified quality about such places, and that those who come to soak up the natural loveliness, fish, picnic, and visit go away blessed.

ALONG THE CREEK

How lovely to see the broad leaves
of the wild grape vine, its tendrils
winding through the branches of a tall
quaking aspen tree, one that sends deep,
dappled shadows across the creek.
Or, wade the ford below the dam,
knee deep in dancing water.
And pick purple-staining berries from
a bramble-bush.

—Jane Watson Hopping

A Fourth of July Picnic on the American River

DURING THE THIRTIES, PEOPLE didn't have much money for recreation, so, as many folks used to say, we made our own fun. And the Fourth of July was surely a day for fun!

First we went eight miles to town to watch the parade, then had a picnic and listened to the old-time fiddlers play—sometimes Uncle Arch played a tune or two with them. We children clogged on the back of a farm truck until we were worn out.

When it got too hot in the late afternoon, we went back home to rest, deep in the cool canyon where we lived. As the late-afternoon temperature began to drop, Mother, Daddy, and Grandpa went out to do chores. When that was done, we gathered up our baskets of prepared food, our bathing suits, towels, and utensils for cooking over an open fire. Grandpa took some of his finely chopped kindling to start the campfire.

By the time we got to the sandbar, a narrow shoal formed by currents along the shore of the river, most of the family—aunts, uncles, cousins, and those friends we called Aunty or Uncle—were already there. Uncle Arch usually built the rock-lined circle for the fire and laid it to be started at dusk. Most of us wore our bathing suits to the river under our clothes, so all we had to do was peel off the outer layer and jump in. That is, most everyone jumped in; our father made us wait until he was ready and then wade in. Then he sat like a vigilant lifeguard while Sheila and I played in the water near the shore. Later, Mother would stand waist-deep between us and the far riverbank so that we could play in deeper water, and so that she could teach us how to swim. Not until the shadows began to fall along the river bank did she lead us out of the water; and only then did our father relax his vigil to swim powerfully back and forth across the river several times.

Just before dark, three planks would be set up on sawhorses for a table; one of the women would put a sheet over them, and soon the festivities would begin. Some women began to cook in the coals of the fire; others had brought cold food. Uncle Arch and Grandpa tended the fire, and one or the other of them stayed with it at all times so that children could not play near it and get hurt, and so that the sparks could be controlled. They made a huge five-gallon pot of coffee, which sent its fragrance all up and down the sandbar. After supper, when the women had put all the food away and we were all out of our wet suits and back into our clothes, the men took out a guitar and a violin, and soon everyone was sitting about the fire singing the old songs—"The Isle of Capri," "Moonlight Bay," "I'll Take You Home Again, Kathleen," and "Sweet Genevieve."

Long after dark, just before the children were put to bed, someone would go down to the river and take out the several gallons of cold milk that had been placed there earlier, and some of the women would set out cookies or a cake for a snack. After that children would be put down near their parents on blankets over the sand, and covered with more blankets. Soon everyone under seven years old was asleep. Older children played cards in the light of the fire, quietly so as not to wake the little ones. Grown-ups often sat around the fire and talked until cool breezes began to blow and the night was still. Then, refreshed by the close companionship, relieved for a while from the burdens of the day, they would quietly pick up their children and possessions and steal away home.

♥

Aunt Sue's Salmon Macaroni Salad

MAKES ABOUT 8 SERVINGS

IN THE THIRTIES, when we were growing up, any dish made with pasta was a treat. Usually Aunt Irene or Aunt Pauline brought such experimental dishes to family picnics or potlucks. All of us enjoyed the newfangled foods, except Grandpa, who with Midwestern bias much preferred corn or potatoes.

2 cups elbow macaroni

About 1½ cups shredded salmon
(the contents of a 1-pound can,
liquid, bones, and skin
removed)

4 tablespoons lemon juice

1 cup sweet pickles, chopped

4 tablespoons chives or scallions,
finely chopped

About ½ cup mayonnaise or salad
dressing, more as desired

1 teaspoon salt

⅛ teaspoon freshly ground black
pepper

⅛ teaspoon paprika

Cook macaroni in boiling salt water until tender. Drain and chill. Add to the chilled macaroni the salmon, lemon juice, pickles, and chives or scallions. Moisten with mayonnaise, stirring gently with two forks. Adjust seasoning to taste with salt, pepper, and paprika. Mix again lightly with forks. Turn into a covered casserole dish. Refrigerate to chill.

♥

Aunt Irene's Stuffed Tomatoes

MAKES 6 SERVINGS

THESE COLORFUL, DELICIOUS STUFFED tomatoes were prepared at the river just before serving. Aunt Irene kept her tomatoes and the filling in an ice chest.

6 medium to large firm-ripe
tomatoes

1 pint cottage cheese, more if you
wish

½ cup celery, finely diced (Aunt
Irene used the light-colored
center stalks for the filling and
reserved the tender young
leaves for garnish)

1-pound can of whole black olives,
finely sliced (reserve 6 whole
olives for garnish)

Peel tomatoes; cut a slice from the top and remove pulp (set pulp aside to use in soups or salads). Chill tomato shells.

Combine cottage cheese, celery, and sliced olives. Chill. Just before serving, fill shells and carefully place on a platter or tray. Top each tomato with a black olive and garnish tray with celery leaves.

♥

Mother's Coconut Angel Cake

MAKES ONE 10-INCH CAKE

IN SPRING AND EARLY summer, Mother made angel cakes of all sorts. We ate them topped with strawberries and whipped cream, and with home-churned ice cream. Sometimes she fancied them up for a special occasion like a summer picnic.

10 egg whites
½ teaspoon salt
1 teaspoon cream of tartar
1½ cups sugar
1¼ cups cake flour, sifted 3 times

1 teaspoon vanilla extract
1 cup coconut, shredded (pulled apart until finely divided)
Thin Powdered-Sugar Glaze (recipe follows)

Preheat oven to 350°F. Set out a 10-inch angel cake pan.

Beat the egg whites with salt until frothy; add the cream of tartar and beat until stiff but not dry. Fold in the sugar, 1 tablespoon at a time. Gradually fold in the flour, then the vanilla.

Cover the bottom of the angel cake pan (unoiled) with cake batter, and sprinkle generously with shredded coconut. Cover with batter, then add a second layer of coconut. Continue layering until all coconut has been used, topping off with a layer of batter.

Bake until well risen, light golden, and firm to the touch, about 1 to 1½ hours. Remove from the oven and immediately turn pan upside down on a wire rack, letting the cake hang in the pan upside down until thoroughly cooled. Using a thin spatula, loosen from outside edge and from center cone, and carefully take the cake out of the pan. Serve as is or topped with Thin Powdered-Sugar Glaze. (If you glaze the cake let some of the glaze stream down the sides.)

♥

Thin Powdered-Sugar Glaze

MAKES JUST ENOUGH TO LIGHTLY GLAZE ONE 10-INCH CAKE

1 cup powdered sugar
1 tablespoon milk, plus 1 more
  tablespoon as needed

½ teaspoon vanilla

Sift sugar into a medium bowl. Add milk and vanilla; stir until well blended, then thin as needed with additional tablespoon of milk.

ð

From AMERICA

HIGH o'erlooking sea and land,
  America!
Trustfully with outheld hand,
  America!
Thou dost welcome all in quest
Of thy freedom, peace and rest
Every exile is thy guest,
  America! America!

—James Whitcomb Riley

An Afternoon Ripe with Heat

ON THE FARM THERE are no endless lazy days of summer. Country folk are wedded to the land, and to the harvest. Even so, when the hot afternoon sun shimmers across the earth, humankind and the beasts of the field all settle down in shaded depths, to sleep, to catch a wayward breeze, or to watch a hawk becalmed in a cloudless azure sky.

Then, refreshed, everyone goes back to work, following where dusty lanes lead, men on foot, on tractors and trucks, or on wagons, and with them women and sometimes children. High above the wayside weeds, grasshoppers leap to cling to ripening grasses and saw out a tune with whirring wings. From the fields there comes the melodious call of a killdee.

ON THE GRASSHOPPER AND THE CRICKET

THE poetry of earth is never dead!
   When all the birds are faint with the hot sun
   And hide in cooling trees, a voice will run
From hedge to hedge about the new-mown mead
   That is the grasshopper's; he takes the lead
   In summer luxury; he has never done
   With his delights, for when tired out with fun
He rests at ease beneath some pleasant weed.
The poetry of earth is ceasing never:
   On a lone winter evening, when the frost
   Has wrought a silence, from the stove there shrills
The cricket's song, in warmth increasing ever,
   And seems to one in drowsiness half lost,
   The grasshopper's among some grassy hills.

—John Keats

JANE WATSON HOPPING

♥

Chilled Baked Salmon

MAKES 8 SERVINGS

THIS IS A DELICIOUS summertime treat. Fish brought back from the rivers or the coast are fresh, brightly colored, and richly flavored. Chill leftovers for making sandwiches or salads.

*3- to 5-pound fish, boned
    (instructions for boning follow)*
*Butter or margarine, softened at
    room temperature*
1½ teaspoons salt

*⅛ teaspoon freshly ground black
    pepper*
¼ cup celery leaves
A generous sprig of parsley
A snippet of chives

Lay out chilled fish and bone it, then refrigerate until ready to bake. Thoroughly butter a heatproof baking dish; set aside.

Preheat oven to 350°F. Brush the boned fish lightly on all sides with melted butter or margarine; sprinkle with salt and pepper. Fill cavity with celery leaves, sprig of parsley, and snippet of chives (don't chop). Place in prepared dish and cover with buttered waxed paper (or a buttered piece of foil).

Bake until the fish flakes or until the internal temperature in the thickest part reaches 140°F.

INSTRUCTIONS FOR BONING

To bone a whole fish, split the body open beginning at the belly side, cutting through the fish to the top of the back; take care not to cut the skin along the bone. Lay the fish out flat, meat side up, still hooked together at the back. Remove the large bones, cutting them free with a sharp, thin-bladed knife. Use tweezers to remove small bones.

When all bones have been removed, lay the two sides of fish together again. Chill. When ready to bake, open the sides of the fish again, just enough to insert herbs.

♥

Dilled Cucumbers and Sweet Onions in Sour Cream

MAKES 6 OR MORE SERVINGS

WHEN THOROUGHLY CHILLED, THIS delicious dish hits the spot on a hot summer evening. Sometimes Mother added a little of the tender tips from her dill weed, finely minced.

6 medium cucumbers, peeled and
   thinly sliced
1 large white, sweet summer onion,
   peeled and thinly sliced
1 pint sour cream

1 tablespoon minced dill weed
   (optional)
1/2 teaspoon salt
1/8 teaspoon white pepper (black
   pepper can be substituted)

Into a medium bowl put prepared cucumbers and onion. Dress with sour cream seasoned with dill weed (if desired), salt, and pepper. Chill thoroughly.

♥

Garden-Fresh Grabbled Potatoes with Herbs

MAKES 4 TO 6 SERVINGS

THERE IS NOTHING MORE delicious than new potatoes, not quite as large as eggs, which have been grabbled out of the hill, preboiled with the skins on, then sautéed with a little butter and fresh herbs.

12 new potatoes (waxy red
   preferred)
2 tablespoons butter or margarine,
   more if desired
1 tablespoon fresh parsley, minced

1 tablespoon fresh chives, minced
1/2 teaspoon fresh thyme, minced
1/4 teaspoon salt
1/8 teaspoon freshly ground black
   pepper

Set out a large, heavy-bottomed frying pan.

Wash new potatoes carefully so as not to scrape the tender skins. Put them in a large saucepan and cover with water; bring to a boil and cook 8 to 10 minutes. Drain.

Turn the potatoes into the frying pan and add butter or margarine; when butter is melted, turn potatoes about in the pan until they are coated. Sprinkle parsley, chives, thyme, salt, and pepper over potatoes and continue cooking until potatoes look a little browned (test with a fork for doneness). When done, transfer to a medium platter. Serve immediately.

Vine-Ripened Red Raspberries Topped with Chilled Heavy Cream

MAKES 6 GENEROUS SERVINGS

WHEN MOTHER SERVED FRESH raspberries, she did not chill them. She thought the flavor was better when they were kept in a cool place until needed, only lightly rinsed, and served at room temperature with very cold cream spooned over them.

3 pints red raspberries *1 pint heavy cream, chilled*
Sugar (optional)

Prepare berries just before dinner; only a very short time should pass between rinsing and eating them.

Put one pint of the berries at a time in a wire sieve; rinse for only a few seconds under cold tap water. Drain. Turn berries into individual 1-cup serving dishes; sweeten if you wish. Place each dish as you fill it on a large tray. When all dishes are filled, put the tray of berries in a cool place. Just before serving, spoon 3 tablespoons icy cream over them.

Beneath a Silver Willow Tree

THERE IS NOTHING QUITE so colorful and zesty as a fair or festival in California. Along with the hurrahs and hoopla, one catches the scent of Mexico, found where gaily dressed women sell enchiladas, burritos, and tamales, the fragrances melding with those of Italy —fresh pork, fennel seed, garlic, and oregano. Hamburger and hot dog stands abound. Everywhere there are vendors making wispy, sweetheart-pink cotton candy, pies and turnovers, doughnuts, fried chicken and corndogs, soda pop and ice cream.

The sound of music fills the air, brass bands play Sousa marches; old-time musicians play venerable mountain ballads that are reminiscent of Tennessee and Kentucky; the jeweled tones of barbershop quartets bring to mind handlebar mustaches and beautiful mustache cups; and in the distance are the sounds of singing and dancing, the joyous melody of melded cultures.

As the late-afternoon sun hangs low in the west, sending hot rays through the crowds of people, men perspire, women complain, and children grow tired and fussy.

Folks of all ages begin to seek out the sheltering canopies of the great weeping willows and the cool dense shade beneath their boughs. It isn't long before children and old men are asleep on blankets on the ground, and old women sit on folding chairs in clusters, chatting with those they know and those whom they have just met, as hours pass and the heat wanes.

When twilight begins to creep in and the loud excitement of the day mellows, one can hear the music of the carousel and watch the moon rise.

❧

REMEMBERING

COME love, along with me
back to the center of memory
where summer was night
beneath a silver willow tree
and music, half-heard,
shimmering across the lake.

Strauss and Romberg, Youmans, Friml,
Hoagy Carmichael and distant Sousa;
fireworks far away, more seen than sound;
bright, then pale, trailing to the ground;
illusions
melting like hand-cranked vanilla on our tongues;
cool and sweet, as innocent and delicious
as an uncut melon newly picked
from a block of ice.
As we did in those days, making memories,
like children, we spit the seeds into summer night.

Share another slice with me
while you read again to me
the latest letter from our grandson.
Come, love, with me
back to the summer of our memory.

—Alvin Reiss

THE LAZY DAYS OF SUMMER COOKBOOK

♥

An Old-Fashioned Cottage Cheese Apple Pie with Butter-Crust Pastry

MAKES ONE 9-INCH PIE

THIS PIE, KEPT CHILLED until the moment it was to be served, was in the past brought on ice to picnics by young women and old to share with men they loved.

Butter-Crust Pastry (recipe follows)
2 eggs, beaten lightly
¾ cup sugar
⅛ teaspoon salt
½ cup heavy cream, scalded
¾ cup milk, scalded

1 teaspoon vanilla extract
1 cup dry-curd cottage cheese
1½ cups apples, thinly sliced
¼ teaspoon ground cinnamon
¼ teaspoon freshly grated nutmeg

Make pastry and chill. Just before preparing the filling, remove from the refrigerator. Set out a 9-inch pie pan.

Turn pastry out onto a lightly floured flat surface. Roll to ⅛ inch thick; fold in half and lay in the pie pan. Trim pastry, leaving a 1-inch overhang. Fold the overhang under until the edge is even with the edge of the pan, and crimp. Set aside while preparing the filling.

In a medium bowl, combine eggs, *½ cup* of the sugar, salt, cream, milk, vanilla, and cottage cheese. In a second medium bowl, combine apples with cinnamon, nutmeg, and remaining *¼ cup sugar*. Turn apples into pastry-lined pan and bake in 425° oven for 15 minutes; reduce heat to 325°F, pour custard mixture over apples, and continue baking until lightly browned and custard is firm (insert a knife blade into the custard; if it comes out clean, the custard is done).

Cool to room temperature and serve. Refrigerate leftovers.

♥

Butter-Crust Pastry

MAKES ENOUGH FOR ONE 9-INCH SINGLE CRUST PIE

1 cup all-purpose flour
½ teaspoon salt

½ cup cold butter

In a medium bowl, combine the flour and salt; cut the butter in until mixture is reduced to pea-size pieces. Sprinkle on *2 tablespoons or more of cold water;* blend with a fork just until all particles cling together, forming a ball. Refrigerate until ready to roll out.

♥

Economical Surprise Pie with Vanilla Wafer Crust

MAKES ONE 9-INCH PIE

GIRLS LIKE YOUNG MARTHA loved to take this pie to a social or some other special event. And no wonder: Young men heaped praise on them, and hung around teasing and trying to persuade the girls to let them have the first big slice of pie.

Vanilla Wafer Crust (recipe
* follows)*
1 ½ cups milk
¼ cup sugar
¼ teaspoon salt
1 ½ tablespoons cornstarch
1 egg yolk

1 tablespoon butter or margarine
½ teaspoon vanilla extract
2 ounces semisweet chocolate
⅓ cup pecans, finely chopped
Sweetened Whipped Cream (recipe
* follows)*

Prepare Vanilla Wafer Crust, line a 9-inch pie pan with it, bake, and cool before making filling.

To make filling, pour *1 cup* of the milk into the top of a double boiler, set over boiling water, and scald. In a small bowl, combine sugar, salt, cornstarch, and *remaining ½ cup* milk. Stirring constantly, add sugar-milk mixture to hot milk, continuing to stir as the filling slowly thickens. When thick, cover; continue cooking without stirring for another 5 minutes.

Meanwhile, put the egg yolk in a small bowl. While stirring constantly, pour about *1 cup* of the hot, thick filling into the yolk and blend well. Return egg-filling mixture to the main batch of filling in the top of the double boiler and cook 1 minute longer. Blend in the butter or margarine and vanilla. Remove the pan of filling from base of double boiler and set aside to cool. While the filling cools, melt chocolate in a small saucepan, spread it over the bottom of the crust, and sprinkle pecans over the chocolate. Pour cooled filling into prepared pie shell and top with Sweetened Whipped Cream. Serve lightly chilled. Refrigerate leftovers.

♥

Vanilla Wafer Crust

1½ cups vanilla wafers, finely crushed

3 tablespoons sugar

⅓ cup butter or margarine, melted

Heat oven to 350°F. In a small bowl, combine ingredients. Press mixture firmly and evenly against bottom and sides of an ungreased 9-inch pie pan.

Bake until crust has firmed up and has begun to brown very lightly, about 10 minutes. Remove from oven and cool before filling.

♥

Sweetened Whipped Cream

MAKES 2⅓ CUPS

1 cup heavy cream
¼ cup sugar

1 teaspoon vanilla

Beat the cream until it is well fluffed and begins to mound. Add sugar a little at a time, beating after each addition. Add the vanilla and beat a few times to blend. Continue beating as necessary until cream is glossy. Serve in dollops on desserts.

♥

Ada's Blueberry Pie with Double-Crust Egg Pastry

MAKES ONE 9-INCH PIE

WHEN BLUEBERRIES WERE IN season, Ada went often to Will Bates' house to visit with the old bachelor, who seldom left his home, and to take him a blueberry pie or two. His old eyes would light up and he would dig into one of the pies with the enthusiasm of a teenage boy.

Double-Crust Egg Pastry (recipe
follows)
4 cups blueberries, rinsed lightly in
a sieve under cold tap water

3 tablespoons tapioca
⅔ cup sugar
¼ teaspoon salt (optional)

Make the pastry and chill before assembling the filling.

Preheat oven to 425°F. Set out a 9-inch pie pan.

In a medium bowl, combine the blueberries and tapioca. Add sugar and stir again. Set aside.

Remove pastry from refrigerator. Turn out onto a lightly floured flat surface. Divide the pastry in half; roll out one piece to ⅛ inch and line the pie pan with it, leaving a 1-inch overhang. Set aside. Roll out the top crust to ⅛ inch. Turn the blueberry filling into the bottom crust, moisten the edge of the crust and fold overhang over; press down with your fingertips. Fold the top crust in half and arrange over the blueberry filling. Moisten again and press edges together to seal. Trim edges even with the outside edge of the pie pan and crimp. Cut slits in the top to let steam escape.

Set the pie in the center of the oven over a baking sheet to catch drips. (Save an old baking sheet to use as a drip pan under fruit pies.) Bake until the crust is golden brown, about 50 minutes. Set on a wire rack to cool to room temperature. Serve warm or cold.

♥

Double-Crust Egg Pastry

MAKES ENOUGH FOR ONE 9-INCH DOUBLE-CRUST PIE

1 cup butter or margarine, chilled
2 cups all-purpose flour, plus flour
for shaping and rolling

1 teaspoon salt
2 eggs
2 teaspoons cider vinegar

In a medium bowl, work the butter or margarine with a pastry cutter or your fingertips into the combined flour and salt until the mixture is coarse, with lumps the size of peas. In a small bowl, beat the eggs, about *4 tablespoons cold water,* and vinegar into a froth, and stir into the flour mixture. Gather the dough roughly into a ball; place on a floured surface and knead just enough to make a smooth ball that can be handled without its sticking to the hands. Cover and chill until needed.

AN OLD FRIEND

HEY, Old Midsummer! are you here again,
     With all your harvest-store of olden joys,—
Vast overhanging meadow-lands of rain,
And drowsy dawns, and noons when golden grain
     Nods in the sun, and lazy truant boys
Drift ever listlessly adown the day,
Too full of joy to rest, and dreams to play.

The same old Summer, with the same old smile
     Beaming upon us in the same old way
We knew in childhood! Though a weary while
Since that far time, yet memories reconcile
     The heart with odorous breaths of clover hay;
And again I hear the doves, and the sun streams through
The old barn door just as it used to do.

And so it seems like welcoming a friend—
     An old, old friend, upon his coming home
From some far country—coming home to spend
Long, loitering days with me: And I extend
     My hand in rapturous glee:—And so you've come!—
Ho, I'm so glad! Come in and take a chair:
Well, this is just like old times, I declare!

—James Whitcomb Riley

A LANGUID
ATMOSPHERE,
A LAZY
BREEZE

~~~~~~~~~~

A dreamy day; and tranquilly I lie
At anchor from all storms of mental strain;
With absent visions, gazing at the sky,
"Like one that hears the rain."

—From A SUMMER AFTERNOON
James Whitcomb Riley

AT THE END OF a warm summer day, various members of the family used to gather to visit, to sit in the shade of our old maple tree and reminisce and share a little, while the sun sank behind the barn and the air began to cool. Sometimes, when conversation failed, Ada would sing some of the old church songs she had learned as a child: "Love Lifted Me," "I've Anchored in Jesus," and "He Keeps Me Singing," at which point most of the family joined in.

THERE'S within my heart a melody
Jesus whispers sweet and low,
Fear not, I am with thee, peace be still,
In all of life's ebb and flow.

Once the music began, there was no stopping it. All of us would coax Uncle Bud to whistle, to make the old tunes dip and trill. Mama's favorites were "Listen to the Mockingbird" and "The Rose of Tralee." Grandpa loved to hear "Annie Laurie" and would hum a counterpoint to the whistling. Sheila and I always coaxed Uncle Bud to whistle every bird call he knew: the song of the whippoorwill, jay, meadowlark, and others. When he stopped, we would coax him to whistle just a little more.

Instead, he would tell us stories about his childhood in the woods, and about his father and mother. Sometimes he would recite his favorite poem, which he said he had learned when he was twelve because it reminded him so much of himself.

And when twilight began to darken and the moon's brilliance shone through the night, young folks gathered up their children, while older folks talked a little longer. Then, calling out a few good-byes, we carefully made our way through the darkness to our cars. As always, someone noted that it was certainly a blessing to have it cool down at night.

An Old-Time Wild Blackberry Social

AUGUST's hottest sun shines down
On the fields and silent river,
And wakes the harvest-fly's shrill song
Where berries in the bushes quiver.

—May Aiken

BY MIDSUMMER, COUNTRY FOLKS, adults and children, were eager to lay the seasonal work aside and socialize a bit. One family or another would begin to call the neighbors and friends to invite them over for a blackberry social.

The host family would put up tables under some trees. Great crocks for the punch would be washed out, and huge coffeepots scrubbed down. On the appointed day, when the sun began to dip into the west and all the chores were finished, company began to arrive, bringing not only berry pies, plain or with lattice crusts, but crunches, cobblers, and any other blackberry dish the women could devise. Those families who didn't have access to wild berries often brought mouth-watering, crisp-crusted peach or apple pies, and a smiling apology.

Children ate pie, played hard, and ate more pie, especially the boys. Girls tended to settle down together to share summer secrets. The laden tables drew the men and boys until all were dipping first into this pie pan and then into the other. Some bragged on their women's pies; others ate quietly and went back for seconds. Needless to say, most of the women were busy, pouring coffee, dipping punch, and wiping children's faces. Even so, their gossip flowed in murmured tones, punctuated with lighthearted laughter.

When no one could eat another bite, the women and girls cleared away the food, traded pies, and gave away the extras to bachelors and older folks who lived alone. Now boxes and baskets of string beans and cucumbers, corn and apples, and early peaches were unloaded and passed around to anyone who wanted them.

Usually someone brought a fiddle or guitar, a mandolin or zither, and in no time music filled the air. Young folks danced a bit, older women talked about family matters, and men talked about the price of hogs, wheat, corn, and livestock—and about the weather. When the women had the children all settled down for the ride home, with many thank-yous to their hosts, all shook hands or hugged each other and went their way.

ॐ

THE HUMAN TOUCH

'TIS the human touch in this world that counts,
The touch of your hand and mine,
Which means far more to the fainting heart
Than shelter and bread and wine;
For shelter is gone when the night is o'er,
And bread lasts only a day,
But the touch of the hand and the sound of the voice
Sing on in the soul alway.

—Spencer Michael Free

♥

Wild Blackberry Pie with Flaky Lattice Crust

MAKES ONE 9-INCH PIE (6 SERVINGS)

By MID-AUGUST, BERRIES ALONG the creek and in the pasture hang ripe, coaxing one to stay and pick enough and then more. In no time, a row of richly colored blackberry jam appears on the pantry shelf, then quarts of berry nectar, and several slowly cooling lattice-crusted pies.

Light Crispy Pie Crust (recipe
follows)
2½ tablespoons tapioca
⅔ cup sugar
3½ cups blackberries, stems
removed, rinsed lightly under a
light stream of cold tap water

1 tablespoon butter, melted
Pinch of salt (optional)

Prepare pastry before assembling pie. Cover and chill until needed.

Preheat oven to 450°F. Set out a 9-inch pie pan.

In a medium bowl, combine tapioca, sugar, berries, butter, and salt; let stand.

Remove dough from refrigerator; turn out onto a lightly floured flat surface. Cut in half; cover one half and return to refrigerator. Roll the other half ⅛ inch thick. Line the pie pan, allowing pastry to extend ½ inch beyond the edge of the pan. Moisten edge and fold inward, even with the rim of the pan. Moisten edge again. Turn berry filling into the lined pan.

Roll remaining chilled half of dough into a rectangular sheet ⅛ inch thick. Cut into strips; lay half the strips across the top of the pie (don't press them down). Weave in the remaining strips to form a lattice. Flute the rim with your fingertips.

Bake in 450°F oven for 10 minutes, then decrease heat to 350°F and bake for 30 minutes more. Serve warm, topped with a scoop of ice cream, if you wish.

♥

Light Crispy Pie Crust

MAKES ENOUGH FOR ONE 9-INCH DOUBLE-CRUST PIE

2½ cups all-purpose flour, sifted
¼ teaspoon baking powder

½ teaspoon salt
⅔ cup chilled butter or margarine

Into a large bowl sift flour a second time with baking powder and salt. Using a pastry cutter or two table knives, cut butter into flour until texture is granular, resembling small peas. Add about ½ cup cold water, a small amount at a time, mixing lightly with a fork. Handling as little as possible, turn dough out onto a lightly floured flat surface. Shape into a ball. Roll in waxed paper and chill thoroughly before rolling.

♥

Deep-Dish Wild Blackberry Crunch with Vanilla Wafer Topping

MAKES 6 SERVINGS

TOWARD THE END OF July, our fields are dappled with berry pickers. Mark and Colleen, my son-in-law and daughter, pick in the back pasture, filling bowls full of thumb-size berries, which Colleen makes into jam, cobblers, and pies for the freezer.

Lisa, a dear friend, comes over after dinner, bringing the children to play beside her while she picks, and to pick a few berries themselves. Rachel, who is five, picks handfuls and drops them into her own or her mother's bucket. Naomi, who at two still has trouble with sentences, grins and joyfully says over and over, "pickun," "pickun." She likes to pull a few berries off the vine, drop them into her bucket, and then eat them immediately, staining her mouth and hands with sweet purple juice. When the berries are gone, she puts the bucket on her head for a hat.

Vanilla Wafer Topping (recipe
    follows)
4 cups fresh blackberries
2 tablespoons lemon juice, strained

⅔ cup sugar
2 tablespoons tapioca
½ teaspoon salt (optional)
1 tablespoon butter

Prepare topping first and set aside until needed.

Preheat oven to 350°F. Thoroughly grease a 1½- to 2-quart casserole dish and set aside.

Gently pour blackberries into a sieve; lightly rinse for a few seconds under a small stream of cold tap water. (Ripe blackberries are very fragile, so handle as little as possible.)

Turn berries into a large bowl and sprinkle lemon juice over them. In a small bowl combine the sugar, tapioca, and salt, and gently fold into the berries. Turn into the prepared casserole dish. Sprinkle Vanilla Wafer Topping liberally over the top. Place in the center of the oven. *(Put a cookie sheet underneath the casserole to catch drips.)*

Bake until berries are bubbling and top is golden brown, about 45 minutes. Serve while still warm.

♥

Vanilla Wafer Topping

MAKES ENOUGH TOPPING FOR ONE CRUNCH

⅓ cup sugar
⅔ cup all-purpose flour
1 cup vanilla wafers, crushed with
*   a rolling pin*

⅓ cup butter or margarine

In a medium bowl combine ingredients. Using your fingertips, work together until butter is well blended with sugar, flour, and wafer crumbs.

♥

Wild Blackberry Cordial

MAKES ABOUT 2 GALLONS

OLD-TIME PEOPLE THOUGHT BLACKBERRY juice was a good tonic in winter; they gave it by the spoonful to children for upset stomachs and drank it hot or cold as a beverage.

*Ripe wild blackberries, lightly
   rinsed, mashed, and strained
   through coarse cheesecloth*
*2 cups sugar for each quart of raw,
   strained juice*

4 teaspoons grated nutmeg
*1 tablespoon crushed stick
   cinnamon*
2 teaspoons whole cloves
4 tablespoons vanilla extract

Measure strained juice into a medium or large saucepan, as needed.

Add sugar (2 cups for each quart of juice). In a thick muslin bag, tie the grated nutmeg, stick cinnamon, and cloves. Simmer juice and spices over low heat until blended, about 25 minutes. Take saucepan off heat and remove the bag of spices. Stir in the vanilla.

Pour into thoroughly scrubbed and sterilized quart jars to ½ inch of the top. Put on lids which have been heated to boiling. Tightly screw on scrubbed and sterilized rings. Process jars in a boiling-water bath (instructions follow) for 15 minutes. Place hot jars on a clean towel (berry juice stains, so use an old towel), away from drafts. If rings seem loose, don't try to tighten them, as that will loosen the seal. When jars are cold and sealed, remove the rings. Wash and dry them to prevent rusting. Store the cordial in a cool, dark place.

To serve, pour as is over ice, or dilute with water to taste before serving over ice.

USING A BOILING-WATER-BATH CANNER

A commercial canner is inexpensive to buy and easy to use. Set the canner, filled about one-third full of hot water, over high heat; bring to a boil. Put a teakettle of water on to heat. When the jars are filled and tightly sealed, place them in the wire basket that came with the canner. Submerge jars in the hot-water bath, leaving room between them for the water to circulate. *If the jars are cold, warm them before placing in the canner to avoid cracking.*

Before starting to count the time (15 minutes for this recipe), let the water return to a rapid boil. Keep it boiling through the entire processing period. If water evaporates, replace it from the teakettle.

The Roadside Produce Stand

NOT LONG AGO, ROADSIDE stands were commonplace along highways and country roads across the nation. Folks who grew vegetables and fruits, even on just a few acres, could make a little income during the harvest seasons of spring, summer, and fall. Daughters not needed for canning and preserving tended the stands. Fathers and sons often ran a little produce route, taking extra produce by the truckload into town to sell from house to house.

Buyers could be sure to find tree-ripened fruit and tender vegetables picked early in the morning while the dew was still on them. In the spring there were freshly pulled carrots, beets, and rhubarb for eating and making pickles, sauces, and pies. In late May there were fresh garden peas, red and green leaf lettuce, turnips, spinach, and Swiss chard. By mid-June there were crisp cabbages and luscious, big strawberries for eating out of hand or making into shortcakes or jam.

By August, tomatoes, summer squash, and cucumbers, both for slicing at table and for making pickles, lay thickly in the field and were picked daily for size and freshness. Sweet peppers, red and yellow, fiery hot peppers, and long yellow mild varieties sat about in baskets. Giant sweet summer onions, pulled only hours before the stand opened, were laid out with the tops still on and left to dry, with a card laid on them that read, "Sweet as an apple!"

Some baskets of red and russet potatoes sat about in the shade, the scent of the earth still clinging to them. Neat stacks of corn lay on tables, and gunnysacks full, three dozen or more in each bag, could be purchased for canning.

After the great squashes, butternut, acorn, Hubbard, were sold (and stored away for family use) and the apples and pears were picked and stored, the stands were closed down for the winter. By late fall rain slanted down over the buildings, rattling on the roofs, gusting in through the wooden slats to dampen empty picking boxes. Then, like the earth itself, the stands would return to life in early spring, the age-old pattern would unfold, the harvests would come again, and so would the crowds. The God-given seasonal bounty was at hand once more.

THE MELON MAN

He came around in childhood summers,
gray, in his chattery truck
covered with canvas,
bringing us vegetables and melons
he grew himself, with his son
and a little help from God.

Then, one year, he didn't come;
just the son, with his son,
selling the sweet taste of summer remembered
to us and our children.

Remember?

—Alvin Reiss

♥

Poached Fresh Peaches

MAKES 6 WHOLE-PEACH SERVINGS, OR 12 HALF-PEACH SERVINGS

OUR FRIEND BILL, WHO raises huge, sun-ripened peaches, tells all the young women who buy his fruit that color alone is not a good indication of ripeness in peaches, especially a pink or reddish blush. He tells them to check for a good peachy fragrance and to squeeze the peach gently in the palm of the hand (never with the fingers, as it bruises the fruit) to test for firmness with a little give.

²/₃ to 1 cup sugar, as desired
2 cups water
Juice of 1 lemon, strained

6 medium to large peaches, peeled
and pitted (Elberta or Hale
Haven preferred)

Prepare peaches a few at a time, just before poaching, to prevent browning.

In a wide, flat saucepan heat the sugar, water, and lemon juice to a boil. When boiling, lower prepared peach halves into the syrup. Adjust the heat so that the syrup barely simmers. Cook the peaches until they are just clear, all the way through—do not let them become limp or mushy.

As the peaches become clear, gently remove the halves from the syrup. Place in heatproof serving dishes, allowing one whole peach for a generous serving, half a peach for smaller servings. Serve hot, if you wish, with a dot of butter and a dusting of cinnamon. Or set aside to cool before serving.

NOTE: If you wish, combine one part wine or brandy with an equal part of syrup. Pour over hot or cooled servings of fruit.

♥

A Summer Garden Casserole

MAKES 6 TO 8 SERVINGS

BY MID-AUGUST, THE SEASON'S bounty can be found everywhere, in the fields, on old-fashioned back porches, in corners of working kitchens, and, vine-ripened and freshly picked, at roadside produce stands.

4 medium tomatoes, peeled and
   sliced
4 medium zucchini, washed,
   blossom and stem ends
   removed, sliced crosswise ¼
   inch thick
2 teaspoons salt
1½ pounds lean ground beef
⅔ cup long-grain rice, uncooked
2 tablespoons fresh parsley, minced

¼ cup green onion, chopped
¼ cup green pepper, chopped
1 cup tomato juice
½ teaspoon ground cinnamon
¼ teaspoon allspice
¼ teaspoon ground nutmeg
¼ teaspoon freshly ground black
   pepper
1 cup Longhorn Colby or American
   cheese, shredded

Preheat oven to 375°F. Thoroughly grease a 9-by-12-by-2-inch baking dish. Set aside.

Arrange half the tomatoes on the bottom of the baking dish. Cover with half the zucchini. Sprinkle over all *½ teaspoon* of the salt. In a large bowl combine ground beef, rice, parsley, onion, green pepper, tomato juice, cinnamon, allspice, nutmeg, *1 teaspoon more* of the salt, and black pepper; mix well. Pat the meat mixture into the casserole over the vegetables. Layer *remaining* tomatoes and zucchini over the meat mixture. Sprinkle *remaining ½ teaspoon* salt over the vegetables.

Cover and bake until vegetables are very tender and meat mixture is done, about 1½ hours. Spread cheese over hot casserole and bake 15 minutes more, uncovered, to melt and brown the cheese.

♥

Effie's Jellied Cucumber Salad

MAKES 8 SERVINGS

THIS COOL, COLORFUL, ZESTY, easy-to-make salad is a midsummer delight, just perfect for a warm-weather potluck, grange supper, or Sunday-afternoon dinner for company.

Just enough salad oil (not olive oil) to thoroughly grease a decorative mold
2 tablespoons (2 envelopes) unflavored gelatin
6 small to medium cucumbers (those with immature seeds preferred), plus ½ medium cucumber to thinly slice for garnish

1½ cups mayonnaise, chilled
2 tablespoons prepared horseradish
2 tablespoons sweet summer onion, grated
½ teaspoon salt
¼ teaspoon white pepper
1 cup whipping cream, chilled
Sprigs of parsley for garnish

Set out and lightly oil a 2-quart mold. Turn upside down to drain excess oil. When well drained, chill the bowl and a rotary beater until needed.

Into a small heatproof bowl pour ½ cup cold water and sprinkle gelatin evenly over the water. Let set until gelatin is softened, about 5 minutes. Set bowl of gelatin in a pan of very hot water until dissolved.

Meanwhile, rinse and pare *the six* cucumbers, cut into halves lengthwise (if seeds are large, remove and discard them). Finely grind cucumbers with the fine blade of a food chopper (for a finer texture use a blender). Set aside.

In a large bowl thoroughly stir dissolved gelatin with mayonnaise, horseradish, onion (a drop or two of green food coloring, optional), salt, and pepper. Refrigerate, stirring occasionally, until mixture is about the thickness of an uncooked egg white. Then, using the chilled beater, whip the cream into soft peaks. Fold into the cucumber mixture and pour into prepared mold. Refrigerate until firm, 1½ hours or more.

Just before serving, peel *remaining* ½ cucumber and score by pulling tines of fork down the sides. Slice thinly. Unmold the salad onto a serving plate and garnish with cucumber slices and parsley.

The Boy 'at Lives on Our Farm

The boy lives on our Farm, he's not
    Afeard o' horses none!
An' he can make 'em lope, er trot,
    Er rack, er pace, er run.
Sometimes he drives two horses, when
    He comes to town an' brings
A wagon-full o' 'taters nen,
    An' roastin'-ears an' things.

Two horses is "a team," he says,
    An' when you drive er hitch,
The right-un's a "near-horse," I guess
    Er "off"—I don't know which—
The boy lives on our Farm, he told
    Me, too, 'at he can see,
By lookin' at their teeth, how old
    A horse is, to a T!

I'd be the gladdest boy alive
    Ef I knowed much as that,
An' could stand up like him an' drive,
    An' ist push back my hat,
Like he comes skallyhootin' through
    Our alley, with one arm
A-wavin' Fare-ye-well! to you—
    The Boy lives on our Farm!

—James Whitcomb Riley

The Boy 'at Lives on Our Farm

IN THE OLD DAYS, when most summer work on the farm was done with horses and by hand, men and boys would trade off, meaning that a boy from one family would go to live with a neighbor or member of the family who needed extra help for the summer, to earn room and board and some money.

Plans for such an arrangement often began at the end of the harvest season, or as soon as a boy was considered old enough to leave home for that long. Over the summer, the two families involved had picnics together and melon feeds so that the boys could visit with their own relatives for a while. The boys learned new skills from their hosts, saw family life from a little different perspective, and earned the affection and admiration of the younger children in the household.

Then just before school began, they packed up their things, threw them into a wagon, and started for home. They took with them sun-browned, hard-muscled bodies, enriched lives, and a summer's worth of wages.

♥

Old-Fashioned Corn Pudding

MAKES 6 SERVINGS

MY GRANDMOTHER USED TO make this old-time corn pudding in a great metal baking pan, which held enough for a family of ten to have seconds, and still left plenty should company stop by.

12 ears sweet corn, uncooked   *½ cup light cream*
1 teaspoon salt, more if desired   *⅔ cup whole milk*

Preheat oven to 350°F. Thoroughly grease a 1½-quart casserole dish. Set aside.

Husk corn and split kernels by running a sharp knife blade lengthwise down the ear. Using the back of the knife, scrape off enough kernels to make 2 cups corn pulp. To the pulp, add salt, cream, and milk. Pour corn mixture into the prepared casserole dish. Place in the center of the middle rack in the oven; set an old baking sheet under the pan to catch spills.

Bake until corn has thickened the pudding, cream and milk have boiled down by half, and the top is lightly browned, about 1 hour. Serve piping hot.

♥

Effie's Stuffed Red Bell Peppers

MAKES 6 OR MORE SERVINGS

ALMOST EVERYONE IN OUR family loves stuffed green bell peppers. Fillings range from all rice to all meat, and sometimes an assortment of vegetables. Effie's favorite, though, was stuffed red peppers. She loved the sweet taste of the mature ripe peppers, and thought they were something special when stuffed with pork or chicken and rice.

Chicken and Rice Filling (recipe
follows)
3 medium sweet red peppers, sliced
in half lengthwise, inner fiber
and seeds removed

½ teaspoon salt
6 thin slices Swiss cheese

Prepare filling before cooking peppers.

Preheat oven to 375°F. Thoroughly grease a 12-by-9-by-2-inch baking dish. Set aside.

In a large saucepan place pepper halves in salted boiling water to cover and cook only 3 minutes. Drain. Sprinkle each half with a few grains of salt. Fill each half with Chicken and Rice Filling and arrange in the prepared baking dish.

Bake until peppers are well done and filling is cooked through, about 25 to 30 minutes. Over each stuffed pepper half lay a thin slice of Swiss cheese. Return to the oven and bake only long enough for the cheese to melt, bubble, and brown lightly. Serve immediately.

♥

Chicken and Rice Filling

MAKES ABOUT 3½ CUPS

2 cups chicken, cooked and minced
1¼ cups cooked rice
¼ teaspoon salt
⅛ teaspoon freshly ground black
pepper

1 tablespoon butter, melted
½ medium onion, minced
1 cup chicken broth

In a medium bowl mix chicken and rice together. Add salt, pepper, butter, and onion. Moisten with chicken broth.

♥

Eggplant with Tomatoes

MAKES 4 TO 6 SERVINGS

MY GRANDFATHER, A STAUNCH Midwesterner, never grew eggplant in his youth—I don't think he even recognized it as a vegetable. However, when all his children settled in California, they liked it and he tolerated it. In time he grew the purple variety in his large vegetable gardens and found a market for his oversupply, which put money in his pocket and changed his attitude a bit.

Eggplants may be round, oblong, or pear-shaped, yellow, purple, white, ash-colored, green, brown, or even variegated. They are harvested while immature; size is not an indication of quality. In our garden we look for a vegetable that has a sleek, shiny skin over taut, firm flesh with light-colored, soft seeds.

2 medium strips bacon
1 small onion, diced
1 clove garlic, crushed
2 to 3 peeled tomatoes
1/2 green bell pepper, diced
1/2 cup celery, chopped
1 tablespoon fresh parsley, finely minced

1 teaspoon sweet basil, dried
1 medium eggplant, peeled and diced
1/2 teaspoon salt, more if desired
1/8 teaspoon freshly ground black pepper

In a large skillet or Dutch oven fry the bacon until crisp and transfer to a small platter. Add the onion and garlic to the fat in the pan and sauté for 3 to 5 minutes. Add tomatoes, pressing them down into the skillet with a spatula or spoon so that they will yield a little juice. Add the green pepper, celery, parsley, basil, eggplant, salt, and pepper. Cover tightly and cook until the eggplant is tender and most of the moisture has converted into sauce, about 25 minutes. Crumble bacon over the top and serve hot.

♥

Ann's Early Peach Ice Cream Shortcake

MAKES 8 TO 10 SERVINGS

EFFIE'S DAUGHTER ANN MADE this deluxe peach shortcake for her mother's birthday. Since then it has been a favorite summer-birthday cake in our family.

4 to 6 large, ripe peaches
2 tablespoons lemon juice
⅓ cup (more if you wish) sugar
Prebaked Sponge Cake (recipe follows)

1 quart (more if you wish) vanilla brick ice cream

Just before serving, peel, pit, and lightly crush the peaches. Add lemon juice and sugar and set aside. Cut cake into 1½-inch wedges. Using two wedges of cake for each serving, lay one slice on a serving dish; place a slice of ice cream on it, then top with a second slice of cake, turning so that the narrow end of the top wedge is above the wide end of the bottom wedge. Spoon crushed, sweetened peaches generously over the top.

♥

Sponge Cake

MAKES ONE 10-INCH CAKE

1 cup cake flour
¼ teaspoon salt
5 eggs, separated

Grated rind of 1 lemon
Juice of 1 lemon, strained
1 cup sugar, sifted

Preheat oven to 325°F. Set out an ungreased 10-inch tube pan.

Into a medium bowl sift flour four times with salt; set aside. In a large bowl beat *egg yolks* until they are thick and light in color. Add grated rind and juice of lemon, and blend well. In a second bowl, beat *egg whites* with a wire whisk into stiff, moist peaks. Fold in the sugar, about *2 tablespoons* at a time, cutting down through the whites with a large spoon, then lifting up and folding over. Using the same careful motion, fold in the yolks. When the yolks have been incorporated and no yellow streaks show, fold in the flour, a small amount at a time, taking care not to lose the spongy lightness of the batter. Spoon the batter into the tube pan.

Bake until cake is well risen, appears spongy, and is a delicate golden brown, about 1 hour (long, even baking in a slow oven ensures tenderness).

Invert the pan on a wire rack, or hang cake upside down on a funnel to cool for about 1 hour or longer if needed. When cake is thoroughly cooled, use a thin spatula to gently loosen cake from sides and from around center cone of pan. Turn upside down onto a cake plate.

&

A Fruit-Piece

THE afternoon of summer folds
Its warm arms round the marigolds,

And, with its gleaming fingers, pets
The watered pinks and violets

That from the casement vases spill,
Over the cottage window-sill,

Their fragrance down the garden walks
Where droop the dry-mouthed hollyhocks.

How vividly the sunshine scrawls
The grape-vine shadows on the walls!

How like a truant swings the breeze
In high boughs of the apple-trees!

The slender "free-stone" lifts aloof,
Full languidly above the roof,

A hoard of fruitage, stamped with gold
And precious mintings manifold.

—James Whitcomb Riley

A
COUNTRY
GROWERS'
MARKET

〰〰〰〰〰

IN OUR TOWN, A gloriously colored Growers' Market blossoms each week in a cool spot on the edge of the town park, shaded by great maples. Tables are set up and covered with fresh vegetables. Baskets full of peppers, grapes, berries, and much more are stacked everywhere. Stands display handcrafted wooden spoons, dippers made of oak and alder to entice women, and rocking horses and clowns that climb a string to delight the young.

Baby's breath and other flowers that traditionally are dried for winter bouquets grace vintage vases or are tucked into grapevine or straw wreaths amid dried roses. Great bundles of statice are everywhere. Women buy it by armfuls to fill crocks or vases for winter bouquets.

Along the edges of the midway, pickup trucks are parked, the beds filled with boxes of peaches—49ers, Elbertas, Hale Haven—and plums, and apples of every ilk—Winesap, Gravenstein, or Yellow Transparent, depending on the time of year.

Here and there are tables, covered with antique lace cloths, on which rest artistically arranged sprays of flowers and bottles of natural scented oils: yellow rose oil, oil of hyacinth, and oil of lavender, for gently rubbing on the wrist or where the pulse beats behind the ear. And there are bottles of clove, peppermint, and other spicy oils for scenting potpourris and sachets.

On special days musicians come to entertain the crowds, sometimes playing the hammer dulcimer and the ancient music of Ireland. On other days, old-time fiddlers play tunes almost forgotten, like "The Wabash Cannonball," or the lovely and haunting "Wildwood Flower," known to be centuries old, which is so beautiful that crowds stand entranced, so quiet that each note can be heard hanging in the air.

Of Statice and Other Beautiful Summer Flowers

ONE OF THE PLEASURES of summer is growing (or buying fresh) flowers that can be dried for winter bouquets. At our house we pick the flowers and hang them in small clusters on the clothesline in the shade. Some women hang flowers under the eaves of the house, where a light breeze dries them and the sun does not fade them.

Statice, which is perfect for fresh or dried arrangements, has petite flowers in various pastel shades, including soft blue and burgundy, on graceful flower sprays. The paperlike blooms are sturdier than they appear, and even when dry, if kept in a protected corner, they will hold their color through two or more seasons.

Candy Tuft, our favorite, is a spectacular shade-lover which grows in a rounded flower mound and when sowed at two- to three-week intervals provides long-lasting color. Even though the stems are short, these flowers can be dried, fastened to florist's wire and used in dried bouquets. Baby's breath produces dainty sprays of delicate snowy-white and pink flowers in early summer, and when dried and tucked into bouquets of other dried flowers adds a fragile beauty to the whole. In Grandma's day, bachelor's

Statice, sinuatum, baby's breath, and love-in-a-mist

buttons were a favorite flower for drying. Growing nearly wild, these soft blue or rose-pink petaled beauties with frilled edges made striking borders and were used in both fresh and dried bouquets.

Old-fashioned strawflowers, members of the genus helichrysum, are reminiscent of the Victorian age. The flower naturally has a strawlike appearance, making it seem almost artificial. When blooms are cut before they are fully developed, the leaves stripped off, and the flowers hung upside down to dry, they become sturdy enough to handle and retain their color for years, even when exposed to light. Helichrysum resembles or at least reminds me of strawflowers, but it grows much taller (three feet). The dazzling mixture of dusty-colored blossoms which develops over a long season is perfect for country decorations.

એ

THE LORD GOD PLANTED A GARDEN

THE Lord God planted a garden
In the first white days of the world,
And he set there an angel warden
In a garment of light enfurled.

So near to the peace of Heaven,
That the hawk might nest with the wren,
For there in the cool of the even'
God walked with the first of men.

The kiss of the sun for pardon,
The song of the birds for mirth—
One is nearer God's heart in a garden
Than anywhere else on earth.

—Dorothy Frances Gurney

♥

Yellow Rose-Petal Sugar

MAKES ABOUT 2½ CUPS

AUNT SUE GATHERED HER BRIGHTEST-COLORED and most fragrant yellow rose petals early in the morning before the dew was off them, and laid them in the shade to dry. When they became crisp, she made Yellow Rose-Petal Sugar, which she spooned over desserts and stirred into her tea.

2 cups crisp-dried yellow rose petals
2 cups sugar
1 drop yellow food coloring
(optional)

1 drop (edible) yellow rose oil
(optional)

Pass dried rose petals and sugar through a sieve several times until the petals are thoroughly pulverized—the coarseness of the sugar will help pulverize the petals. If you wish, add a drop of yellow food coloring and one of yellow rose oil to the rose petal and sugar mixture. *(Do not use rose oil made for toiletries! Use only oil purchased at a specialty food shop for culinary purposes!)*

Pour the flavored, scented sugar into a glass bottle or jar that has a tight cork or lid. Set containers of Yellow Rose-Petal Sugar away in a cool, dark place to protect color, fragrance, and flavor. Rose sugar can be sprinkled over the top of ice cream, an unfrosted cake, or glazed cookies, and can be used to sweeten tea.

♥

Candied Red Rose Petals

MAKES ENOUGH TO SHARE WITH FRIENDS

FOR GENERATIONS, FLOWER CONFECTIONS have been served at ladies' teas and other elegant affairs, along with tea cakes and miniature sandwiches. They are delightful to the eye and leave the fragrance of roses on the palate.

2 cups of richly scented red rose
petals

1 egg white
About ½ cup sugar

Early in the morning, pick rose petals. Put them in a sieve and rinse no more than a second under cold tap water (over-rinsing will remove the scented oils). Lay out on a towel to dry.

Meanwhile, whip the egg white to a froth (don't beat). Put sugar in a small flat dish. Dip each petal first into the egg white, then into the sugar, taking care not to get too much sugar on the rose petal (it should be coated lightly). Lay out on a piece of waxed paper to dry.

When all petals are dry, layer them in a container with a tight-fitting lid between layers of waxed paper. The container should fit the petals snugly, without much air space left.

NOTE: When tightly sealed, petals last for a remarkably long time and retain their subtle fragrance and taste.

Serve on a glass plate as you would candy, or use to decorate the top of a cake or a dish of ice cream.

♥

Mock Capers

MAKES ABOUT 8 HALF-PINTS

OLD-FASHIONED WOMEN PICKED THE pods of their nasturtiums just as soon as the blossoms dropped and pickled them to use as a substitute for capers.

1 quart green nasturtium seedpods,   *One 3-ounce stick cinnamon*
full grown, but not yellow,   *2 teaspoons whole cloves*
dried for a day in the sun   *1 teaspoon ground allspice*
1 quart cider vinegar

Put seeds in scrubbed, sterilized ½-pint jars, filling about ½ inch from the top. Pour vinegar into a large saucepan. Tie whole spices in a clean cotton cloth (or in a muslin bag); add them to vinegar and boil 5 minutes. Remove bag, add ground allspice, stir, and pour spiced vinegar over the seeds. Seal immediately with hot, scrubbed, sterilized lids and rings. Set on a folded towel to cool; store in a cool, dry place.

♥

Nasturtium Salad

MAKES 8 TO 10 SERVINGS

FRAGRANT NASTURTIUM FLOWERS, WHICH bloom above the foliage in sunshine shades of orange and gold, have for generations been used for colorful garden beds and borders and for bouquets. But both leaves and flowers have also been added to salads and used as garnishes.

1 head Boston lettuce, rinsed, air-dried, and torn into bite-size bits

1 head curly green leaf lettuce, rinsed, air-dried, and torn into bite-size bits

1 head red leaf lettuce, rinsed, air-dried, and torn into bite-size bits

1/4 cup nasturtium leaves, minced

1 1/2 cups nasturtium flowers, left whole

Lemon Vinaigrette (recipe follows)

Into a large bowl turn the lettuces, nasturtium leaves, and flowers (retain a few flowers to garnish the top of the salad). Toss with just enough Lemon Vinaigrette to coat. Chill for a few minutes and serve.

♥

Lemon Vinaigrette

MAKES ABOUT 2 CUPS

1 cup salad oil
2/3 cup fresh lemon juice, strained
1/4 cup chives, minced

1/4 teaspoon salt
1/8 teaspoon white pepper

In a jar with a tight-fitting lid combine ingredients. Chill until needed. Shake thoroughly before using.

JANE WATSON HOPPING

Jane and Raymond

HUMMINGBIRDS

SPLINTERING sunlight
in colors as thoughts of God;
flowers spread dream wings.

—Alvin Reiss

Lemon Cucumbers and Footlong Beans

AT ABOUT SEVEN OR eight o'clock in the evening, I love to walk in the vegetable garden. I always feel my grandfather's spirit is there among the lush plants, the lavender and purple eggplant bushes, and the deep green pepper plants, with their hanging globes, thick-meated and sweet to the taste. Ace and Romano tomatoes litter the ground, in shades of green, pink, and ripe red. The corn won't be ready for harvest until later, but the silk is as soft as a woman's hair, and the ears become fuller almost day by day. In among fingered leaves lie fast-developing rattlesnake watermelons, and, nearby, ribbed cantaloupe, and, farther out in the field, dozens of butternut squash. All of these have curlicues near the stem that turn brown when the melon or squash is ripe.

As dusk comes on and shadows fall, and the air gets cool, I wander back toward the house, taking with me a sense of having been in touch with all that is fragile and yet bountiful, all that sustains us. And then, I hear a night bird call.

♥

Lemon-Cucumber Cottage Cheese Salad

MAKES 4 SERVINGS

2 cups (1 pint) cottage cheese,
    small-curd preferred
1/2 cup sour cream
1/4 cup chives, chopped
1/2 cup cucumber, peeled and diced
1 tablespoon parsley, minced, plus
    a few sprigs for garnish

1/8 teaspoon salt
Pinch of white pepper (black can be
    substituted)
Crisp Bibb lettuce

In a large bowl, stir cottage cheese and sour cream together lightly with a fork. Blend in chives, cucumber, parsley, salt, and pepper. Divide into four equal portions and shape into mounds. Arrange on lettuce leaves and garnish with sprigs of parsley.

Hot Footlong Beans and Bacon Salad

MAKES 6 SERVINGS

GRANDPA LOVED TO PLANT newfangled and old-fashioned vegetables. He would watch the garden giants grow—foot- and yard-long beans, forty-five-pound watermelons, banana squash that grew four or more feet long and as he often said "weighed a short ton," huge, thirty-five-pound-plus sauerkraut cabbages, and pumpkins that weighed up to five hundred pounds and sometimes more. He would take us out to measure "the giants" and would have us write down the circumferences and guess what the total weight and size would be by harvest time.

*2 pounds fresh footlong beans
(fresh green beans can be
substituted)*
3 slices uncooked bacon, diced
*1 medium sweet onion, peeled and
diced*

½ cup cider vinegar
*Dusting of freshly ground black
pepper*

Wash the beans, string them if needed, and cut into diagonal strips.

Place beans in a medium saucepan and fill pan about 2 inches deep with hot water; cover and boil just until the beans are tender-crisp, about 15 to 25 minutes. Remove from heat and drain; cover to keep hot. In a skillet fry bacon until crisp (if there are more than 2 tablespoons of fat in the skillet, pour out enough to leave only 2 tablespoons). Add onion, stir for a minute, then add vinegar and let the mixture boil up once. Pour vinegar mixture over the beans. Dust with pepper and serve hot.

♥

A Medley of Watermelons

MAKES ABOUT 8 TO IO SERVINGS

WATERMELONS GROW IN VARIOUS shades of red and crimson, gold, and light and dark shades of pink. Grandpa, who loved melons, grew great patches of them, to eat, sell, and share with neighbors and friends.

*1 quart crimson-fleshed
    watermelon balls
1 quart golden-fleshed
    watermelon balls
1 quart deep-pink-fleshed
    watermelon balls*

*One head pale green leaf lettuce,
    divided into individual leaves,
    rinsed, air-dried, and
    refrigerated until needed
Cream Cheese Mayonnaise
    (recipe follows)*

All melons should be served very cold. Using a melon baller or a teaspoon, cut melon balls out of the heart of the melon (the center without seeds).

Line individual serving bowls with pale green leaf lettuce. Arrange the melon balls on the lettuce. Serve with Cream Cheese Mayonnaise.

♥

Cream Cheese Mayonnaise

MAKES ENOUGH FOR 8 TO 10 SERVINGS

*3 ounces cream cheese, softened at
  room temperature*
1 tablespoon lemon juice
1 cup heavy cream, whipped

2 tablespoons powdered sugar
*⅔ cup toasted almonds, chopped,
  plus ½ cup for garnish*

In a small bowl, work cream cheese with a fork until light. Blend in the lemon juice; fold in whipped cream which has been sweetened with powdered sugar. Fold in the *⅔ cup* toasted almonds, reserving the *½ cup* for garnishing the medley.

From THE OLD SWIMMIN' HOLE

Oh! the old swimmin'-hole! whare the crick so still and deep
Looked like a baby-river that was laying half asleep,
And the gurgle of the worter round the drift jest below
Sounded like the laugh of something we onc't ust to know
Before we could remember anything but the eyes
Of the angels lookin' out as we left Paradise;
But the merry days of youth is beyond our control
And it's hard to part ferever with the old swimmin'-hole.

—James Whitcomb Riley

THE CRICK
SO STILL
AND
DEEP

~~~~~~~~~~

WHEN SUMMER NIGHTS WERE so hot that it was hard to sleep, my future husband, Raymond, age twelve or thirteen, his buddies Dick Whiteman and Gene Sanders, and his younger brother Walter would slip out about eleven o'clock and by the light of the moon make their way through a field rampant with stinkweed to the spot where Cripple Creek made a bend, leaving a swirled-out pond about four feet deep. Around the swimming-hole stood several giant oak trees. In one of them, Raymond and his friends had tied a rope swing on which they could fly out over the water and drop *kersplash* into the center of the pond.

When they got tired, they crawled out of the water and lay on a bed of crushed grass, sharing secrets and telling each other those jokes which have always been the province of twelve-year-old boys. About two o'clock, they would wend their way home, crawl into bed and sleep the sleep of good health and innocence.

A WARM SUMMER'S DAY

A WARM summer's day—
The wind blows;
The sun is hot.
My feet feel good
In the cool grass,
The birds are singing;
The toads are croaking.
The horses are galloping
Through the green fields.
Summer is special to me!

—Katie Schuler (age 8)

A Children's Country Poetry Contest

HISTORIC JACKSONVILLE, OREGON, LITTLE changed since the turn of the century, is nestled among forested mountains just over the hill from our farm. From the top of the incline, the distant mountains come into view, making you catch your breath with their softened blue hues. Downhill, the rolling, patchwork valley stretches all the way to the nearby town of Medford.

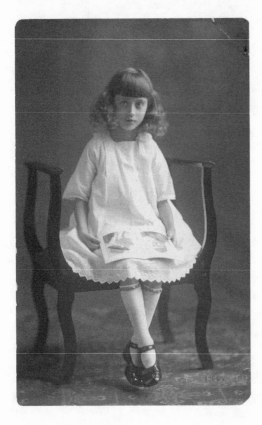

Just a short distance inside the Jacksonville city limits, the old Beekman house still stands on the left side of the street, testimony to the enterprise of that family. On the corner of California and Third streets in the center of town, the restored Beekman Bank is a tourist attraction. Turn-of-the-century buildings, nostalgia-inducing shops, and eating establishments line the ancient streets. Kitty-corner from the bank, Jacksonville Books invites readers to cross its well-worn threshold, passing through the aged doors, to browse among new and old books, and to look with wonder at artifacts of yesteryear: lanterns, harnesses, baskets, tins, and much more.

Nearby, on flat land at the base of a hill on which the old school still stands, is the new Jacksonville Elementary School, whose wide halls are graced with children's work: drawings, paintings, photographs, poetry, and papers.

SUMMERTIME IN THE VALLEY

SUMMERTIME is here now.
I just want to sit around,
Be lazy, or maybe—
Just go to the pond,
Take off my shoes and then—
Get on the old wooden swing
To glide over the pond.

I can feel my feet passing through the water
As I hear the distant croaking of frogs,
Sitting on their lily pads,
Also, the buzzing of bees gathering
Nectar for honey.
I see the butterflies fluttering above.
It's summertime in the valley.

—Johnnie Stevens (age 8½)

A SUMMER AFTERNOON

HOT summer afternoon—
The sun is shining and
I lie in the hot grass.
The sky is my window
Through which I see birds
And butterflies.
I pick flowers for my mother—
Build a tree fort for myself.
I help my mother do the chores.
And then, ride my horse, swim
In the lake, and go fishing
With my dad.

—Stephanie Stebbins (age 9)

SUMMER

IT was summer
I went to play.
Then went to the farm
To cut some hay.
Looking around,
I spied a big pit.
As I started down this hole,
I saw a mole.
Then I left and lay in the grass,
And saw a zooming car pass.

—Ben Taft (age 9)

Climbing Trees, Catching Butterflies

Climbing trees, catching butterflies
Camping, reading, and relaxing
Fishing with my dad and brother,
Family picnics and ladybugs,
Then it's time for chores

The day is over—
Now, it's time to say goodnight.

—Courtney Kingston (age 9)

Summer Evening Sounds

Summer evening sounds,
Crickets chirping, frogs croaking.
Late at night we go to the barn dance.
Do whatever you please
But do not sneeze!

—Shauna Stanley (age 8)

Loving Is a Two-Way Street!

LUCKY THE BOY TO have an uncle in his life, for uncles can play fun games and tell you wonderful stories:

Johnny Webster, Grandpa's friend, always said that it was from his uncle that he learned to love his father, to know him as a person, as a boy who got into trouble like any might do, and as a young man trying to court the girls.

It was his uncle who talked to him when he was still quite small about a man's responsibilities in the world, about doing his job well, giving full measure to those who put their confidence in him, about the extra mile his father went every day to see to his and his mother's and sister's welfare and to share his love with them all.

Old uncle taught him young to talk to his father about good and bad things, about feelings, and about people and the world as he saw it, all of which stood him in good stead throughout his lifetime.

And as he became a man, a husband and father, Johnny would talk to his own children about his childhood, and reminisce about the closeness that had grown between him and his dad. And he would tell the children, boys and girls alike, that it was his Uncle Joe who had taught him that loving is a two-way street!

THE SQUIRT-GUN UNCLE MAKED ME

UNCLE Sidney, when he was here,
Maked me a squirt-gun out o' some
Elder-bushes 'at growed out near
Where wuz the brick-yard—'way out clear
  To where the Toll-Gate come!

So when we walked back home again,
 He maked it, out in our woodhouse where
Wuz the old work-bench, an' the old jack-plane,
An' the old 'poke-shave, an' the tools all lay'n'
  Ist like he wants 'em there.

He sawed it first with the old hand-saw;
 An' nen he peeled off the bark, an' got
Some glass an' scraped it; an' told 'bout Pa,
When he wuz a boy an' fooled his Ma,
  An' the whippin' 'at he caught.

Nen Uncle Sidney, he took an' filed
 A' old arn ramrod; an' one o' the ends
He screwed fast into the vise; an' smiled,
Thinkin', he said, o' when he wuz a child,
  'Fore him an' Pa wuz mens.

He punched out the peth, an' nen he putt
 A plug in the end with a hole notched through;
Nen took the old drawey-knife an' cut
An' maked a handle 'at shoved clean shut
  But ist where yer hand held to.

An' he wropt th'uther end with some string an' white
 Piece o' the sleeve of a' old tored shirt;
An' nen he showed me to hold it tight,
An' suck in the water an' work it right.—
  An' it 'ud ist squirt an' squirt!

—James Whitcomb Riley

♥

Salmon Wiggle

MAKES 6 SERVINGS

WHEN I WAS A child, the women at Uncle Bud's house served canned salmon, bread and butter with tea for lunch. They made salmon patties, loaves, croquettes, puffs, and salads; creamed, molded, and scalloped salmon; and a dish called Salmon Wiggle.

24 soda or whole-wheat crackers, crumbled

2 cups Medium White Sauce (recipe follows)

2 cups (about ½ pound) salmon, poached until tender, chilled, skin and bones removed

2 cups peas (about 2 pounds), shelled and cooked (a 16-ounce can of tender, small salad peas can be substituted)

A dusting of paprika

Finely minced parsley, if desired

Set out six shallow bowls, or six medium salad or luncheon plates. Cover the bottom of the plates with cracker crumbs. Set aside.

Make the Medium White Sauce. To the cooked sauce still on the stove, add salmon and peas; fold gently together. When the whole is medium-hot, spoon the creamed salmon and peas over the cracker base. Sprinkle with paprika and freshly minced parsley. Serve immediately. Refrigerate any leftovers.

♥

Medium White Sauce

MAKES 2 CUPS

4 tablespoons butter or margarine

4 tablespoons all-purpose flour

2 cups milk

1 teaspoon salt

¼ teaspoon white pepper (black pepper can be used)

In a small saucepan over medium heat, melt butter or margarine and blend in flour, whisking to a smooth consistency. Add milk gradually, stirring constantly until mixture boils. Reduce the heat and continue cooking for 3 minutes longer over low heat. Add salt and pepper and blend.

NOTE: If the sauce must stand for any length of time, cover the pan to keep a film from coating the top of the sauce.

♥

Mid-Season Corn

MAKES 6 SERVINGS

ALONG ABOUT MID-TO-LATE AUGUST, corn reaches the height of production and roasting ears sit about in boxes, baskets, and buckets. Women are canning, freezing, and pickling the bounteous supply, as well as preparing it for meals in many different ways.

4 cups corn, shucked, cleaned, cooked in lightly salted water, and cut off the cob
1/4 cup onion, minced
2 tablespoons butter or margarine, softened at room temperature

Dash of freshly ground black pepper
1/2 teaspoon sugar
1 teaspoon lemon juice
3 tablespoons parsley, minced
1 tablespoon pimiento, chopped

To the hot corn, add onion which has been sautéed until clear in the butter or margarine. Add pepper, sugar, lemon juice, parsley, and pimiento. Toss with a fork to blend. Serve hot.

♥

Ada's Favorite Snap-Bean Dish

MAKES 4 TO 6 SERVINGS

GREEN BEANS, EVEN THE stringless bush varieties, are a trial to pick. Fortunately, at our house, our son-in-law, Mark, loves green beans no matter how we cook them. And he will continue to pick them by the bucketful while we put them up for winter meals.

1 pound stringless green beans, washed and cut crosswise into 1-inch pieces
1/4 cup butter or margarine, softened at room temperature
3/4 cup sweet summer onion, diced
1 clove garlic, minced
1/2 cup celery, minced

3 tablespoons parsley, minced (stems discarded)
1/4 teaspoon dried rosemary
1/4 teaspoon dried basil
3/4 teaspoon salt
Juice of 1 lemon, strained (optional)

JANE WATSON HOPPING

In a medium saucepan cook beans in 1 inch of salted boiling water (use ½ teaspoon salt for each cup boiling water) until tender-crisp, 15 to 20 minutes. Cover to keep warm. Meanwhile, melt butter or margarine in a small saucepan; sauté onion, garlic, and celery for about 3 to 5 minutes, then add parsley, rosemary, basil, and salt and simmer for about 8 minutes more. When done, add lemon juice and toss with green beans and serve immediately.

♥

Blueberry and Almond Muffins

MAKES 10 LARGE MUFFINS

THESE MUFFINS WIN LOTS of compliments for the cook. The recipe is simple enough that a young girl can make them. They are just right for a breakfast treat, a sweet to be tucked into a school lunch bag, or for an after-school or bedtime snack.

2 cups all-purpose flour, sifted
2½ teaspoons baking powder
3 tablespoons sugar
¾ teaspoon salt
½ cup butter or margarine,
    softened at room temperature

1 egg, well beaten
¾ cup milk
1 cup blueberries
½ cup shaved almonds

Preheat oven to 400°F. Thoroughly grease a 10-cup (large) muffin tin. Set aside.

Into a large bowl sift flour a second time with baking powder, sugar, and salt. Using a pastry cutter or your fingertips, cut or work butter or margarine into flour mixture. Combine egg and milk and add all at once to flour mixture. To mix, draw a spoon from the side of the bowl to the center ten to fifteen times; then chop the spoon through the batter eight to ten times (don't beat). Finally, *stir* about five strokes, only until flour is dampened. Fold in blueberries and almonds (don't overwork batter). Turn into the prepared muffin cups, filling each about two-thirds full.

Bake until well risen, firm to the touch, and golden brown. Remove from oven; let stand in tin about 5 minutes; then turn out onto a wire rack to cool. Serve hot or cold.

THE GAZEBO

A CONFECTION of white lattice
in a world of color and green,
a covered harbor sheltering
summer days and dreams,
this rounded wooden work of ours
floats in a windbent river of phlox,
foxglove, stocks, hollyhocks
and the murmur of sunblown bees,
landbound, yet never still.

Come sit with me, love, here,
and talk with me. Sing with me
and share your music while streams
wind beyond the hedge
carrying our whispers and melodies
from the edge of our sunlit garden
toward October twilight,
past Cahokia memories
to the Mississippi of others' muses,
lyrics and lovesongs
from the center of their lattice worlds,
floating into the heart of ours.

—Alvin Reiss

Effie's Gazebo

IN 1915 EFFIE WENT to visit friends in St. Louis, Missouri, where she saw for the first time a gazebo, an elegant little shell of a building, painted brilliant white with gingerbread trim, enhanced with dove-grey steps, floors, and benches on which were scattered striped and floral cushions. The gazebo was set in a well-tended garden; yellow roses twined over one side, hydrangeas and other shade plants clustered about its base.

When Effie arrived home she enthusiastically told everyone about the lovely little summer building she had seen. She tried to tell the menfolk in her family just what it was like so that they could build one for her.

But no matter how hard she tried to make them understand that a gazebo was just a small shell of a room, without true walls, fixed up so you could sit in it and gaze at the surrounding scenery, or serve a little iced tea while you visited with friends and admired the flowers, the men couldn't seem to picture it. They kept asking why she couldn't just sit on the porch and look around . . . much to Effie's disgust!

Finally, her brother-in-law Bill said he would build her one if she'd choose the spot, draw him a picture of the gol-darn thing . . . and paint it herself. That was enough for Effie.

Once the foundation was laid, the building started to take shape. Family and neighbors began to drop by to look at it. The women thought it was a mite out of place, sitting there as it was between the house and the orchard gate, but, undaunted, Effie assured them all that it would be beautiful when she got it painted and the flowers planted around it.

After the first week, men from nearby farms and family began to drift in after supper, bringing with them hammers and other tools, so's they could help Bill finish up Effie's gazebo.

It wasn't long before town and country folks alike began to drive past the farm to look at the glistening white building with latticework along the sides and rosebushes planted on each side of the dove-grey steps. Occasionally women would step down out of their buggies and take a few minutes to stroll through Effie's flower beds, and sit a spell in the gazebo and look around the farm, at the great poplar trees blowing in a breeze near the pond which was alive with mallard ducks, or out over the endless cornfields. They would admire her giant hollyhocks. Some of them even told her that it was a pleasant place to rest a mite.

In time, Effie invited the banker's wife, the minister's wife, and two other ladies from the church to a little social affair in her new gazebo. She served them elegant foods she had learned to make in St. Louis.

♥

Effie's Watercress Sandwiches

MAKES ABOUT 40 TEA SANDWICHES

WHEN "THE LADIES" CAME to visit, Effie loved to serve these fancy little tea sandwiches. All the other women in the family used this recipe, but added ingredients other than watercress, such as pimiento, parsley, finely chopped sweet herbs, bits of pickles and olives, even fruit and nuts.

*8 ounces cream cheese, softened at
    room temperature*
1 teaspoon chives, minced
1 tablespoon lemon juice, strained
2 tablespoons mayonnaise

*½ cup watercress, finely chopped,
    more if desired*
*1 (or more) loaves whole-wheat
    bread, thinly sliced*

In a small bowl blend softened cream cheese, chives, lemon juice, and mayonnaise together to a spreadable consistency. Add just enough watercress to enhance the filling. Cover and hold at room temperature (75°F).

Meanwhile, remove crust from slices of bread and cut in half to make triangles. (Cover prepared bread with a clean dishtowel to keep it from drying out.)

Spread each triangular slice of bread lightly with cream cheese filling. Place second slice on top. Gently lay small sandwiches in a waxed-paper-lined box. Continue to assemble sandwiches and put them in the box, placing a piece of waxed paper between each layer. Top off with a final piece of waxed paper. Refrigerate until needed, but not more than an hour or so. If sandwiches are to be served immediately, put them directly onto the tray and not into the box.

JANE WATSON HOPPING

♥

Almond Wafers

MAKES ABOUT 3 DOZEN WAFERS

EFFIE THOUGHT THESE CRISP cookies were just right for serving with tea. She usually made two batches, one for her women friends and another to serve to their children as they played nearby.

⅓ cup butter, softened
⅓ cup vegetable shortening
1 cup sugar
1 egg, well beaten
¼ cup milk

1½ teaspoons almond extract
2 cups all-purpose flour, sifted
2 teaspoons baking powder
½ teaspoon salt

Preheat oven to 400°F. Thoroughly grease a large baking sheet. Set aside.

In a large bowl cream butter and shortening together until light. Add sugar gradually; cream until fluffy. Blend in the egg, milk, and almond extract. Sift flour a second time with the baking powder and salt. Stir into the butter-sugar mixture. Cover and chill thoroughly, 1 hour or more.

Remove from refrigerator, remove one fourth of the mixture from the bowl, and turn out onto a lightly floured flat surface. Cover *remaining* dough and return to the refrigerator.

NOTE: If unused portion of dough is left out to warm at room temperature, additional flour will have to be added before rolling, which makes the wafers hard rather than crisp.

Roll first portion of dough as thinly as possible; shape with a small round cutter, 1½ inches or slightly more in diameter, dipped in flour. Place wafers close together on prepared baking sheet. Set the first batch in the oven to bake, meanwhile gathering up the trimmings to roll with another portion of dough. Bake until wafers are crisp and lightly browned, about 8 minutes.

While the first batch bakes, roll out about one third of the remaining chilled dough; refrigerate unused portion. Cut out the next batch of wafers. Bake. Continue until dough is used up.

♥

Russian Tea with Preserved Strawberries

MAKES 4 SERVINGS

WHEN EFFIE VISITED ST. LOUIS her cousin told her that in Russia tea was never served with milk or cream, but instead was often flavored and sweetened with preserved strawberries.

6 teaspoons loose black tea from China

Effie's Preserved Whole Strawberries (recipe follows)

Scald an earthenware or china teapot. Put in the tea and pour on 4 cups boiling water. Let stand in a warm place for 5 minutes. Strain and serve hot, pouring over a preserved strawberry in the bottom of the cup.

♥

Effie's Preserved Whole Strawberries

MAKES ABOUT 4 HALF-PINTS

1 pound strawberries　　　　*1 pound sugar*

Rinse strawberries quickly under cold tap water. Hull and set aside.

Put the sugar in a large saucepan. Add *1 cup water* and boil until a thick syrup is formed (224°F on a candy thermometer). Put the whole ripe fruit into the syrup and allow the mixture to boil up just once. Remove from heat and pour onto a deep earthenware platter, or into a flat baking dish; cover with glass. Set in direct sunlight for three days, taking the platters of fruit in at night.

NOTE: Natural heat draws out the flavor of the berries better than other preserving methods. The fruit holds its shape perfectly.

Put preserves into thoroughly scrubbed and scalded pint or half-pint canning jars, top with sterilized lids and scrubbed and sterilized rings. Simmer in a boiling-water bath for 15 minutes to kill mold spores. (See instructions for using a boiling-water bath, page 128.)

An Old-Time Ice Cream Social at the Schoolhouse

BY THE MIDDLE OF summer, farm people had the crops pretty well laid by and could take a little time out on a Sunday afternoon before the evening church services to enjoy an ice cream social.

People gathered from miles around, since women and children and most of the men had not seen their friends for several months. The event was always a great success, an outpouring of socializing and sharing. The children were so excited they could not contain themselves; the men, who were thoroughly enjoying themselves, talked too loud; and the women couldn't seem to keep their minds on the children or the ice cream.

After some of the initial clamor subsided, men took out the twenty-five- or fifty-pound blocks of ice they had brought from the icehouse in town, and bags of rock salt.

They twisted the sacks of ice tightly shut and crushed each with a sledgehammer or the side of an ax. The women brought out the milk and cream, eggs and vanilla, strawberries and peaches, and sometimes custard which had been chilled and brought from home ready to churn.

Soon the buckets were full, and men and teenage boys offered to do the churning while the women set the tables, laid the cookies out on platters, and brought out cakes.

The children, guided by their fathers, lined up with plates and bowls in hand. Soon they sat on blankets and quilts, sharing bites and bragging on their mother's or sister's cookies or cake. Boys and men piled their plates to the rims with goodies and filled the ice-cream bowls to overflowing. In time, women helped themselves and sat down to eat and visit some more.

When everyone was sated, all began to talk about the good time they'd had; women holding small children on their laps looked tired; men made last-minute deals and wives could see that they were getting restless.

About four-thirty, everyone began to pick things up and get ready to go home; there were evening chores to do, cows to milk, lambs and pigs to feed, watering troughs to fill, and babies to bathe and put to bed. Younger folks left early so that they could get their work done in time to go to the evening service at the church.

ॐ

To a Boy Whistling

THE smiling face of a happy boy
*   With its enchanted key*
Is now unlocking in memory
My store of heartiest joy.

And my lost life again today,
*   In pleasant colors all aglow,*
*   From rainbow tints, to pure white snow,*
Is a panorama sliding away.

The whistled air of a simple tune
*   Eddies and whirls my thought around*
*   As fairy balloons of thistle-down*
Sail through the air of June.

O happy boy with untaught grace!
*   What is there in the world to give*
*   That can buy one hour of the life you live*
Or the trivial cause of your smiling face!

—James Whitcomb Riley

♥

Old-Fashioned Peach Ice Cream

MAKES I GALLON

THIS VELVETY, DELICIOUS HOME-CHURNED ice cream has always been a favorite at summertime ice cream socials, where children beg to eat the ice cream which clings to the paddle, and half-grown boys eat so many servings they develop headaches.

1 quart skim milk
1½ cups sugar, plus ¾ cup for
*   sweetening peaches*
¼ cup all-purpose flour
½ teaspoon salt

4 eggs, lightly beaten
1 tablespoon vanilla
3 cups light cream (or
*   half-and-half)*
1 quart crushed fresh peaches

In a medium saucepan scald milk; set aside. Combine thoroughly the *1½ cups sugar,* flour, and salt. Add enough hot milk to the sugar-flour mixture to make a paste. Stir paste into the *remaining* hot milk. Cook over low heat, stirring constantly until mixture thickens slightly, about 15 minutes.

Remove saucepan from heat. Pour some of the hot mixture gradually into beaten eggs, blend, then return the thickened mixture to the saucepan. Set the saucepan over low heat and continue cooking until eggs are cooked through and mixture has thickened further, about 2 minutes.

Remove from heat and refrigerate immediately—do not cool at room temperature. When mixture is thoroughly chilled, or just before churning the ice cream, add vanilla and light cream or half-and-half and blend thoroughly. At this point, the *¾ cup of sugar* may be added to the peaches and the sweetened fruit folded into the ice cream base. Or, the peaches may be prepared and sweetened just before adding to half-frozen ice cream. (Churning instructions follow.)

♥

Luscious Frozen Strawberry Custard

MAKES I GALLON

EFFIE LOVED THIS LIGHT frozen dessert, which was delicious but not as rich as ice cream. She usually brought a large plate of old-fashioned soft sugar cookies to eat with it.

2 quarts milk

4 eggs, lightly beaten

2 cups sugar, plus ½ cup sugar for sweetening berries

2½ to 3 cups heavy cream (additional ½ cup cream makes richer custard)

1 tablespoon vanilla extract

¼ teaspoon salt

3 drops lemon extract

1 quart washed and hulled strawberries

Scald 1 quart of the milk in a large saucepan.

In a large bowl, combine the eggs and *2 cups* sugar. Immediately, while scalded milk is still hot, pour it slowly into the egg-sugar mixture, stir until blended, then pour mixture back into saucepan and cook over low heat until thickened, stirring constantly.

Set the pan in a basin of cold water to slowly cool contents. When cool, add cream, *remaining 1 quart cold milk,* vanilla, salt, and lemon extract; blend until smooth. Fold in strawberries sweetened with the *½ cup* sugar. (See churning instructions, page 171.)

NOTE: For coloring custard pink, use 2 to 3 drops of red food coloring.

♥

Old-Time Soft Sugar Cookies

MAKES ABOUT 2½ DOZEN COOKIES

THESE SIMPLE SUGAR COOKIES, not too rich, not too sweet, were a part of the weekly baking in most old-fashioned homes. They were packed in lard-tin lunch buckets, wrapped in napkins and sent with children on their way to school with instructions not to lay the packet down or drop it on the ground.

2¾ cups all-purpose flour, sifted
2¾ teaspoons baking powder
½ teaspoon salt
½ cup butter or margarine,
  softened

1 cup sugar, plus about ⅓ cup
  sugar for sprinkling on cookies
2 eggs, well beaten
1 teaspoon vanilla

Preheat oven to 400°F. Set out and lightly grease a large baking sheet.

Into a medium bowl sift flour a second time with baking powder and salt. In a large bowl cream butter or margarine thoroughly; add 1 cup sugar gradually and cream together until light. Add eggs to butter-cream mixture and beat well. Stir in vanilla. Turn the flour mixture into the combined other ingredients and stir to blend.

Chill until dough is firm enough to roll, about 20 to 30 minutes. Turn onto a lightly floured flat surface. Roll ⅛ inch thick and cut with a 3½-inch floured cutter. Sprinkle each cookie with remaining sugar.

Set pan in center of oven. Bake until cookies are well risen, firm to the touch, and golden brown, 10 to 12 minutes. With a spatula remove cookies from pan immediately and transfer to a wire rack or a piece of brown paper to cool. Store in an airtight container.

♥

Churning Instructions

To make home-churned ice cream, begin by checking the equipment. Wash the can and dasher in hot soapy water and rinse. Allow them to cool thoroughly. Then prepare ice cream recipe and chill until you are ready to churn it.

When making a *4-quart freezer can* of ice cream, use *about 20 pounds of crushed ice*. Measure out *about 2½ cups of rock salt* for making the ice cream and *another 2½ cups* for ripening it. When using *table salt*, use *1½ cups* for making the ice cream and *another 1½ cups* for ripening it.

Fill the freezer can only about three-fourths full of the chilled ice cream mixture. (Don't overfill it or the texture of the ice cream will not be as smooth.) Set the can in the freezer pail and insert the dasher. Be sure the can is centered on the pivot in the bottom of the pail and the dasher is correctly in place. Put the lid securely on the can; set the hand-crank unit in place over the top of the dasher and lock it in place.

To pack with ice and salt, first fill the bucket about one-third full of ice, sprinkle with salt, then add ice and salt in layers until the pail is full. More salt and ice may have to be added during the freezing period. After the bucket is full, wait about 3 to 4 minutes before starting to churn.

When using a hand-cranked freezer, turn slowly at first until you feel a pull, then triple the speed for about 5 to 10 minutes. About 20 minutes of steady cranking in all is necessary. When ice cream has frozen to the consistency of mush, it is ready.

If the ice cream freezes too quickly (if the crank is difficult to turn after a very short time), too much salt has been added. A solid layer has formed on the inside walls of the can, leaving the center unfrozen. To correct the situation take the freezer apart, remove the dasher, stir the frozen ice cream back down into the unfrozen mixture, put the dasher back in place, and reassemble the freezer. Remove the salt and ice from the bucket, repack with the correct proportions of ice and salt, and start churning again. Be certain the drain hole is clear.

Usually ice cream is then "packed" for at least two hours to harden it. (For immediate use, churn until the ice cream is a little harder.) To pack it, clean the salt and ice away from the top of the can, pour off the salt water from the bucket, and wipe off the lid. Carefully remove the lid and take the dasher out, being careful not to get any salt water in the ice cream. Scrape the ice cream down from the sides of the can and replace the lid. Place a cork in the hole of the lid where the dasher was. Repack the bucket with salt and ice, in the same proportions that were used for the initial packing, until the bucket is again full and the ice is piled up over the lid of the can. Cover the bucket with newspaper or two or three grocery bags. Throw a heavy piece of material (an old blanket will do) over the bucket and let it stand.

❧

THE CAT IN THE WINDOW

EMERALD independence winks slowly,
shining disinterest on passersby.
Lovers walk in summer twilight,
equally indifferent to her knowing eye.

—Alvin Reiss

JOYFUL

MEMORIES

REVIVED

~~~~~~~~~~

IT IS NOT TOO uncommon to see older couples strolling through Ashland Park, enjoying its serenity, feeding Pekin and mallard ducks small pieces of bread, and looking to see if the swans are still there. These couples stand on the various bridges that cross the rippling creek, or just settle in some sheltered spot to talk and reminisce. Sometimes they take a drink of Lithia Water, and make faces at its mineral taste. Strangers, couples too, stop to comment on the lovely flower beds and ask if they too saw the glorious display of azaleas and rhododendrons in the spring.

Sometimes the older couples can be found near the play yard, sitting on benches, watching the children slide, climb the steps and slide again, or swing higher and higher, pumping with all their might. If little ones seem lost or begin to cry, these older folks will look for the parent; all their own familial skills, the instinctive response to a child who seems to be in trouble, revives in an instant. When a dashing young mother or father arrives on the scene, they sag back into their own comfortable selves.

After a while, with joyful memories revived, they walk on hand in hand, until they are out of sight, together among the trees.

From OH, HER BEAUTY

OH her beauty was such that I fancied her hair
Was a cloud of the tempest, tied up with a glare
Of pale purple lightning, that darted and ran
Through the coils like the blood in the veins of a man:
And from dark silken billows that girdled her free,
Her shoulders welled up like the moon from the sea.

—James Whitcomb Riley

My Love Is Like a Wild, Wild Rose

MARY BETH, AUNT SUE AND Uncle Bud's youngest child, so often spoke of the love her parents had for each other.

Dad was a romantic, she would recall. He loved to get out the old photograph albums and pore over them. He would linger over pictures of himself and Mother when they were young. "Come and look at this old sweetheart of mine!" he'd call to her.

And he would pull her down beside him and tease her with loving remembrances, recalling youthful dreams, memories as mellow as elderberry wine. They would drift into conversation about the days when all they had was each other and the babies who brought joy with them into the world. They would talk about the tiny cabin they had, and the orchard that miraculously flourished in hard clay soil, and the one cow whose milk kept them all well fed and healthy.

They would hold each other, as they had throughout the years, and speak with gratitude for a love that had grown, blossomed, and mellowed richly for so long.

♥

Effie's Sweetheart Cake with Lemon-Flavored Seven-Minute Frosting

MAKES ONE 3-LAYER CAKE

EFFIE LOVED TO MAKE this light-textured white cake for occasions like weddings, anniversaries, and such. She often baked two or three cakes for these affairs, to serve with hot coffee, tea, or iced punch.

3 cups cake flour, sifted
1 tablespoon baking powder
½ teaspoon salt
⅔ cup butter or margarine,
    softened at room temperature
2 cups sugar

1 cup milk
1 teaspoon vanilla
5 egg whites, beaten until stiff
Lemon-Flavored Seven-Minute
    Frosting (recipe follows)

Preheat oven to 325°F. Thoroughly grease three 9-inch layer cake pans. Set aside.

Into a large bowl, sift flour a second and third time with baking powder and salt. In a second large bowl cream butter or margarine thoroughly, add sugar gradually, and cream together until light and fluffy. Add flour mixture alternately with milk, a small amount at a time, beating well after each addition. Blend in the vanilla. Fold in the beaten egg whites. Spoon equal amounts of batter into each of the three prepared pans. For even baking, place pans in the oven so that they do not touch each other and are not close to the sides of the oven.

Bake at 325°F for 15 minutes; then increase heat to 350°F and bake 15 minutes longer, until layers are well risen, firm to the touch, and light golden brown.

Let layers stand for about 8 minutes in the pans; then turn out onto a wire rack to cool completely. Fill layers and frost with Lemon-Flavored Seven-Minute Frosting.

NOTE: Effie often arranged a small bouquet of rinsed and air-dried miniature roses in the center of the cake.

♥

Lemon-Flavored Seven-Minute Frosting

MAKES ENOUGH TO LIGHTLY FILL AND FROST A 3-LAYER CAKE

2 egg whites
1½ cups sugar
2 tablespoons lemon juice, strained

¼ teaspoon lemon rind, grated
¼ teaspoon cream of tartar
1½ teaspoons light corn syrup

In the top of a double boiler place egg whites, sugar, 3 tablespoons cold water, lemon juice and grated rind, cream of tartar, and corn syrup. Set top pan in place over rapidly boiling water in lower pan.

Using a rotary beater or wire whisk, beat ingredients constantly for 7 minutes. Remove icing from heat and continue beating until icing is of a spreading consistency, about 3 to 5 minutes longer.

Summer's Wanderlust

UNCLE VERNON, MORE THAN most, loved to go on summer vacations while all his children were out of school. He worked for the Southern Pacific Railroad out of Roseville, California, and thus had a "railroad pass" which allowed him and his family to travel on Southern Pacific and other trains for free.

Using his pass, he and Aunt Margaret, with four young children—Phillip, Lawrence, Donald, and Virginia—in tow, visited Niagara Falls and other points east, the West Coast, and many other parts of the country—wherever the railroad lines ran. They saw America pass by outside their windows: plains, mountains, deserts, small and large towns. And when the trains stopped they took endless pictures, which today they share with their grandchildren, and tomorrow, no doubt, with their great-grandchildren.

Uncle Vernon, Aunt Margaret, and children

JANE WATSON HOPPING

SUMMER IN STOCKBRIDGE

THROUGH a July afternoon
the spirit of Norman Rockwell
still walks this town.
Heat and humidity circle
antique streets
like spotted, tongue-lolling pups
waiting for the people's artist
to immortalize them.

On the long, shaded porch
of the Red Lion Inn, behind
a sign that says 1793,
people sit, and sip,
and shed the cares of New York
like winter clothes,
like years. Main Street
passes before us and we
are younger than the country,
and our country is new again.
Every year should have a summer.

—Alvin Reiss

♥

New England Hot Pot

MAKES 6 SERVINGS

THIS EASY-TO-MAKE DISH IS a meal in one; when a good salad and a little dessert are added the meal becomes an old-fashioned feast.

6 potatoes, peeled and sliced
1½ pounds lamb shoulder or
    breast, cubed
1 large onion, sliced
1½ teaspoons salt

⅛ teaspoon freshly ground black
    pepper
1 cup Homemade Chicken Broth
    (recipe follows)
2 tablespoons butter, melted

Preheat oven to 350°F. Grease a 2-quart casserole. Place *half* the potatoes in casserole; add meat. Cover with sliced onion and season with salt and pepper. Add chicken broth (water can be substituted); arrange *remaining* potatoes on top, covering the meat completely. Brush with melted butter. Bake until meat is tender and hot pot is browned, about 2 hours.

♥

Homemade Chicken Broth

MAKES I QUART

*2 quarts chicken backs, necks, and
   wings*
4 black peppercorns
A small bay leaf
½ teaspoon crushed thyme
3 or 4 generous sprigs of parsley

*Half a medium onion, peeled and
   chopped*
2 small whole peeled carrots
*3 stalks of celery, cut in 3- or
   4-inch lengths*

Wash chicken parts in cold water. Put them in a large kettle; add cold water to cover, about 1½ to 2 quarts, and add the rest of the ingredients. Over high heat, bring liquid to a boil; reduce heat and simmer about 2½ hours or until liquid is reduced by half. Strain broth; remove meat from chicken bones. Return meat to broth if you wish to make a light soup; otherwise, use only the broth (all other ingredients removed) in soups or other dishes that call for it.

Cook and chill broth, remove fat, then freeze in cup or pint containers. (Use empty, clean 1-cup yogurt and 1-pint cottage cheese cartons for containers. Fill with cold broth, set on a flat surface in freezer until frozen, then package several containers in a plastic bag.)

Caroline

Magnolias and Moss-Draped Pines

UNCLE HENRY BEECHER NEVER forgot his beloved home state of Georgia, nor did his Southern accent ever leave him. On sunny days he loved to tell us all about flowering magnolias, moss-draped pines, and poinsettias. When feeling in fine fettle, he would brag about the richness of the Georgia soil, favorable growing climate, and the traditions of the people.

Then in 1938, longing for the familiarity of home and the people he had known since birth, he took a train south to Atlanta. For a few days he saw the city sights and listened to some Dixieland jazz, and then, taking a bus, hitchhiking, and walking, he worked his way into the wild and beautiful highlands of his childhood.

He stayed all night with a cousin and feasted on 'possum and sweet taters, fried okra, and Georgia Belle peach cobbler. The next day, his cousin took him deeper into the wooded foothills of the Blue Ridge Mountains to the old home place, where his father still lived and farmed. Nearby his three sisters and five brothers had apple orchards, cattle, hogs, and broods of children.

After about a month, he walked into our house one day, beaming and looking hale and well fed. "Child," he said to me, "it does a body good to be back home fer a while, in the embrace of kith and kin!" to see the sights, hear the sounds, and breathe in the fragrances of childhood.

DIXIELAND JAZZ

GEORGIA.
The summer night spreads a note
from Sweet Auburn Avenue to Peachtree.
Martin sleeps, but the dream goes on
through the blue note of the summer night.
Scarlett and Rhett dance the night away
raising money for the boys in gray.

Georgia. Georgia,

immortalized in the words of the immortal Ray.

Geo-ja.

Over in Marietta pickups angle around the square,
pointing their dreaming lights toward the fountain
cascading lazy water lace down a mountain of bronze
green as kudzu. The summer night sticks to you
like wet magnolias,
like honey rolling off a honey tongue,
like Coca-Cola.
Beyond the fountain, off center-square, unseen,
the band spreads notes
that wake up Jelly Roll, and Satchmo, and Pee Wee,
and the immortal Ray.

Marietta   Atlanta   Five Points   Savannah   Marietta

Jahw-ja.
Jaaahw-Jaaah.

Honey and magnolia, an unseen song.
The music goes round, a lifetime long.

What a great day for a summer night.

Jaaaahw—juuhhhh . . .

—Alvin Reiss

♥

Georgia Belle Peach Cobbler

MAKES 6 SERVINGS

THE GEORGIA BELLE, SOMETIMES called the Belle of Georgia, is an excellent white-fleshed freestone grown commercially in the South. It is the most important of the white varieties and rivals the yellow freestones for flavor and juiciness. Like all other white varieties, it is very hardy.

*4 cups peeled, pitted, sliced fresh
    Georgia Belle peaches (7 to 8
    peaches)
1 tablespoon lemon juice, strained
½ cup sugar
1 tablespoon tapioca
2 tablespoons butter or margarine,
    melted, plus ¼ cup chilled*

*1 cup all-purpose flour, sifted
1½ teaspoons baking powder
1 tablespoon sugar for batter, plus
    1 tablespoon for sprinkling on
    top of batter
½ teaspoon salt
1 egg, beaten to a froth
¼ cup milk*

Preheat oven to 350°F. Set out and thoroughly grease a 12-by-8-by-2-inch baking dish.

In a large bowl, combine prepared peaches, lemon juice, sugar, tapioca, and melted butter or margarine. Set aside.

Immediately, into a medium bowl sift flour a second time with baking powder, *1 tablespoon* sugar, and salt. Work butter into flour mixture with two knives or a pastry blender to a consistency like cornmeal. With a fork stir in combined egg and milk. Turn peaches into prepared baking dish and spread the batter thinly over them. Sprinkle the *remaining 1 tablespoon* sugar over the batter.

Bake until crust is golden brown, peaches are tender, and juice is bubbling, about 40 to 45 minutes. Set cobbler on a wire rack to cool. Serve warm, cut into squares, plain, or with a little heavy cream spooned over the top, or with a scoop of ice cream.

WARM-WEATHER
PLEASURES
THAT LAST
A LIFETIME

~~~~~~~~~~

ONE OF THE GREATEST joys of summer is that the children are out of school, home to play for hours uninterrupted, to draw and paint in the shade of a tree, or to read a book from cover to cover. Arlene, my dear friend, and her sisters loved to do embroidery during the summers of their youth, stitching flowers and butterflies on new pillowcases for their winter beds.

In our family, on long warm afternoons, mothers and aunts taught us to crochet, or to sing old-fashioned songs and recite poetry. When the men came home from work, and supper was over and the evening cooled down a bit, there would sometimes be inter-family baseball games, or a four-cornered game of catch. When it got too dark to play in the yard, little groups settled down under the lights on the porch to play chess or checkers.

Whatever the pastimes, just being together, sharing thoughts and feelings, filled us with memories vivid enough to last a lifetime. And I have often thought that the warmth and laughter, the storytelling, riddles and jokes, the hugs, the swinging together on an old porch swing, singing and giggling when the harmony was off-key, gave us all the strength to face the less joyful times of life.

THE JOYS OF SUMMER

LOVELY the sights and sounds of summer, the taste and feel of warm weather, joyful and sensuous, playful and uninhibited, ripened in the sun.

—Alvin Reiss

This Funny Little Friend of Mine

MOTHER LEARNED TO RECITE this poem when she was a little girl. When Sheila and I were small, she would sit with us on warm summer days in the shade of a big oak tree, share milk and cookies, and teach us to recite her poem. That was fifty and more years ago. Sometimes I can remember all of the poem, sometimes I can't. But I have never forgotten those precious hours spent with my mother and sister.

ॐ

My Shadow

I'VE a funny little playmate,
    Who lives upon the wall,
Sometimes he's very short,
    Sometimes he's very tall.

But the funniest thing about him,
    As I think you will agree,
Is that when I stand close to him,
    He looks so much like me.

He grows so very quickly,
    This playmate dear of mine,
That he grows clear to the ceiling,
    Without taking any time.

For when I run away from him,
    He shoots up straight and tall,
Does this funny little friend of mine,
    My shadow on the wall.

—Words by Alice C. D. Riley

♥

Sand Tarts

MAKES 6 DOZEN COOKIES

WHEN SHEILA WAS A little girl she refused to eat these cookies because she thought they were made of sand, the way her own mud-pies were made of mud. Our father finally persuaded her to try one, and after that she thought Mother should always bake Sand Tarts.

2 cups all-purpose flour, sifted
1½ teaspoons baking powder
½ teaspoon salt
½ cup butter or margarine,
    softened at room temperature

1 cup sugar
1 whole egg, well beaten, and
    1 egg white, beaten to a froth
1 tablespoon sugar
¼ teaspoon cinnamon
1 cup blanched almond halves

Into a medium bowl sift flour a second time with baking powder and salt. In a large bowl cream butter or margarine thoroughly, add sugar gradually, and cream together until light. Add *whole egg* and blend into the butter mixture. Add flour mixture to butter-sugar mixture about one quarter at a time, until well incorporated (don't beat this dough). Refrigerate until dough is firm, 2 to 3 hours or overnight.

Preheat oven to 375°F. Set out one or two ungreased cookie sheets.

Cut dough in half and return half to refrigerator. Roll other half out on a lightly floured flat surface to ⅛ inch thick. Using a doughnut cutter dipped in flour, cut out cookies and lay them on the cookie sheets. Brush with egg white and sprinkle with the combined sugar and cinnamon. Arrange 3 almond halves on each cookie.

Bake until lightly browned and done throughout, about 10 minutes (don't over-bake). Transfer immediately with a spatula to brown paper or a wire rack to cool. Roll out, cut, and bake second half of dough. When all cookies are thoroughly cooled, store in an airtight container.

♥

Chocolaty Pecan Dollars

MAKES ABOUT 8 DOZEN COOKIES

ONE SUMMER DAY UNCLE Joe came to visit Grandpa and brought with him a large bag of pecans, a nut we seldom saw in the gold country of California. Mother was delighted with her gift, and told the old man how much she missed the nuts of the Midwest and South for her baking.

2½ cups all-purpose flour, sifted
1 teaspoon baking powder
½ teaspoon cinnamon
1 egg, beaten to a froth
1 cup sugar
½ cup butter or margarine,
*   softened at room temperature*

2 tablespoons milk
2 squares unsweetened baking
*   chocolate, melted*
1 teaspoon vanilla extract
½ cup pecans, chopped

Into a medium bowl sift flour a second and a third time with baking powder and cinnamon. In a large bowl combine remaining ingredients. Stir until well blended. Add flour mixture one quarter at a time, mixing well. (If dough is crumbly, work with the back of a wooden spoon.) Fold in pecans. Gather dough into a ball. Divide dough in half. Working with half of the dough at a time, fold waxed paper over the dough and lightly press into a roll 2 inches in diameter. Tightly wrap waxed paper around rolls and pat to smooth and shape evenly. Put both rolls in the refrigerator for 2 to 3 hours or overnight, or until both rolls are firm enough to slice.

Preheat oven to 400°F. Set out and thoroughly grease one or two large cookie sheets.

Working with one chilled roll at a time, unwrap, lay out on a lightly floured flat surface, and, holding the roll gently, slice ⅛ inch thick, using a long, sharp, thin-bladed knife (press down lightly and use a sawing motion).

Bake until cookies are well puffed and done throughout, about 5 minutes. Transfer to brown paper or a wire rack to cool. Store in an airtight container.

♥

Slice-and-Bake Vanilla Walnut Cookies

MAKES 6 DOZEN COOKIES

MOTHER LOVED THESE NO-ROLLING-NEEDED, no-cookie-cutters-to-wash cookies. Aunt Mabel found the basic recipe in a 1933 cookbook and thought it a modern, convenient way to make cookies. Needless to say, Mother changed the recipe a little to suit herself.

4 cups all-purpose flour, sifted
4 teaspoons baking powder
½ teaspoon salt
¾ cup butter or margarine, softened
½ cup light (or dark) brown sugar, firmly packed

2 cups granulated sugar
2 eggs, well beaten
1 cup walnuts, chopped
1 tablespoon vanilla extract

Into a medium bowl sift flour a second time with baking powder and salt. In a large bowl cream butter or margarine until waxy, add brown and granulated sugar gradually, and cream until light. Add eggs, nuts, and vanilla, and blend thoroughly. Add flour mixture gradually about one quarter at a time, blending well. (If mixture becomes stiff, work the last of the flour in with the back of a wooden spoon.) Using your hands, gather loose particles and press lightly into one large piece of dough.

Divide in half. Working with one half at a time, press lightly together and mold into a roll about 1½ inches in diameter, lengthening as you shape. When roll is shaped, wrap waxed paper tightly around it and pat until roll is smooth and evenly shaped. Repeat with the second half of the dough. Chill both rolls 2 to 3 hours or overnight, or until firm enough to slice.

Preheat oven to 425°F. Set out one or two ungreased cookie sheets.

Remove one portion of dough from refrigerator and unwrap. Lay on a very lightly floured flat surface. Gently hold dough with one hand and, using a long, sharp-bladed knife, press down gently and use a sawing motion to cut into slices ⅛ inch thick. (If cookies are to retain their shape, you must work the dough while it is thoroughly chilled and firm, with light, even pressure.) Lay slices as you cut them on cookie sheets, leaving ½ inch between cookies.

Bake until puffed, lightly browned, and firm to the touch, about 10 minutes. Transfer warm cookies to brown paper or a wire rack to cool. Store in an airtight container.

You Can't Climb Our Apple Tree

EFFIE LOVED THE OLD song, "I Don't Want to Play in Your Yard"; she sang it in a playful little child's voice to the children when they were arguing outside in the yard. In a minute, they would be laughing and could be persuaded to sit down under the trees and have a picnic, which in the thirties might have been only cold milk with homemade bread and butter, or Apricot Nectar Ice Cubes, made of home-canned juice.

&

I DON'T WANT TO PLAY IN YOUR YARD

I DON'T want to play in your yard,
  I don't like you any more
You'll be sorry when you see me,
  Sliding down our cellar door
You can't holler down our rain barrel,
  You can't climb our apple tree.
I don't want to play in your yard,
  If you won't be good to me.

—Words by H. W. Petrie

♥

Effie's Homemade Graham Bread

MAKES 1 LOAF

EFFIE BAKED BREAD—NOT one loaf, but several—every Saturday morning, and it seemed as though all the children and many of the old men in the neighborhood could smell it baking, for they came in a steady stream to bring her goodies—a basket of figs or peaches, a few cucumbers, fresh butter. She gave them each a warm loaf of bread wrapped in a napkin and thanked them for their gifts.

2 tablespoons granulated yeast
1 cup lukewarm milk (only raw
   milk need be scalded, then
   cooled to lukewarm)
1 tablespoon sugar
2 teaspoons salt
¼ cup molasses

2 tablespoons butter or margarine,
   softened at room temperature,
   plus 1 tablespoon or more for
   brushing top of loaf
2 cups all-purpose flour, plus
   ½ cup or more for kneading
2½ to 3 cups whole-wheat flour

Thoroughly grease a large bowl and a 9-by-5-by-3-inch bread pan. Set aside.

In a small bowl blend yeast with ½ cup warm water (105° to 115°F). Set aside until a frothy head has formed, 5 or more minutes.

In a large bowl combine milk, sugar, salt, molasses, the *2 tablespoons* butter or margarine, and the all-purpose flour. Beat until smooth. Mix in *enough* of the whole-wheat flour to make a dough that is easy to handle.

Turn the dough onto a lightly floured flat surface. Knead, using more flour as needed, until dough is smooth and elastic, about 5 minutes. Place dough in greased bowl, gently move about, then turn greased side up. Cover and let rise in a warm place until doubled in bulk, about 50 to 60 minutes.

NOTE: To test, touch dough with finger; if the impression remains, dough is adequately risen.

Punch down dough with fingers or fist (don't overwork). Turn out onto a lightly floured flat surface and roll into a 9-by-5-by-3-inch rectangle. Beginning at the short end, roll up the sheet of dough, and press sides and ends together with the side of your hand to seal the loaf. Turn the ends back under the loaf; then place seam side down in prepared pan. Brush the top with softened butter or margarine. Set in a warm spot to rise a second time, until light and doubled in bulk, 50 to 60 minutes.

Preheat oven to 400°F. Set risen loaf in the center of the oven. Bake until loaf is puffed, golden brown, and sounds hollow when tapped, about 30 to 35 minutes.

♥

Apricot Nectar Ice Cubes

MAKES ENOUGH FRUIT CUBES TO PLEASE HALF A DOZEN OR MORE CHILDREN

THESE NATURAL FRUIT-JUICE TREATS are easy to make. Serve to one or more children on a hot day. Be sure to give each a washcloth rinsed in cold water for continual wiping of hands and faces.

> **3 cups apricots, washed, pitted,**   **Sugar to taste**
>   **and sliced (be sure to use only**
>   **sound, ripe fruit)**

In a large saucepan, heat apricots and 2 cups water to simmering. Turn off heat and press through a fine sieve. Return to washed and scalded saucepan. Bring to a simmer a second time and add sugar to taste; stir until sugar is dissolved. Cool to room temperature, then pour into two ice cube trays. (If there is not quite enough juice, dilute the nectar enough to fill the trays.) Freeze.

NOTE: Some varieties of apricots are juicier than others.

JANE WATSON HOPPING

BENEATH

A

CHINABERRY

TREE

~~~~~~~~

Alvin Reiss

Mabel Reiss

DURING THE HOT SUMMER months, in the Oklahoma of his childhood, my good friend Al Reiss reveled in Sunday dinners at his grandparents' house, filling up on acceptance, nostalgia, recollections of his old folks, the love of kith and kin—and on fried spring chicken, vegetables right out of the garden, and all the watermelon he could eat. Now, looking back, he recalls the wealth of such times, the wonder, and the deep-down pleasure that has lasted a lifetime.

From GRANDFIELD

GRANDFIELD was the name; I never questioned that:
logical enough; a town where my grandparents lived
in a one-room house unencumbered
by running water, electricity, or paper on the wall,
a gray-board house in a red-clay field
of weeds and chiggers and friendly snakes;
a room of two beds and a big round table
resting on a pedestal, and chairs
wooden and old even then
that antique shops now sell dearly.
When we went to visit,
maybe to stay a week, it was always summer.
We never went in the winter.
Maybe we went in the winter,
but I think we never did;
the summer of the open cabin; of mosquitos,
the unfinished quilt in the frame against the ceiling;
to be lowered for blocking and gossip.
Apple pie Sundays around that old table; the family down
from Lawton, talking, eating in shifts and talking
around that old table.

—Alvin Reiss

♥

Mabel Reiss's Apple Pie

MAKES ONE 9-INCH PIE

BY EARLY JULY, APPLE lovers looked forward to the first fruits of the season. Stark's Earliest, picked hard-ripe, crisp, and juicy, are devoured out of hand, or made into a thick, tart, light-yellow applesauce or into a pie like this one. The flesh of such apples is tender, the color pleasing to the eye, and unlike some summer apples, the slices retain their shape when baked.

Double-Crust Flaky Pastry
(page 15)
6 or 7 medium apples, peeled,
cored, and thinly sliced (if you
don't want them to turn
brown, coat slices with lemon
juice or a fruit freshener)

³/₄ cup sugar
¹/₂ teaspoon ground cinnamon
¹/₄ teaspoon apple pie spice
¹/₈ teaspoon ground nutmeg
¹/₈ teaspoon salt
1 tablespoon butter
2¹/₂ tablespoons flour

Because apple slices may darken, prepare crust before making filling, and line the 9-inch pie pan (glass pie plate preferred).

Preheat oven to 425°F.

In a large bowl combine apple slices, sugar, cinnamon, apple pie spice, nutmeg, and salt. Stir gently together. Turn into prepared pie crust. Dot with butter. Add 2 tablespoons water and sprinkle lightly with flour.

Immediately roll out top crust; fold in quarters or halves to transfer to top of pie. Moisten edges of bottom crust with cold water; arrange top crust over filling. Flute the edges or press crusts together with wide-tined fork.

Bake in 425°F oven for 15 minutes, then reduce heat to 350°F and bake until crust is golden brown and apple filling is clear and bubbly, about 45 minutes.

Serve lukewarm or a little warmer, or cold. Spoon a little heavy cream over the top if you wish.

Apple Pie Sundays

THERE IS A NOTE of pride in my friend Al's voice when he tells about his mother, who from eight years of age to eighteen helped pick cotton to sustain her family. He grows more than a little nostalgic when he talks about visiting his grandparents in Grandfield, and about meeting the relatives at a soul-satisfying reunion.

ॐ

From ON LEARNING MY MOTHER HAS CHEROKEE BLOOD

I should have known that the earth said more
in those Oklahoma days than childish ears could hear,
when a summer noon was shirtless on a cot
beneath a chinaberry tree in a breeze too hot
and thick with Red River mud
to blow brown from the hopper-popping grass.
The nights tried to say it; the one-room nights;
bat-and-board nights of June bugs on the screen,
(didn't they know it was July?);
of lying awake and looking out, and up at ten-year
stars so close they fell through weeds, beyond
the hogwire fence.
Silly little stars.
What was it in the veins that told me then
to scoop them from the ground?
They were nearer in the night than the lights in Burkburnett,
forty miles away in Texas.

—Alvin Reiss

♥

Mabel's Luscious Divinity

MAKES ABOUT 36 PIECES

AL'S MOTHER USUALLY MADE this candy for Christmas, but at our house we decided it was an easy-to-make, all-occasion treat. It would be just right to sell at a candy sale, or at an apple blossom festival.

2½ cups sugar
½ cup white corn syrup
2 egg whites, beaten until stiff
1 teaspoon vanilla

⅔ cup Spanish peanuts (broken
   pecans or walnuts can be
   substituted)

In a large saucepan boil sugar, syrup, and ½ cup water until a soft ball forms (234° to 238°F on a candy thermometer).

NOTE: To test, remove syrup from heat; pour about ½ teaspoon of the syrup into 1 cup of cold water. Pick the candy up in your fingers and try to roll it into a ball. It should quickly lose its shape after being removed from the water.

Beating constantly, pour half the syrup in a thin stream into the stiff egg whites (an electric beater makes this process easier); add the vanilla and beat just enough to blend.

Return the remaining syrup to the heat, and boil over high heat, testing often until it reaches the crackle stage (275°F).

NOTE: Remove from heat while testing. When the correct temperature is reached, the syrup will form brittle threads, which will soften on removal from the water.

Beating continually, pour the hot syrup in a thin stream into the first mixture. Continue beating until the syrup is all gone and the candy holds in soft peaks (beat the last few strokes by hand). Gently fold in nuts. Immediately drop by teaspoonsful onto waxed paper. Pieces should hold their form without flattening.

A Boy's Favorite Peanut Butter Cookies

MAKES 7 DOZEN COOKIES

THIS RECIPE, SHARED BY Mabel Reiss, yields crisp, nut-flavored cookies that can't be beat.

1 cup sugar

1 cup light brown sugar

1 cup creamy peanut butter

2 eggs, lightly beaten

1 teaspoon vanilla

3 cups flour, sifted

1 teaspoon soda

1 teaspoon salt

*1 cup vegetable shortening, melted
    and cooled to lukewarm*

Preheat oven to 350°F. Set out two large cookie sheets.

In a large bowl, cream both sugars with the peanut butter. Add eggs and vanilla to the mixture and thoroughly blend. Sift flour a second time with soda and salt. Add flour mixture alternately with melted shortening to creamed mixture. Stir into a dough which can be molded with your hands. Roll between your fingertips into walnut-size balls. Space 2 inches apart on cookie sheets. Mash flat with tines of a fork in a criss-cross pattern.

Bake until firm, light golden, and crisp, 12 to 15 minutes. With a spatula transfer onto a wire rack or piece of brown paper to cool. Store in an airtight container (or seal in plastic bags and freeze).

Summer Saturdays in Oklahoma

ALMOST EVERY WOMAN WOULD agree that there is something wonderful about men and boys, large and small, playing in the yard. The expended energy seems to hang in the air. High-pitched boyish laughter and shouts at times are overwhelmed by excited, loud, deep-throated voices, and inevitably the babies start to cry.

Even so, women and girls are always drawn to watch and enjoy the rough play. In our family the women of the house bring out a plate of cookies or a cake, some cold milk, tea, and a beer or two (when asked), and pour when a red-faced boy or sweating man drops on the porch to "set this one out" and brag about his prowess.

When it's over and neighbors, friends, and family wander off home, and everyone talks about the great plays made, a special sort of bonding has come about that will last a lifetime.

ॐ

THE PRINCE, AFTER THE RAIN

ON summer Saturdays in Oklahoma it never rained,
Except that once, and as a child, I never knew why.
Since, and long since, I have learned.
The rain was a gift of wet diamonds.
God, not Abner Doubleday, invented baseball.
Abner was the designated hitter.

On that Saturday so long ago, The Prince was to come.
Al Schacht, The Clown Prince of Baseball, would entertain us,
coming down to us from Valhalla, and Ebbets Field,
and Oklahoma City, on the Rock Island Line.
But the rain came first, a gray and thunderous watery wall
washing our dreams to dust, and our diamond to mud.
Uncle Ed, the groundskeeper, certified the funereal pall,
shrouding the mound and home in futile canvas.
I remember looking up from the belt-level of my father,
there on the diamond edge, up at the falling sky,
toward Dad and Uncle Ed, and The Prince himself.
Giants, There were giants in those days.
First The Prince looked solemn. Then he smiled.

"The sky is breaking," he said. "See the blue."
"Not in time for the diamond," said Uncle Ed.
"There is always tomorrow," said The Prince. "I have no plans
and one day to be a clown is as good as another."
With the afternoon drowned, Dad invited the princely clown
to our home. Four of us rode in our rocking Chev.
I sat in the car, a listener at court,
hearing but not understanding the language between words.
They pitched names across the motor drone:
Hornsby and Dizzy and Murderers' Row;
Dickey and Rickey and DiMaggio;
Walter Johnson, "The Iron Train";
Gehrig, who would never be home on first again;
Connie Mack, whose name was McGillicuddy.
Mel Ott, Greenberg, Feller, and the immortal Babe.
Giants lived in those days. And Yankees. And Sox.
Then the Prince looked at me.
"Does your kid play catch?" he asked my dad.

Out in our yard in the new-washed sun,
under trees dripping diamonds the color of dreams,
four-cornered catch in the afternoon.
The ball went around:
Thock, Thock, Thock, Thock.
Tinker to Evers to Chance to me.
Thock, Thock, Thock, Thock.
Dad to Uncle Ed to Schacht to me.
Thock, Thock, Thock, Thock.
Afternoon, to twilight, to eternity.

The earth still smells of youth after rain.
Down the block, in the long ago distance,
I hear voices of kids playing our game.

—Alvin Reiss

♥

Spice Drops with Creamy Orange Icing

MAKES ABOUT 7 DOZEN 5-INCH COOKIES

THIS OLD-FASHIONED COOKIE KEEPS well and is delicious. Ada found the handwritten recipe among her mother's things, and through the years has shared it with young women, both in and out of the family.

1 cup light cream
1 tablespoon vinegar
½ cup butter or margarine,
    softened at room temperature
2 cups light brown sugar
2 eggs, beaten until frothy
2 cups all-purpose flour, sifted
1 teaspoon soda
½ teaspoon salt
1 teaspoon ground cinnamon

1 teaspoon ground cloves
1 teaspoon allspice
¼ teaspoon nutmeg
2 cups golden raisins (dark raisins
    can be substituted)
1 cup quick-cooking rolled oats
1 cup nuts, chopped (walnuts or
    pecans preferred)
Creamy Orange Icing (recipe
    follows)

Preheat oven to 325°F. Grease two baking sheets. Set aside.

In a small bowl combine light cream and vinegar; set aside to sour. In a large bowl blend butter or margarine, sugar, and eggs until light. Add soured cream and mix well. Into a medium bowl sift flour a second time with soda, salt, cinnamon, cloves, allspice, and nutmeg. Add flour mixture, raisins, oats, and nuts to butter-sugar mixture. Stir until well blended. Drop by teaspoons onto prepared baking sheets.

Bake until risen, firm to the touch, and lightly browned, about 15 minutes. Transfer with a spatula to wire racks or to a large piece of brown paper to cool. Top with Creamy Orange Icing.

♥

Creamy Orange Icing

MAKES ABOUT 1¾ CUPS

¼ cup light cream
2 tablespoons orange juice
1 tablespoon grated orange rind
A few grains of salt (less than ⅛
  teaspoon)

3 cups powdered sugar, sifted
¼ cup butter or margarine,
  softened at room temperature

In a medium bowl combine cream, orange juice and rind, salt, and powdered sugar. Add butter or margarine and beat until icing is creamy. Spread on top of cookies. Don't stack until frosting has set.

♥

Katrina, Katrina

AUNT MARY'S FRIEND KATRINA came to this country when she was just nine years old. She and her family lived down the road from Uncle Bud's place. The children got acquainted late in the summer. That year, 1921, many German immigrants moved into the area. War memories had not yet faded, and it took all summer for the neighbors to realize that those who had come to America were hardworking men, women, and children in search of freedom and a new and better life.

When the children went to school that fall, there was some concern among the parents. But Ann White, the teacher, did much to bring her classes into harmony with each other. Aunty recalls having to copy a bit of verse off the blackboard written by Alice C. D. Riley:

> DEAR little child, the God above
> Made me as well as you . . .

KATRINA

KATRINA came to our school,—
    Her seat is next to mine,—
She used to live in Germany,
    Beside the river Rhine.

Her cheeks are pink as cherry blooms,
    Her lips ten times as red;
But none of us could understand
    A word Katrina said.

Her eyes are like my best big doll's,
    Her hair is just the same;
I'm sure I never could pronounce
    Her father's funny name.

She's such a different kind of girl
    And from so far away
You'd think she would feel sad and strange
    And lonely all the day.

But no! Katrina always smiles;
    She's made us all her friends,—
When anybody's pencil breaks
    Her own she always lends.

She fixes our hair ribbons straight,
    She pins us when we tear,
I never saw a little girl
    So useful everywhere.

She always comes to school on time;
    Her desk is just as neat!
I'm sure I'm twice as careful
    Since Katrina shares my seat.

It makes me have some new, new thoughts,—
    Some kindlier thoughts!—to know
That, though I cannot speak to her,
    I love Katrina so.

—Stella George Stern

♥

Ada's Jeweled Cookies

MAKES ABOUT 40 COOKIES

ADA'S CHILDREN AND ALL the neighbors' children loved these jelly-filled cookies. Besides making them for the pleasure of it, Ada often took these treats to bazaars or church affairs, where she sold them to raise money for good causes. Sometimes she took a couple of gallons of icy milk and a big batch of her cookies to the school as a midmorning treat for the children, who had been up since shortly after dawn and had done their chores before coming to school.

2½ cups all-purpose flour, sifted
1 teaspoon soda
1 teaspoon salt
1 cup light brown sugar, firmly
*   packed*
1 cup butter or margarine, softened
*   at room temperature*

2½ cups quick-cooking rolled oats
About 1 cup powdered sugar for
*   sprinkling on rolling surface*
½ cup strawberry jelly

Preheat oven to 350°F. Lightly grease a large baking sheet. Set aside.

Into a large bowl sift flour a second time with soda and salt. Add sugar, butter or margarine, and *½ cup water;* beat until batter is smooth, about 2 minutes. Fold in rolled oats.

Sprinkle a flat, smooth surface generously with powdered sugar. Turn dough out onto surface and roll quite thin. Cut into rounds with a 2- or 2½-inch cookie cutter, then cut a design in the center of half the cookies. (The halves with the design will be the tops, and the plain halves will be the bottoms of the filled cookies.)

Place plain cookie bottoms on prepared baking sheet, top each with *½ teaspoon* of the jelly, and cover with cookie tops. Lightly press edges together.

Bake until cookies are risen and light brown in color, about 10 to 12 minutes.

A Day at the Beach

WHEN THE CHILDREN WERE small, we used to go often to the beach. We would take the binoculars for watching birds, seals, and—we hoped—whales. Sometimes we just lay in the sun and talked, or watched the children flying kites. Colleen liked to take lots of pictures to capture the beauty of the ocean; Randy, who was older, played nearer the water's edge.

All of us walked for hours, looking in tide pools, searching for bits of driftwood and shells, stopping to talk with others who had lost themselves among awesome polished banks of driftwood, or among rocks and miniature dunes of sand.

By noon, the children were always ready to picnic, which meant snacking ended and eating the "good stuff" began. Raymond usually spread a tarp over the sand in a sheltered place, then threw an old quilt over that to make a comfortable place to sit and eat. I spread out the tablecloth and set out the food, all the while warning the children not to scuffle sand into it.

By late afternoon our inland family was ready to move away from the waves and wind, sand and seagulls to a state park set in a grove of giant redwoods. The children laughed and ran about the place while Raymond made coffee on a coin-operated hot plate and I spread the picnic table with supper.

After eating and picking up, I put the children down to sleep in the back seat of the car. Raymond and I wound our way over a two-lane road, through a grove of giant redwoods and scented myrtle-wood trees. There were springs and damp, grassy plots, and many large and small ferns. Eventually we reached the highway, familiar territory, and then under a bright summer moon turned into our own drive-way.

It was a very different day for us, a joyful day and an adventure, but we were all glad to be back on the farm.

JANE WATSON HOPPING

♥

Aunt Mabel's Braised Chilled Chicken

MAKES 8 TO 10 SERVINGS

AUNT MABEL ALWAYS BROUGHT chicken to family gatherings, picnics, and summer potlucks. This chilled chicken was a favorite when we gathered far from home because it held up well when kept in an ice chest.

Two 4-pound frying chickens
2½ teaspoons salt, more if desired
½ teaspoon freshly ground black pepper, more if desired

2 teaspoons oregano, slightly more if desired
2 cloves garlic, peeled

Preheat oven to 400°F. Set out a large covered roasting pan.

Remove giblets and necks from birds; discard the livers and cook the hearts, gizzards, and necks with the chicken if you wish. Using *about ½ teaspoon* salt, *⅛ teaspoon* pepper, and *½ teaspoon* oregano for each bird, sprinkle seasonings in the cavities. Put *1 whole garlic clove* in the cavity of each bird.

Place birds in roasting pan and sprinkle *remaining* salt, pepper, and oregano over the tops and sides of both birds. Pour 1 cup boiling water around the base of the birds. Check now and again to see that some water remains in the pan; if necessary, add more. Roast until chickens are tender and browned, about 50 minutes (don't overcook). Temperature on a meat thermometer should read 170° to 180°F.

Immediately transfer chickens from pan to a large platter. Set out uncovered in a cool place. When most of the heat is gone, refrigerate until thoroughly chilled. Discard pan drippings or freeze for later use in soups or as flavoring for casseroles.

♥

Lima Bean Salad

MAKES 8 SERVINGS

As the summer begins to wane and gardens begin to mature, this salad is very popular, being made first with small tender green lima beans and then, as the season wears on, with those that fill the pods to bursting.

3 cups green lima beans, cooked
1½ cups sweet pickles, finely
    chopped
½ cup celery, diced
½ cup stuffed green olives, chopped

¾ cup mayonnaise, chilled
½ teaspoon salt
A few grains of freshly ground
    black pepper

In a large bowl toss lima beans, pickles, celery, and olives with chilled mayonnaise, and season with salt and pepper. Toss again lightly to blend. For picnics, serve as is, chilled. For home dinners, serve on a lettuce leaf.

♥

Our Favorite Buttermilk Rolls

MAKES ABOUT 48 SMALL ROLLS

When I was a little girl, Mother milked two cows morning and night. She sold icy-cold milk by the gallon and fresh sweet butter, salted or unsalted, to nearby families and single men who worked at the Sugar Rock Quarry.

1 tablespoon (1 envelope)
    granulated yeast
2 cups buttermilk, heated to
    lukewarm (only raw milk need
    be scalded)
1 tablespoon sugar

2 teaspoons salt
¼ teaspoon soda
4 tablespoons butter or margarine,
    melted
5 cups all-purpose flour, plus ½
    cup flour or more for kneading

In a small bowl soften yeast in ¼ cup warm water (105° to 115°F). Set aside until it forms a foamy head. Set out and thoroughly grease a large baking sheet.

In a larger bowl combine lukewarm buttermilk, sugar, salt, soda, and melted butter or margarine, stirring until sugar is dissolved. Add *2½ cups* of the flour and beat well. Add enough of the *remaining* flour to make a soft dough (one that is quite pliable but does not stick to the hands). Lightly flour a flat surface; turn out dough and knead until shiny, about 5 or more minutes. Shape dough into a ball, then pinch off small round balls of dough about the size of an extra-large egg. Place balls on greased baking sheet, tucking them close together. Cover and let rise until double in bulk, about 1½ hours (this single-rising method requires a little longer rising time).

About 15 to 20 minutes before the rising time is up, preheat oven to 400°F. Set the pan of rolls in the center of the preheated oven and bake until they are well puffed, golden brown, and firm to the touch, about 15 to 20 minutes.

ૐ

From THE SANDPIPER

Across the lonely beach we flit,
One little sandpiper and I,
And fast I gather, bit by bit,
The scattered drift-wood, bleached and dry.
The wild waves reach their hands for it,
The wild wind raves, the tide runs high,
As up and down the beach we flit,
One little sandpiper and I.

I watch him as he skims along,
Uttering his sweet and mournful cry;
He starts not at my fitful song,
Nor flash of fluttering drapery.
He has no thought of any wrong,
He scans me with a fearless eye;
Staunch friends are we, well tried and strong,
The little sandpiper and I.

—Celia Thaxter

♥

Orange Tea Cakes with Orange Butter Frosting

MAKES 24 MEDIUM TEA CAKES

THESE LITTLE CAKES TRAVEL well and can be eaten out of hand by children and adults alike. Ada and Effie served them at picnics and other outings with milk and fresh fruit.

2 cups cake flour, sifted
2 teaspoons baking powder
¼ teaspoon salt
1 tablespoon grated orange rind
2½ tablespoons butter or margarine, softened at room temperature

1 cup sugar
1 egg
¼ cup milk
½ cup orange juice
Orange Butter Frosting (recipe follows)

Preheat oven to 375°F. Set out and thoroughly grease two cupcake pans (24 medium cups).

Sift flour a second and third time with baking powder and salt. In a medium bowl cream orange rind and butter or margarine until waxy. Add sugar gradually, blend well, then add egg and beat until light. Add flour alternately with milk and orange juice, a small amount at a time, beating after each addition until batter is smooth. Spoon or pour into prepared cups, filling them two-thirds full.

Set in the center of the oven and bake until well risen, golden brown, and firm to the touch, about 20 minutes. Set on a wire rack to cool for 5 to 8 minutes; then turn tea cakes out onto brown paper or a wire rack to cool thoroughly. For picnics serve without frosting; for suppertime desserts or party fare, frost with Orange Butter Frosting.

♥

Orange Butter Frosting

MAKES ENOUGH TO LIGHTLY COVER TOPS OF 24 MEDIUM TEA CAKES

3 teaspoons grated orange rind
½ teaspoon grated lemon rind
4 tablespoons orange juice
2 teaspoons lemon juice

¼ cup butter, softened
A few grains of salt
3 cups powdered sugar

In a small bowl combine grated orange and lemon rind with orange and lemon juice. Let stand about 10 minutes, then strain.

In a medium bowl cream butter and salt together. Add 2 cups sugar, a small amount at a time, blending well after each addition. Add remaining 1 cup sugar alternately with fruit juice mixture, beating until frosting is of a smooth spreading consistency.

❦

THE USED-TO-BE

BEYOND the purple, hazy trees
Of summer's utmost boundaries;
Beyond the sands—beyond the seas—
Beyond the range of eyes like these,
And only in the reach of the
Enraptured gaze of Memory,
There lies a land, long lost to me,—
The land of Used-to-be!

James Whitcomb Riley

ON
BRIDGES
OF
MEMORY

〰〰〰〰〰

AUNT CLARY USED TO tell us that memories hang on silken cords 'twixt Heaven and earth. That they rise in dreamlike sequences, bringing to mind the scenes of our life past. The best recollections, she would tell us, are warmed until sadness and anger are forgotten, and only memories that are bright and filled with love and pleasure remain.

Softly she would talk of home and her mother and father, her grandparents and many brothers and sisters. In the mind, she would say, orchards bloom again, and the ruby-and-white cattle still graze on the green sod. The old house, ripe with age, still stands, and the walls are saturated with the laughter of all the children who grew up there. Mother's ancient rose garden, yellow, peach, pink, and white, is blooming yet, and the remembered fragrance tantalizes the senses until tender memories come tumbling to the fore.

Once while we were talking, she spoke of a young beau who had gone a-sailing and had not come home for two years, and how he brought her silk from China. They had stood in the rose garden, where the lifetime embrace of a giant fir and a cedar tree had prompted the young man to declare his troth. She had, she said, as gently as possible sent him on his way, because she had long since decided that she did not want to marry a man whose first love was the sea.

Off Old Point Comfort

Born and bred on the Chesapeake, Old Man Lawson liked to talk about raising boys. He vowed that his daddy knew more about that than any man alive—and why not? He himself had raised seven, and his father, Old Man Lawson's grandpap, had raised twelve sons, and none of them had gone astray.

Old Man Lawson would allow that his grandpap never judged a man by his race or creed, nor by the gold he'd put aside, nor by his piety. It was the character of a man that mattered.

When he was really wound up, he'd tell every male in sight that a man has got to be judged by his sense of justice and fair play, squareness in all his dealings, and his honest and straightforward way. Yes sir! The measure of a man can be taken right off by the way he treats his fellow man.

♥

Oven-Fried Sea Bream

MAKES 6 SERVINGS

This simple oven-frying method is a quick and easy one that requires less fat than traditional pan-frying methods. Wives and daughters of fishermen often adapted it to any of various saltwater fish, and to small freshwater fish like perch, trout, and sunfish.

> 6 small sea bream, whole or cut
> into serving-size pieces (allow
> about ½ pound of unboned
> fish or ⅓ pound of fillets
> per person)
> ¼ cup light cream or rich milk

> About 2 cups seasoned bread
> crumbs (season with salt,
> pepper, and herbs to taste)
> ¼ cup butter for basting, more or
> less, as desired

Preheat oven to 350°F. Set out an ungreased baking sheet.

Scale, if necessary, and clean fish. Wash and drain each fish or piece of fish. Pour cream or milk into a 9-inch pie tin or deep platter. Into a second pie tin or platter turn *1 cup* of the crumbs. Dip fish, or pieces of fish one at a time, first in the cream, then in the crumbs to coat each side. Lay coated fish or pieces on the baking sheet, leaving a small amount of space between each portion.

Set pan in center of preheated oven and bake until fish are about *half* done, then baste with melted butter; carefully turn over and baste on the other side (do not turn again). The fish is done when it feels firm to the touch, flakes when pricked with a fork, and is golden brown. Transfer to a platter and serve piping hot.

ð

TIDEWATERS

SUMMER Saturdays on the Virginia peninsula
we fished those rivers wedded to the ocean;
the Warwick, the York, the James.
From boats and beaches we cast our lines
into Chesapeake Bay.

We caught Flounder and Flukes
and Drums that made strange noises
on the stringer under the boat;
sometimes a sand shark,
and off Old Point Comfort, Bream.

While boats at anchor turned bows to the tide
you told me about the myriad
shapes of life and fortune.
We saw water rise to cover marshes,
lifting our boat to newer places,
You counseled me as a father should
in the breath of those three short summers.

At night, after a day on the bay or river,
with eyes closed in my bed, I felt the gentle sway
of water, waves, turning bows.
Inland now and years away from childhood tides
I feel it still.

—Alvin Reiss

The Last Blacksmith on Nantucket

MEG'S GREAT-GRANDFATHER, THOMAS RUPERT Warren, was a native and longtime resident of Nantucket Island, off the coast of Massachusetts. During his early years, in the late 1800s, he worked on a horse breeding and training farm at Ponkapog in Milton. Upon his return to Nantucket he followed his father's trade as a blacksmith, and when he retired in 1938 he was the last of the Nantucket blacksmiths.

THE MIGHTY BLACKSMITH

CLING! Clang! goes the blacksmith's hammer,
Cling! Clang! hot the anvil rings,
As he shapes the curving horseshoe,
Hear the song the blacksmith sings:
Blow bellows, Heat iron, Burn my fire a
Blazing red.
Strike hammer, Ring anvil, shape the iron
While 'tis red,
Cling! Clang! Cling! Clang! Cling! Clang!

—Words by Alice C. D. Riley

♥

New England Doughnuts

MAKES 2 DOZEN DOUGHNUTS

THESE SIMPLE-TO-MAKE DOUGHNUTS ARE just right for serving with tea. Our Aunt Mae and her friends set platters of them out when the men came in tired and hungry, ready for a little refreshment.

1 tablespoon butter or margarine,
*   softened at room temperature*
1 cup sugar
1 egg, well beaten
1 cup milk
2 cups all-purpose flour, sifted

1 tablespoon baking powder
½ teaspoon salt
½ teaspoon nutmeg
Shortening or vegetable oil for
*   deep-frying*

In a large bowl cream butter or margarine and sugar together until light. Add egg and milk and stir until well blended. Sift flour a second time with baking powder, salt, and nutmeg. Add enough of the flour mixture to the butter-sugar mixture to make a soft dough (one which can be handled and rolled). Cover and refrigerate about 20 to 30 minutes.

Turn onto a lightly floured flat surface and roll into a sheet ⅓ inch thick. Cut with a doughnut cutter.

In a deep skillet or deep-fryer, heat the shortening or oil to 365°F. Fry doughnuts in the hot fat until golden brown on both sides; do not crowd. Drain both sides on absorbent paper until the surface is dry, then dust with powdered sugar.

♥

Apple Turnovers with a Simple Powdered-Sugar Glaze

MAKES 6 TURNOVERS

WHEN WILL BATES WAS a little boy, he learned this rhyme from his grandfather. He loved to recite it for the children when summer apple turnovers were served for dessert. (He also loved to recite it in fall and winter!)

> THERE was an old lady of Dover
> Who baked a fine apple turnover.
> But the cat came that way,
> And she watched with dismay
> The overturn of her turnover.
>
> —THE OLD LADY FROM DOVER
> Carolyn Wells

2 cups all-purpose flour
1 teaspoon salt
¾ cup butter or margarine, plus 3
    tablespoons divided into 6 pats
    to flavor filling
3 cups (about 1 pound) apples
    (Early McIntosh or
    Gravenstein)

⅔ cup sugar
2 teaspoons ground cinnamon
¼ teaspoon freshly grated nutmeg
1 tablespoon minute tapioca
Simple Powdered-Sugar Glaze
    (recipe follows)

Preheat oven to 400°F. Set out a large ungreased baking sheet.

In a medium bowl combine flour and salt. With fingertips work butter or margarine into flour until mixture has the consistency of meal. Add enough ice water (about ⅓ cup) to form a dough that barely sticks together. Turn dough out onto a lightly floured flat surface. Knead 4 or 5 times, roll dough about ¼ inch thick, and, using a saucer, cut into 6-inch circles. (Reserve dough scraps; roll out into a circle to make a smaller or larger turnover.) Cover circles with a clean kitchen towel while making filling.

TO MAKE FILLING

Combine thin-sliced apples, sugar, cinnamon, nutmeg, and tapioca in a medium bowl. Stir until well blended. Spoon 3 to 4 tablespoons of apple filling into the center of each circle of dough. Moisten the edges of the pastry circle; fold circle in half over the filling (filling should come within about 1 inch of the edge). Press edges together to seal, and crimp. Score top of each turnover to let steam escape while baking. Place on baking sheet.

Bake at 400°F for 15 minutes; then reduce heat to 350°F and continue baking until turnover tops are golden brown, about 30 minutes.

Transfer turnovers to brown paper or a wire rack to cool. Drizzle a little Simple Powdered-Sugar Glaze over the tops of the cooled turnovers.

♥

Simple Powdered-Sugar Glaze

MAKES ENOUGH TO LIGHTLY GLAZE 6 TURNOVERS

1 cup powdered sugar
1 tablespoon milk, a little more
   if needed

Drop of vanilla extract (optional)

In a small bowl, blend sugar and milk together until smooth. Add a drop of vanilla if you wish.

This Summer of the Heart

HOME RESIDES IN THE heart of the child within, nourished by memories and visions indelibly wrought upon the mind, creating bonds that survive throughout our lives—so much so that the moment we gather with our grandparents, parents, and siblings, it's as though time stands still, and we are young again, sharing all the good and some of the bad times. We find ourselves filling each other in, passing the continuing story of our personal lives and experiences around so that there is among us more continuity in the memories of our shared lives.

And when we part, the hugs, reassurances of affection and love, and the sense of roots, home, family, and identity strengthen and enrich us.

JANE WATSON HOPPING

Salad Days

This summer was so beautiful, sisters,
because you spent your vacation time with me,
crossing seven years on silver wings,
and we built such bridges of memory, we sisters.

The night before you left for home
we sat at table in the garden, we three,
laughing again like schoolgirls,
talking about Mum and Dad, and then to them,
and they laughed with us
and shared our meal of salads.
You always loved salads, sisters;
and I made them just for you:
potato, tomato, orange, three bean and green.

The next day, at the parting gate,
people must have wondered
who were those three middle-aged women
and why were those three
hugging and crying and laughing
like schoolgirls seeing a friend
off to a weekend in the country.
They couldn't see our greentimes.
We could see nothing else.
This summer was so wonderful, sisters.

—Alvin Reiss

♥

Easy-to-Make Potato Salad

MAKES 4 SERVINGS

WHEN THE TEMPERATURE SOARS, this salad, chilled, is delicious. And since it contains no mayonnaise and the eggs are served separately, it is safer than others to serve in hot weather.

2 cups boiled potatoes, peeled and diced into ¼-inch cubes
1 teaspoon salt
⅛ teaspoon freshly ground black pepper
A few drops of onion juice
1 tablespoon parsley, minced

About 3 tablespoons olive oil
1 tablespoon vinegar
4 red lettuce leaves
2 hard-boiled eggs
Whole tiny salad tomatoes (larger tomatoes cut into eighths can be substituted)

Put prepared potatoes into a medium bowl. Add salt, pepper, onion juice, and parsley. Blend in just as much olive oil as the potatoes will absorb. Stir in the vinegar, mixing only until it too is absorbed.

Line a shallow glass serving dish with washed and towel-dried lettuce. Mound the potato mixture on the lettuce bed (salad can also be divided into 4 individual servings). Garnish with eggs cut into eighths lengthwise, and whole tiny tomatoes.

♥

Sliced Tomato Salad

MAKES 6 SERVINGS

ON HOT SUMMER DAYS this colorful salad not only looks appetizing, but when chilled is absolutely delicious.

4 medium-size tomatoes
Juice of 1 lemon
Salt and pepper to taste
8 ounces cream cheese, softened at room temperature
1 slicing cucumber, grated (discard seeds if you wish)
2 teaspoons onion juice

1 tablespoon parsley, minced
About ¼ teaspoon salt
About ⅛ teaspoon freshly ground black pepper
Dash of paprika
About ⅔ cup mayonnaise
½ cup heavy cream, whipped
Green leaf lettuce

Fill a large saucepan full of hot water and bring to a boil. Carefully plunge tomatoes into boiling water. When the skin just begins to split, immediately, using a slotted spoon, remove tomatoes from water and plunge them into cold tap water (tomatoes should not be cooked). Peel at once and set aside to cool; then cut each tomato into three thick slices. Sprinkle on *a little* lemon juice, salt, and pepper; chill thoroughly.

Mix cream cheese, grated cucumber, onion juice, minced parsley, salt, pepper, and paprika with *3 tablespoons* of the mayonnaise, beating into a thick, creamy paste. Spread a generous layer of filling on one slice of chilled tomato and place another slice of tomato on top (three or even four thinner slices of tomato can be layered into these individual salads). Carefully arrange tomato layers on a bed of light-green leaf lettuce. Blend remaining mayonnaise with whipped cream and spoon over prepared tomatoes.

♥

A Simple Three-Bean Salad

MAKES 4 TO 6 SERVINGS

THIS TASTY SALAD GOES well with almost any picnic or summer fare. Serve it chilled and mounded on a bed of leaf lettuce. When the women in our family first made it, they laughed about using all canned ingredients except one small onion and a fresh pepper.

*8-ounce can cut green beans,
    drained*
8-ounce can cut wax beans, drained
*8-ounce can red kidney beans,
    drained*
*1 small onion, thinly sliced and
    separated into rings*

*½ cup chopped red sweet pepper
    (green sweet pepper can be
    substituted)*
*½ cup Homemade Sweet French
    Dressing (recipe follows)*
4 to 6 leaves red lettuce

In a medium bowl combine green, wax, and kidney beans. Add onion rings and sweet peppers; toss. Marinate beans overnight in ½ cup Homemade Sweet French Dressing. Arrange lettuce leaves on four or six salad plates as desired. Spoon chilled salad onto lettuce.

♥

Homemade Sweet French Dressing

MAKES ABOUT I CUP DRESSING

⅔ cup salad oil
*2 tablespoons tarragon vinegar
    (cider vinegar can be
    substituted)*
2 tablespoons lemon juice

¼ cup sugar
1½ teaspoons salt
½ teaspoon paprika
½ teaspoon dry mustard
White (or black) pepper as desired

Measure all ingredients into a jar or bottle with a tight-fitting lid. Cover and chill. Shake well just before serving.

♥

Fresh Spinach Salad

MAKES 4 TO 6 SERVINGS

THIS IS A FAVORITE early-summer salad which old-time women thought was very good for you. And they were right! They planted a row of spinach in the fall garden so that dishes like this one could be enjoyed into late autumn.

6 cups tender leaves of spinach
1½ cups Homemade French
  Dressing (recipe follows)

1 pimiento, cut into strips (store-
  bought will do)
1 hard-boiled egg, sliced crosswise

Pick over the spinach, sorting out the small tender leaves. Break off any thick stems. Wash and towel dry. In a flat bowl marinate spinach 10 minutes in Homemade French Dressing. Serve on salad plates, garnished with stripes of pimiento and a slice of hard-boiled egg.

♥

Homemade French Dressing

MAKES ABOUT 1½ CUPS

1 clove garlic, cut in half
½ cup olive oil
½ cup salad oil
½ cup cider vinegar
1 teaspoon sugar

½ cup tomato catsup
¼ teaspoon salt
Dash of freshly ground black
  pepper
Dash of paprika

Set out a glass jar or bottle that has a tight-fitting cover. Drop cut clove of garlic in the bottle and add remaining ingredients. Cover and refrigerate. Shake well just before using.

♥

Luscious Orange Sponge

MAKES 6 GENEROUS SERVINGS

THIS CITRUS-FLAVORED MOLDED SALAD is delicious when served alone or served with or at the end of a summertime meal.

1 cup sugar
3 tablespoons (3 envelopes)
    unflavored gelatin
2 tablespoons lemon juice
1 cup orange juice
Shredded pulp of 1 orange
    (about ¼ cup)
1 cup heavy cream, whipped

12 large marshmallows, quartered
    (or 1½ to 2 cups small
    marshmallows)
1½ dozen fingers of leftover sponge
    or plain yellow cake
8-ounce can drained mandarin
    orange sections for garnish
    (optional)

In a medium saucepan cook sugar and *1 cup water* together to make a syrup, about 15 minutes. Meanwhile soak gelatin in *½ cup cold water;* set aside. When syrup is done, add gelatin and stir until it is dissolved. Add lemon juice and cool at room temperature. Add orange juice and pulp. Fold in whipped cream and marshmallows.

Pour into a 1½-quart mold which has been rinsed in cold water and lined with fingers of cake. Chill until firm. Unmold just before serving and garnish, if you wish, with orange sections.

A Pine Bed Under the Trees

WHEN THE CHILDREN WERE small, we would pack our gear and head for the hills to spend a night or a weekend. Once we made camp we would hike through the woods and sometimes walk as far as a nearby lake. In the evening we would cook chili, our favorite iron-kettle supper, over a campfire. Great dishesful served with warmed bread and cold milk settled us down for the night.

Wrapped in blankets, looking up at the stars, Raymond and I often thought that the woods must have been God's first cathedral. The silence, the softness of night-bird calls, and the whispering in the fir trees, left us full of tender emotions, a thankfulness for our two lovely children, for each other, for the beauty around us, and for all living creatures.

The Woods in Autumn

THE woods in Autumn are a wordless song
That floods my heart with throbbing melody;
Colors of flame and bronze the notes prolong,
And russet and red complete the harmony.

The woods in Autumn are as paintings hung
Against the sky, with colors bold and bright;
The creeks are silver ribbons, deftly flung
Across the foreground, spreading left and right.

The woods in Autumn are an artist's store
Of treasures, laid upon a thousand hills;
October opens wide the magic door
Into the great salon, that charms and thrills.

And woods in Autumn are a sermon, too,
Teaching that death must come to everything;
But that when death and earth-decay are through,
We shall be called——to greet another Spring.

—Grace E. Hall

JANE WATSON HOPPING

Marly, 1933

When You and I Were Young

PAPA LOWERY, A GOOD neighbor and a hardworking farmer who lived in the hill country of Missouri when Mother was a child, was a great bear of a man whose devoted love for his wife and children tended toward actions and not words. Sometimes, though, he would cut up and in a self-conscious way, sing little songs, or at least a part of a song, to them, letting the verses tell them what he would like to say himself. Off key he would sing:

> IF a body meet a body
> Comin' thro the rye
> If a body kiss a body
> Need a body cry?

And he would grab his wife and kiss her and hug her so tight that all their children who stood around to watch the loving playfulness of their parents at first scolded, then laughed with glee.

When You and I Were Young, Maggie

I WANDERED today to the hill, Maggie,
To watch the scene below,
The creek and the rusty old mill, Maggie,
Where we sat in the long, long ago.
The green grove is gone from the hill, Maggie,
Where first the daisies sprung;
The old rusty mill is still, Maggie,
Since you and I were young.

They say I am feeble with age, Maggie,
My steps are less sprightly than then;
My face is a well-written page, Maggie,
But time alone was the pen.
They say we are aged and gray, Maggie,
As spray by the white breakers flung,
But to me you're as fair as you were, Maggie,
When you and I were young.

And now we are aged and gray, Maggie,
The trials of life nearly done,
Let us sing of the days that are gone, Maggie,
When you and I were young.

—George W. Johnson and J. A. Butterfield

♥

An Old-Fashioned Elberta Peach Pie

MAKES ONE 9-INCH PIE

THE ELBERTA PEACH, SOMETIMES called Yellow Freestone Elberta because of its color and rich flavor, is one of the most popular peaches grown. It is widely adapted all across the country, and a sure bearer. Delicious when eaten fresh, it is also among the best freestones for canning and drying.

*Double-Crust Flaky Pastry
    (page 15)*
*8 peaches (Elberta preferred),
    pared, pitted, and sliced in
    eighths*
3 tablespoons lemon juice
*¹/₂ cup sugar, more if desired,
    and a little more to sprinkle
    on crust*

2 tablespoons tapioca
¹/₈ teaspoon salt (optional)
*About 2 tablespoons light cream
    or milk*

Make pastry and chill before assembling pie. Allow an extra ¼ cup flour for rolling out dough.

Preheat oven to 450°F. Set out a 9-inch pie pan.

Turn peaches into a medium bowl and stir in lemon juice to keep them from darkening. Stir in sugar, tapioca, and salt, folding gently together until peaches are thoroughly coated.

Remove pie crust from refrigerator. Cut in half. Place one half on a lightly floured flat surface; using about ¼ *cup* flour, roll pastry out ⅛ inch thick and line the pie pan, leaving about a 1-inch overhang. Moisten the edge of the pastry that lies on the edge of the pan and fold the overhang toward the center of the pan until the outside edge of pastry is even with the edge of the pan. Fill with peach mixture. Roll out the *remaining* pastry to ⅛ inch. Moisten the edge of the pastry in the pan a second time and lay the top crust over the filling. Using a sharp knife, trim the top crust even with the edge of the pan. Flute the edges. Cut decorative steam vents in the top crust. Brush a coating of light cream or milk over the crust and sprinkle on *a little* sugar.

Bake in 450°F oven for 15 minutes, reduce temperature to 350°F, and bake 35 minutes longer.

♥

An Apple Brown Betty

MAKES 4 SERVINGS

In July and August summer apples hang hard-ripe on the trees. Ada always loved this time of year, spending hours in the kitchen canning and preserving the season's bounty, hoarding away apple butter and golden applesauce for winter, and when begged by her family, making this old-fashioned dessert for late snacking.

$\frac{1}{3}$ cup sugar
$\frac{1}{2}$ teaspoon ground cinnamon
$\frac{1}{4}$ teaspoon salt
2 cups (white or whole-wheat) fine
    dry bread crumbs

4 hard-ripe apples (Early McIntosh
    or Gravenstein preferred),
    pared, cored, and diced
3 tablespoons butter or margarine,
    melted

Preheat oven to 375°F. Thoroughly grease a 1½- to 2-quart covered casserole dish. Set aside.

In a small bowl, combine sugar, cinnamon, and salt. To assemble, spread *one third* of the bread crumbs in the baking dish. Cover with *half* the apples and sprinkle with *half* the sugar mixture. Continue until all ingredients are used, topping with a layer of bread crumbs. Pour melted butter or margarine over crumbs and cover the dish.

Bake until fruit is tender and bread crumbs are slightly puffed, 30 minutes. Remove the cover and bake 10 minutes longer to brown the top.

♥

A Ginger-Flavored Fig Cake

MAKES ONE 3-LAYER CAKE

This is an antique cake recipe. Aunt Mae loved to make it for holidays, winter and summer. She would bake it early before dawn in summer, on her old black woodstove, so that the house would not be too hot by midday.

1½ cups dried figs
½ cup butter or margarine,
    softened at room temperature
1 cup sugar
2 eggs, lightly beaten
1 cup light corn syrup (Aunt Mae
    sometimes used sorghum)
3 cups cake flour, sifted
1 teaspoon baking powder
1 teaspoon baking soda

½ teaspoon salt
1 teaspoon ground ginger
½ teaspoon cinnamon
½ teaspoon cloves
½ cup buttermilk
1 teaspoon lemon extract
½ cup nuts, chopped (walnuts or
    pecans preferred)
Ginger Icing (recipe follows)

Boil figs 10 minutes in water to cover, drain, and slice fine. Set aside until needed.

Preheat oven to 375°F. Thoroughly grease three 9-inch layer cake pans. Set aside.

In a large bowl cream butter or margarine and sugar until light; add eggs and corn syrup. Sift flour a second time with baking powder, soda, salt, ginger, cinnamon, and cloves. Add flour mixture alternately with milk to the butter-sugar mixture, blending well after each addition. Stir in lemon extract and blend thoroughly. Fold in cooked, sliced figs and nuts. Beat thoroughly. Pour into prepared cake pans.

Bake until well risen, browned, and firm to the touch, about 20 minutes. Turn out onto a wire rack to cool. Ice with Ginger Icing.

♥

Ginger Icing

MAKES ENOUGH TO THINLY FILL LAYERS AND DRIZZLE ON TOP OF CAKE

2½ cups powdered sugar, sifted
2 teaspoons lemon juice
⅓ teaspoon ground ginger, more
    or less to taste

About 3 tablespoons sour cream

In a medium bowl combine ingredients and stir to blend. Add more sour cream if needed to give icing a smooth, spreadable consistency.

The Mountains

GOD loved the mountains best, be very sure;
He kept the tallest, straightest trees to trim
The rugged brown façades, and to secure
Immunity from trespassers within
The cool, deep-shadowed places, interlaced
Vine maples in a network strong and fine;
Then side by side artistically He placed
The multitudinous shrub and clinging vine.

He built the mountains rough and very high,
And laid hewn rocks along the canyon walls;
Upon a green moss carpet soft and dry,
The oreads dance to music of the falls;
The sun's too-eager rays He screened away
With canopies of deeply tinted leaves;
And Zephyrus and Notus gently sway
The tesselated awning in the breeze.

God loved the mountains best. He made no road
In all that vast domain for man to tread;
Here wild free creatures find a safe abode,
And luscious fruit is hanging ripe and red;
The ax-man's blows have cleft and cleared a way,
The noisome, shrieking things go hurrying through;
But God forgives, and in the twilight gray
This alien path He dampens down with dew.

But oh, that they might be as He had planned—
Untrodden save by those who seek repose!
His thaumaturgy few can understand;
The thallium on the banks where swiftly flows
The nectar of the gods in murmuring streams—
Ah, who is passing notes that it is there?
Yet God is patient, and His sunshine gleams
Across each new-made trail that men prepare.

—Grace E. Hall

MOUNTAIN
MEMORIES
MUSIC
FESTIVAL

~~~~~~~~~~

NOT SO LONG AGO, my people were Midwestern farm folk, tied to kith and kin who lived in the Ozark Mountains of southwestern Missouri. Theirs was a life still wedded to the past, to the traditions of hillfolk who had come into Missouri in the late 1800s from Kentucky, Tennessee, and Virginia. My grandmother, a Lester, was a playful woman, with masses of brown hair, who was skilled in mountain ways. My grandfather was a natural man, knowledgeable about wild critters, woods, plants, the stars, and much more. His was a body of survival knowledge that is virtually unknown today. My grandparents, and most everyone they knew, loved old-time music, ballads, and the like, kept alive in the hills and hollers of the South from one generation to the next. It was considered a real treat to go by wagon to a get-together to sing and play or just to listen to old-time fiddlers play for a square or round dance.

Some of the family usually sat in. Uncle Arch was a pretty good fiddler, and Uncle Ben played guitar. Mother loved to hear them play "The Orange Blossom Special," bowing the strings to make an old steam-engine sound, then drawing out the lonesome whistle.

Women and men alike would sing when they played "Sourwood Mountain":

> CHICKENS crowin' on Sourwood mountain,
> Hey deing dang diddle ally day.
> So many pretty girls I can't count 'em,
> Hey deing dang diddle ally day.
> My true love she lives in Letcher,
> Hey deing dang diddle ally day.
> She won't come and I won't fetch her,
> Hey deing dang diddle ally day.

Sometimes a man would ask the musicians to play "Shuckin' of the Corn," an old Tennessee folk song, or "Pretty Saro," one from Kentucky, sung quite slowly and with feeling:

> DOWN in some lone valley is a lonesome place,
> Where the wild birds do whistle, and their notes do increase
> Farewell, pretty Saro, I bid you adieu,
> And I'll dream of pretty Saro wherever I go.

Women tended to like the Southern folk hymns like "Wayfaring Stranger," "Wondrous Love," and "Lonesome Valley," a white spiritual from the Southern Highlands, sung in a moderate walking time.

Jesus walk'd this lonesome valley,
He had to walk it by Himself,
Oh—nobody else could walk it for Him,
He had to walk it by Himself.

You must go and stand your trial,
Stand it by yourself,
Oh—nobody else can stand it for you,
You have to stand it by yourself.

We must walk this lonesome valley—
We have to walk it by ourselves,
Oh—nobody else can walk it for us
We have to walk it by ourselves.

THE LAZY DAYS OF SUMMER COOKBOOK

By midday, there were groups of musicians all about the farm place, some over near the barns, practicing for the late-afternoon and evening sessions. Jewel McCord, as always, sat in the shade near the house, playing tunes for young folks on her zither, whose melodious tones so much resemble the lute or harp. Everyone's favorite was "Wild Wood Flower."

After the women had the food for the evening meal prepared, they took off their aprons and gathered in groups to practice for the evening gospel singing. You could hear them testing the harmony, singing "Praise Him, Praise Him," over several times to get it just right. And then "Sing O Earth," "In the Garden," "The Old Rugged Cross," and "Amazing Grace," their voices blended, rich, filled with joy.

ða

MY DANCIN'-DAYS IS OVER

WHAT is it in old fiddle-chunes 'at makes me ketch my breath
And ripples up my backbone tel I'm tickled most to death?—
Kind o' like that sweet-sick feelin', in the long sweep of a swing,
The first you ever swung in, with yer first sweet-heart, i jing!—
Yer first picnic—yer first ice-cream—yer first o' ever'thing
'At happened 'fore yer dancin'-days wuz over!

I never understood it—and I s'pose I never can,—
But right in town here, yisterd'y I heard a pore blind man
A-fiddlin' old "Gray Eagle"—And-sir! I jes' stopped my load
O' hay and listened at him—yes, and watched the way he "bow'd,"—
And back I went, plum forty year', with boys and girls I knowed
And loved, long 'fore my dancin'-days wuz over!—

—James Whitcomb Riley

The Darkness and the Dew

BORN IN 1841, FLOYD, Aunt Clary's friend, lived in Indiana when he was twenty. He admitted himself that he was a wild country lad who loved dancing, fiddle music, and girls. He bragged that he could lift more, run faster, and work harder than any man in his part of the country.

Then when Fort Sumter was fired on, he, like most of the young and some older men, joined up with the Union Army to help Old Abe out. Much to his mother's distress, he wrapped up his fiddle in his blanket roll and walked away from the family farm, not even taking one of the horses, which he knew were badly needed by his young brother and Pa to keep the farm going without his help.

Aunt Clary recalls that Floyd could play you any tune you could think of right into his old age. All through the war, and, as he often said, from Atlanty to the sea, he played stomping music, songs of home, and those he learned along the way. The miracle of it was that when the war was over, he walked back home through the woods, across the pastures, and as he often told Aunt Clary, made a beeline for the house, where he swore to his mother that he could never leave again.

The war, however, had left him with a wandering foot. For several years, he moved from place to place, until he finally settled in Missouri with his good wife, Hannah, down the road a piece from Aunt Clary and Uncle John.

It wasn't long before he was playing again for dances. Clary recalls that his neighbors in Missouri loved to hear his new fiddle tunes and songs about different parts of the country. A favorite was "Elanoy":

WAY down on the Wabash,   *She's bounded by the Wabash,*
Sich land was never known;   *The Ohio and the Lakes;*
If Adam had passed over it,   *She's crawfish in the marshes,*
The soil he'd surely own;   *The milk-sick and the shakes,*
He'd think it was the garden——   *But these are slight diversions,*
He'd play'd in as a boy,   *And take not from the joy,*
And straight pronounce it   *Of living in this garden land,*
Eden in the state of Elanoy.   *The state of Elanoy.*

—A song of the pioneers

Sometimes, when shadows began to fall, Floyd would softly play sentimental tunes he'd learned long before the war, while Aunt Clary would sit quietly and listen. Then, as darkness drew nigh and hid his face from view, he would play and sing the laments of men with whom he had served, among them a ballad called "Love Lies Bleeding," named, he thought, after a flower or bush.

♥

Ada's Harvest Salad

MAKES 6 SERVINGS

ADA WAS NOT ONLY an excellent gardener, but also a fine cook. She loved to grow Ace tomatoes. All through the fall her vines hung full of ripening fruit, some tomatoes weighing as much as a pound. The flesh, deep red and thick, has a delicious sweet flavor. Like other women of the day, Ada canned them, and put them in endless salads. She also scooped the center out of them and filled them with any number of hearty, marinated vegetable stuffings. This harvest salad was a family favorite.

1 cup fresh peas, shelled and cooked until tender in lightly salted water (store-bought salad peas will do nicely)

1 cup fresh green beans, washed, strings removed, cooked until tender in lightly salted water (store-bought beans can be used)

1 cup carrots, peeled, thinly sliced, and cooked until tender in lightly salted water

1 cup uncooked cauliflower, broken into small flowerets

1 cup celery, diced

French dressing, homemade (page 225) or store-bought, as preferred

6 large tomatoes (Ace preferred)

½ teaspoon salt

1 head leaf lettuce, red or green as desired

Mayonnaise for garnish

6 or more sprigs of parsley for garnish

In a medium bowl combine peas, green beans, carrots, cauliflower, and celery with French dressing. Chill. Peel tomatoes, sprinkle with salt, invert, and chill. Just before serving, remove tomatoes from refrigerator and drain. Cut each into five sections, leaving stem end whole and cut sections attached. Place each tomato cup on a nest of lettuce and fill with marinated vegetables. Top each salad with a dollop of mayonnaise and garnish with parsley.

♥

Easy-to-Make Dill Pickles

MAKES 7 QUARTS

BY LATE AUGUST, OLD-TIME women had jars of cucumbers stored under the house, or fermenting out back in sheds. In three weeks to a month they would turn into mouth-watering dill pickles, to be served with meals.

*14 grape leaves, washed and
    air-dried*
14 or more slices of garlic
*About 8 teaspoons prepared
    horseradish*
*14 generous sprays of washed
    dill head*

*7 quarts small to medium
    cucumbers*
7 or more small hot red peppers
Brine (recipe follows)

Put some of the grape leaves in the bottom of each quart canning jar. Add 1 or more slices of garlic, ½ teaspoon horseradish, and a good spray of prepared dill head. Loosely-pack in the cucumbers. Cover with more dill, pack in more grape leaves, and add more garlic. Tuck in 1 hot red pepper to flavor pickles.

NOTE: If you want the pickles to be hotter, add 1 to 4 hot red peppers.

Make the Brine, and when it is boiling pour over the cucumbers, cover with sterilized lids, and screw on rings. Gently immerse the jars of pickles in a simmering water bath—the water should be only hot enough to send up bubbles. Leave for 8 to 10 minutes. As the object is to heat the contents without cooking them, don't boil. Such heating will seal the jars tightly. The pickles will be ready to eat in about 3 weeks.

JANE WATSON HOPPING

Brine

½ cup vinegar   1 cup sauerkraut juice
¼ cup salt

In a large saucepan, heat 4 cups water, vinegar, and salt until boiling. Add the sauerkraut juice and stir to blend.

♥

Country-Fried Sweet Potatoes

MAKES ABOUT 6 SERVINGS

FLOYD WAS A GOOD gardener. Like other farmers in Missouri, he always raised a large patch of "sweet taters" for winter use. His wife, Hannah, made all sorts of dishes out of them, plain and sweet. These "country-fried sweets," as Floyd called them, could not be beat!

3 tablespoons butter or margarine   ¾ teaspoon salt
6 medium to large sweet potatoes,   ⅛ teaspoon freshly ground black
    boiled, chilled, peeled, and   pepper
    sliced

Set out a large skillet. Melt butter or margarine in pan; when fat is hot, add prepared potatoes. Turn heat to medium and cook without stirring until lightly browned and golden on the underside. Turn and brown the top side. Season with salt and pepper and serve piping hot.

♥

Sour Cream Swiss Steak

MAKES 4 LARGE SERVINGS, WITH ENOUGH LEFT OVER FOR A SNACK

FLOYD'S WIFE, HANNAH, OFTEN prepared this tender beef dish. Floyd loved it and so did Uncle John, so the women would plan to have supper together. Hannah would fix the meat and vegetables and Aunt Clary would make a cake or pie.

2 pounds round steak, cut about 1 inch thick
Salt
Freshly ground pepper

1 cup flour, more or less as needed
⅓ cup lard or shortening, just enough for browning steak
1 cup sour cream

Set out a large heavy skillet. Wipe the meat with a damp cloth, then salt and pepper both sides. On a hard surface, pound all the flour possible into it. (Hannah used the side of a heavy saucer to work the flour into the meat.)

Heat the fat in the skillet and sear both sides of the steak. Turn the heat down. Add ½ cup or more of boiling water. Cover. Simmer until meat is becoming tender; about 30 minutes; during the last 15 to 20 minutes of cooking time, add the sour cream. Continue cooking until the meat feels tender when poked with a fork. Serve piping hot.

♥

Aunt Clary's Plain Gingerbread

MAKES 12 SERVINGS

AUNT CLARY SELDOM DRANK coffee, but she thoroughly enjoyed a cup of mild brew with this gingerbread. Since Floyd and Hannah always drank coffee, Clary often made her gingerbread to top off their shared supper.

2½ cups all-purpose flour, sifted	½ teaspoon cloves
1½ teaspoons baking soda	½ cup butter or margarine
½ teaspoon salt	½ cup sugar
1½ teaspoons ginger	1 egg, beaten to a froth
1 teaspoon cinnamon	1 cup sorghum molasses

Preheat oven to 375°F. Set out and thoroughly grease and flour a 9-by-5-by-2¾-inch baking dish.

Into a medium bowl sift flour a second time with baking soda, salt, ginger, cinnamon, and cloves. Set aside. In a large bowl cream butter or margarine and sugar together until light. Add beaten egg and molasses to the butter-sugar mixture and stir to blend. Add combined flour and spices alternately with *1 cup hot water,* beating after each addition until a smooth batter is formed. Pour into prepared pan.

Bake until well risen, browned, and just firm to the touch, about 40 to 45 minutes.

THE
SPAN
OF OWL'S
WINGS

〰〰〰〰〰

BORN AND REARED IN the woods, Uncle Bud, like his father before him, spent as much time as he could wandering through the forest, hunting, fishing, or just marveling at God's creation. He often slipped away to camp out along Deer Creek, and Aunt Sue let him go, knowing his need was great.

He would sit for hours, watching snipe, killdees, and water bugs scooting this way and that over glittering pools of clear water. At night he stargazed, traced the moon's path, listened to bullfrogs, and followed the flicker of lightning bugs.

Come morning, he would head for home, his long, powerful legs striding through the woods, and Aunty, who knew him through and through, would tell folks who passed by or dropped in, "Bud's on his way home, he'll be here by dark."

JANE WATSON HOPPING

Cloud Nocturne

THE span of owl's wings
measures me.
Does' infinite eyes
mirror me.

From Evening Star
to Dawn I ride
in valleys outside the sun.

Diana's Wheel
shining silver light
webs over me,
enchants my tryst with night.

—Alvin Reiss

¿&

WOODEN SPOONS

HERMAN made the spoons of ice cream woods:
Butternut, Maple, Black Walnut, Pecan.
Then he carved forks and added new woods:
Chinquapin, Myrtlewood, Birdseye Pine.

Wooden spoons and forks, salad sets that fit wooden bowls,
serving summer picnics on wooden tables and checkered cloths;
spoons and forks that lay in plates in honeysuckle twilight,
absorbing conversations and memories and family talk;
tracing these times into their grain, like the taste
of Aunt's secret salad oil, the recipe passed
to the eldest daughter, and then to hers;
the lingering taste of generations.

Herman carved them to fit our hands, these spoons and forks,
carved them with his own working hands, carving and sanding
to the shape of their grain, to the pattern of summer rain.

People sent him woods from many lands.
He gave new life to fallen trees:
Butternut, Black Walnut, Oak and Yew.
Now they belong to our gathering, serving us
salad from the miraculous Earth, serving us
remembered stories, the warmth of their own living.

Care for them. Use them gently, as Herman did.
Pass them on. Pass them down.
Share them carefully, like Aunt's secret recipe.
Taste them.

—Alvin Reiss

Herman's Wooden Spoons, Miniature Rocking Horses, and Other Lovely Handmade Things

ABOUT THIRTY YEARS AGO, my husband, Raymond, and I met Herman and Vera Kamping at the Sam's Valley Grange. As we stood outside after the evening's fun, enjoying the warm night air and each other's company, we found that we had much in common. We talked about Kansas and Missouri, about children we had loved and lost, about crops and cattle, and despite the age difference between us, in those few minutes we became friends for life.

Through the years Herman and Vera have raised a nice family and farmed eighty acres and more—growing vegetables of every sort, melons, and fruit from a well-tended orchard for their roadside stand. They have also become a beloved part of our extended family.

Now that they are older, they have developed a new way of life: They work in wood. All about the Rogue Valley, you can find them at growers' markets and fairs, showing off their wares: hardwood spoons, ladles, and dippers all in richly colored oaks,

Herman Kamping

maple, light and black walnut; and other pieces made of fruit woods like apricot and cherry. Amid the array of spoons and such are cunningly wrought toys: miniature rocking horses, clowns that crawl up a string, hardwood hearts, and much more.

As busy as we all seem to be, we still find time for a Sunday dinner together and a good long visit. Debbie and Loretta—young mothers in Vera's family—bring the children over and we get to see how special they are, and how fast they are growing up. Sometimes we take a smoked turkey for supper, and often Vera makes her delicious raisin cake.

♥

Vera's Raisin Cake with Brandy-Flavored Powdered-Sugar Glaze

MAKES ONE LOAF OR ONE MEDIUM TUBE CAKE

THIS EASY-TO-MAKE, delicious, eggless, and almost butterless cake is moist, rich in flavor, and freezes well. Vera sometimes glazes it, but most often it is served plain.

1 cup dark raisins	*½ teaspoon cloves*
2 cups all-purpose flour, sifted	*1 teaspoon baking soda*
1 cup sugar	*1½ teaspoons melted butter*
½ teaspoon salt	*½ cup nutmeats*
1 teaspoon cinnamon	*Brandy-Flavored Powdered-Sugar*
½ teaspoon freshly grated nutmeg	*Glaze (recipe follows)*

Preheat oven to 350°F. Thoroughly grease and flour a loaf or tube pan.

Soak or cook the raisins with *1½ cups of water* until they are plump. Drain and reserve 1 cup liquid for use in the recipe (if there isn't enough, add a little water).

In a large mixing bowl, combine the flour, sugar, salt, cinnamon, nutmeg, cloves, and baking soda. In another medium bowl, combine melted butter and juice from the raisins. Pour the liquid ingredients into the dry flour mixture; stir until well blended. Add raisins. Dust nuts lightly with *2 tablespoons of flour,* then fold into batter until they are well distributed. Pour batter into prepared pan.

Bake until well risen, lightly browned, and firm to the touch, and a toothpick inserted into the cake comes out clean. Set on a wire rack to partially cool. While still warm, glaze if you wish with Brandy-Flavored Powdered-Sugar Glaze.

♥

Brandy-Flavored Powdered-Sugar Glaze

MAKES ½ CUP OR LESS GLAZE

1 cup powdered sugar
1 tablespoon milk

1½ teaspoons brandy flavoring

In a small bowl, combine powdered sugar, milk, and brandy flavoring; beat until smooth. Immediately brush or dribble glaze over the still-hot cake, using it all.

♥

Easy-to-Make Refrigerator Ginger Cookies

MAKES ABOUT 80 COOKIES

THIS SCRUMPTIOUS AND SIMPLE-TO-MAKE cookie is perfect for taking to large gatherings at grange, church, or school. It has an old-fashioned fragrance and flavor that bring to mind country kitchens, grandmothers, and woodstoves.

1 cup butter or margarine, softened
    at room temperature
1 cup sugar
1 cup molasses, warmed to room
    temperature
1 egg, beaten to a froth

5½ cups flour, sifted
2 teaspoons baking powder
½ teaspoon baking soda
½ teaspoon salt
1 tablespoon ginger

In a large bowl, blend butter or margarine, sugar, and molasses together until light. Add the egg and continue blending. In a medium bowl sift flour a second time with baking powder, baking soda, salt, and ginger. Add flour mixture to the butter-sugar mixture, and stir to blend. Chill until dough firms up enough to handle. Turn out onto a lightly floured flat surface and shape into rolls (logs). Wrap in waxed paper and refrigerate for 24 hours.

Preheat oven to 400°F. Set out an ungreased baking sheet. Remove dough from refrigerator and slice into rounds ⅛ inch thick. Bake until cookies are lightly browned and firm to the touch, about 10 to 12 minutes. With a spatula transfer cookies to brown paper or a wire rack to cool. Store cookies in an airtight container.

♥

Sweet Buns with Fruit Filling

MAKES 36 BUNS

OLD-FASHIONED LADIES SERVED THESE delicious buns with tea or coffee. They are easy to make and not too sweet.

2 tablespoons (one package)
  granulated yeast
2¾ cups lukewarm milk, plus
  ¼ cup for softening yeast
1 cup sugar
3 eggs, well beaten
1 cup butter or margarine, melted
  and cooled to lukewarm

8 cups all-purpose flour
2 teaspoons salt
2 cups cooked sweetened prunes
  (reconstituted dried apricots
  can be substituted)
Powdered sugar for sifting over
  the buns

In a large bowl soften dry yeast in the ¼ cup of lukewarm milk. When yeast is soft and bubbly, add remaining milk, sugar, eggs, and melted butter or margarine and stir until well blended. Add 2 cups of the flour, and salt. Stir until well incorporated into the batter. Add remaining flour until a soft dough forms, one that is not sticky yet is just firm enough to knead.

Turn out onto a lightly floured flat surface and knead until a smooth ball forms. Wash the bread bowl in hot soapy water and rinse in very hot water. Dry immediately and grease lightly. Place the dough in the bowl, cover with a damp cloth, and set in a warm place to rise. When dough is doubled in bulk, turn onto a lightly floured surface, pinch off 36 balls of equal size, and shape into 36 buns. Place on a well-greased baking sheet. Cover and let rise until trebled in bulk. When buns are almost risen, make a hole in the center of each bun with a knife handle. Fill with sweetened fruit (or preserves).

Preheat oven to 400°F. Bake until buns are well risen and golden brown, 15 to 20 minutes. Sprinkle or sift powdered sugar over the tops of the hot buns.

♥

Cinnamon-Topped Oatmeal Muffins

MAKES 12 MUFFINS

FOR MOST OF THEIR lives, Herman and Vera got up early, had breakfast before daylight, and were out doing chores shortly after sunrise. Delicious hot muffins like these were a treat. Men and boys would down them with hot coffee and ham and eggs, and then take a couple along in their pockets to eat in the barns and shops.

1 cup all-purpose flour, sifted
¼ cup sugar
1 tablespoon baking powder
½ teaspoon salt
3 tablespoons butter or margarine,
  cold

1 cup oats, quick-cooking preferred
1 egg, beaten
1 cup milk
Cinnamon Topping (recipe follows)

Preheat oven to 425°F. Grease a 12-cup muffin pan. Set aside.

In a large bowl sift flour a second time with sugar, baking powder, and salt. Using a pastry blender or your fingertips, work in the butter until the mixture resembles cornmeal. Add oats and blend thoroughly. Combine egg and milk and stir lightly into the flour mixture, just enough to moisten. Fill muffin cups two-thirds full and sprinkle Cinnamon Topping over muffins.

Bake until muffins are well browned and firm to the touch, about 15 to 20 minutes.

♥

Cinnamon Topping

MAKES ENOUGH FOR 12 MUFFINS

⅓ cup light brown sugar
1 tablespoon all-purpose flour

2 teaspoons ground cinnamon
1 tablespoon butter, melted

In a small bowl combine ingredients.

AN AUTUMNAL TONIC

WHAT mystery is it? The morning as rare
   As the Indian Summer may bring!
A tang in the frost and a spice in the air
   That no city poet can sing!
The crimson and amber and gold of the leaves,
   As they loosen and flutter and fall
In the path of the park, as it rustlingly weaves
Its way through the maples and under the eaves
   Of the sparrows that chatter and call.

What hint of delight is it tingles me through?—
   What vague, indefinable joy?
What yearning for something divine that I knew
   When a wayward and wood-roving boy?
Ah-ha! and Oho! but I have it, I say—
   Oh, the mystery brightens at last,—
'Tis the longing and zest of the far, far away,
For a bountiful, old-fashioned dinner to-day,
   With the hale harvest-hands of the past.

—James Whitcomb Riley

Faring Down Some Wooded Trail

WHEN OUR CHILDREN WERE young, we loved to wander through the mountains along a winding pathway. Now and again, we would trespass into the territory of chipmunks, which darted up onto nearby mounds or logs to scold us and frighten us into moving on.

If by chance a garter snake crossed our path and slithered into a patch of wild strawberries, pandemonium broke out. Randy, yowling with glee, wanted to go dashing after the snake, pick it up, and scare his sister with it. Colleen, small though she was, stood glaring, entrenched. While I watched, Raymond would coax them both on down the path to see a small creek go dashing down the mountainside toward a fast-running river.

I would follow after my exuberant loved ones, stopping here and there to look at wildflowers and the manzanita's delicate waxy-pink cups. Should I come upon the whirring flight of a quail, my heart would beat faster, and pleasure would race all through my mind and body. Sometimes, wild blackberry vines growing along the small creek would reach out and capture my skirt in a thorny embrace. And more than once, I softly and quickly moved along, leaving great bumblebees behind.

In time, we would all find ourselves deep in the realm of tall timber, great fir, and pines, with fern-green young clustered about their bases. The path seemed to dwindle in size and like a thin thread led us downward until we could hear the river's song. Raymond would run on ahead with the children while I picked up a few small cones for my pocket, memories of a lovely day that would soon be over.

As I came out of the woods, the fast-tumbling river came into view. I found a place on a sun-heated rock and sat down near the children. For some time we reveled in the sight of the cascading water as it danced over hidden rocks, cast up white foam, and raced over ripples on toward the sea.

HUNTING WEATHER

WHEN misty misty mornings come,
When wild geese low are flying,
And down along the reedy marsh
The mallard drakes are crying;
When cattle leave the highest hills,
And blackbirds flock together—
By all these signs the hunter knows
Has come good hunting weather.

—Mary Austin

A Hunter's Moon Potluck

WHEN WE WERE GROWING up we were taught that a true hunter has a primitive awe and respect for the animals with which he lives, and that it is shameful to despoil the wilds. My father and grandfather, and those who went before them, believed that poachers and those who killed an animal for its loin or hindquarters alone were butchers.

Grandpa, like other men of his era, hunted because wild meat contributed to the welfare of his family. He loved the woods and the wild critters; he liked to stride over the hills and hunch beside a campfire.

Today, in our area, true hunters consider the fall hunt a harvesting operation, one that thins out the herd so that winter hunger does not kill off animals.

♥

A Hunter's Moon Venison Roast

MAKES 10 TO 12 SERVINGS, WITH SOME LEFT OVER FOR SANDWICHES

MAMA LOWERY WAS A good cook who always brought extra to potluck dinners because her family was so large. The girls baked pies and cakes; she usually roasted both venison and elk. From their large garden they brought boxes of vegetables to cook fresh for the dinner and to share with relatives and friends.

5- to 7-pound venison rump roast
1 clove garlic, more if needed,
*   peeled and slivered*
Butter or bacon grease, warmed to
*   room temperature*
Salt, about 1 teaspoon per pound of
*   meat, less if you wish*

Pepper, ¼ teaspoon per pound of
*   meat*
2 teaspoons crushed dried
*   marjoram leaves*
1 or more green onions (rings of
*   dry onions can be substituted)*
Bacon or salt pork, as needed

Preheat oven to 450°F. Set out a large, shallow roasting pan with a rack.

With a sharp knife, make several long, narrow slits in the meat. Run slivers of garlic down into the slits. Rub the meat with butter or bacon grease and season with salt and pepper. Sprinkle the marjoram over the roast and lay one or more green onions over the top. If the meat does not have a thin coating of fat, bacon or salt pork can be laid over the top to keep it from drying out. Insert a meat thermometer into the thickest part, close to the bone, but not touching it. Place in the oven and turn the temperature down to 350°F.

The meat will be rare at 140°F, medium at 160°F, and well-done at 170°F. Remove the roast from the oven at the desired stage.

NOTE: The meat continues to cook after it is out of the oven.

♥

Baby Beets in Vinegar

MAKES 6 TO 8 SERVINGS

BEETS ARE A COLD-WEATHER vegetable. The first crop is planted early in the spring, the second in late July or early August. If the weather cools down and the beets have plenty of water and potash, tender baby beets can be pulled out of the row halfway through the growing season, leaving more than enough plants to produce a main crop.

12 baby beets about the size of a walnut or a little larger, fresh or canned

1 cup vinegar
⅓ cup sugar
½ teaspoon salt

Wash beets thoroughly. Leave 3 inches of stem and the roots attached. Put cleaned beets into a large saucepan and cover with water. Boil until tender when pierced with a fork, about 20 to 25 minutes. Drain and cover with cold water. When beets are cool enough to handle, slip off skins, stems, and roots. Leave whole (or slice). Combine vinegar, sugar, and salt; heat and pour over beets and let stand for at least 1 hour. Serve as a side dish.

♥

Our Favorite Chinese-Cabbage Salad

MAKES 4 GENEROUS SERVINGS

AT OUR HOUSE WE serve this late-summer salad with smoked sausages, tender yeast rolls, and ripe, deep-red watermelon. Raymond likes the salad with lots of raisins in it, more than the recipe calls for; Colleen prefers shaved almonds; and the rest of us like it any way it's made.

3 cups Chinese cabbage, finely
shredded and chopped
1 large Golden Delicious apple,
peeled, cored, and chopped
½ cup golden raisins, more if
desired

½ cup slivered almonds
½ cup mayonnaise, chilled
¼ cup lemon juice, strained

Turn shredded cabbage into a medium bowl. Add chopped apple, golden raisins, and almonds. Fold in thoroughly blended mayonnaise and lemon juice. Chill for about 20 minutes and serve.

♥

Baked Butternut Squash

MAKES 6 SERVINGS

IN LATE SUMMER WHEN there is a nip in the night air, squash great and small lie abundantly in the fields, soon to be picked up and put in storage for winter. At a hunter's moon potluck, the ladies serve squash breads, cakes, puddings, and other delicious squash dishes, including this simple baked butternut squash.

1 large butternut squash, pared,
pulp and seeds removed, and
cut into 2½-inch cubes
¼ cup or less butter or margarine,
softened at room temperature

½ cup or more light brown sugar
Dusting of nutmeg

Preheat oven to 375°F. Thoroughly grease a 1½- to 2-quart casserole dish.

Layer squash in prepared casserole dish, dotting each layer with bits of butter and brown sugar. Dust top with nutmeg. Bake until brown sugar and butter are bubbling and squash feels tender when poked with a fork, about 30 minutes. (If squash seems dry, add a tablespoon of hot water to the dish.)

♥

Mother's Cloverleaf Rolls

MAKES 24 ROLLS

FOR SPECIAL GET-TOGETHERS LIKE a hunter's moon potluck, Mother often made these light rolls. Grandpa liked them right out of the oven with homemade butter tucked between the "cloverleaves."

2 tablespoons granulated yeast
6 tablespoons sugar
1¾ teaspoons salt
¼ cup butter or margarine, melted

1 egg, well beaten
5 to 5¼ cups flour, plus a little
    more for kneading

Thoroughly grease two 12-cup muffin tins and set aside.

In a large bowl soften yeast in *1½ cups lukewarm water (105° to 115°F).* Let stand for 5 minutes. Add sugar, salt, butter or margarine, and egg. Beat until well blended. Add flour a little at a time, beating thoroughly after each addition until dough is just stiff enough to knead.

Turn dough onto a lightly floured flat surface and knead until smooth and elastic.

NOTE: This dough should be slightly softer than bread dough.

Grease a large bowl, place dough in the bowl and move it about to grease the underside; then turn greased side up. Cover and set in a warm place to rise until doubled in bulk, about 45 minutes.

Punch down with fingers or fist and turn out onto lightly floured flat surface. Shape dough into walnut-size balls; place three in each cup of prepared muffin pan. Cover and let rise until trebled in bulk, about 30 minutes.

Preheat oven to 450°F. Place rolls in the center of the oven and bake until well puffed, firm to the touch, and golden brown, about 15 minutes. Turn rolls out onto a piece of brown paper or a wire rack. Serve piping hot.

♥

Uncle Bill's Sour Cream Raisin Cake

MAKES ONE 9-INCH 2-LAYER CAKE

At eighty, Uncle Bill still went hunting with the boys, some of them forty years old or more. He kept the camp clean, and passed on ancestral hunting lore. Through him our young folks learned about the early days, when hunting was an integral part of survival, and through his eyes they saw the woods about them in a different light.

1 cup sugar
1 cup heavy cream, soured by
    adding 1 tablespoon lemon
    juice
2 eggs, separated (yolks well
    beaten, whites beaten until
    stiff)
2 cups all-purpose flour, sifted
1 teaspoon baking powder

½ teaspoon baking soda
½ teaspoon salt
1 teaspoon ground cinnamon
½ teaspoon freshly grated nutmeg
½ teaspoon ground cloves
1 teaspoon vanilla
1 cup raisins, chopped
Almond Filling and Frosting
    (recipe follows)

Preheat oven to 375°F. Thoroughly grease two 9-inch cake pans. Set aside.

In a large bowl combine sugar, soured cream, and beaten egg yolks. Sift flour a second time with baking powder, baking soda, salt, cinnamon, nutmeg, and cloves. Add flour mixture to sugar-sour cream mixture a little at a time, beating lightly after each addition. Add vanilla and stir to combine thoroughly with other ingredients. Fold in raisins. Fold in the beaten egg whites and pour into prepared cake pans.

Bake until layers are well risen, firm to the touch, and golden brown, about 30 minutes. Fill and top with Almond Filling and Frosting.

❤

Almond Filling and Frosting

MAKES ENOUGH FOR A 9-INCH, 2-LAYER CAKE

2 cups powdered sugar
½ cup sour cream

1 teaspoon vanilla
¾ cup almonds, chopped

Sift powdered sugar into a medium bowl, add sour cream and vanilla, and beat to a spreading consistency.

TO FILL AND TOP CAKE

Place first layer on a cake plate. Spread with frosting and sprinkle half the nuts over the frosting. Place second layer over first. Spread top with frosting and sprinkle *remaining* nuts over top of cake. (The sides are left unfrosted.)

Roberta and Mary

PERSEIDS

THE August night spreads a handmade quilt.
Dew rises through the grass, still smelling of mowing.
The grown-ups sit or lie on quilts or blankets,
or sit in low lawnchairs, wooden, built in a workshop.
They talk in low tones about the job, the trip, old friends.
They drink lemonade, or ice tea, or beer from a brown bottle.
The heat of the day lingers into night.
Locusts in unseen trees fire the distance with melodies.
Crickets, nearer, answer;
between them, the voices of kids
playing hide-and-go-seek with memories;
cousins, children of neighbors,
hiding and finding in a world of backyards without fences.
Auntie, lying on the blanket,
rubbing the undershirted back of Uncle,
who sits beside her holding a cold beer,
talking to a neighbor, sees a falling star.
She thinks of it as a sudden thought of heaven,
an impulse of joy delighting the night sky.
She wishes she had made a wish.
She sees another and makes a wish,
but says nothing, keeping it
inside her heart, with the night,
with memories of unexpected stars.

—Alvin Reiss

JANE WATSON HOPPING

A SUDDEN
THOUGHT
OF
HEAVEN

~~~~~~~~~~~

PERHAPS I'LL NEVER UNDERSTAND why abundant crops lying in the fields, ripe for picking; the sudden chill in the night air when the sun goes down; the wind in a frolic, sending dancing leaves twirling about the home place; rain blowing over the mountaintops and down into the valley, remind me so vividly of early summer, of youth, infatuation, love, and the mid-season's warm and glowing rays of sunshine.

Could it be that the changing season, the flicker of a firefly at dusk, the call of birds gathering to fly south, the chattering of raccoons—wild, masked bandits raiding in the dried cornfield—softens my heart, sending tender memories to flood my soul, and prepares me for the slower pace of winter?

Index

A

Ada's apple crisp, 89
Ada's blueberry pie with double-crust egg pastry, 118–19
Ada's favorite snap-bean dish, 160–61
Ada's harvest salad, 241
Ada's jeweled cookies, 205
Ada's poppyseed pound cake with tangy lemon-orange glaze, 26–27
Ada's rosy rhubarb pie, 15
Aiken, May, 37, 123
Aldrich, Thomas Bailey, 51
Alexander, Cecil Frances, 8
"All Things Bright and Beautiful" (Alexander), 8
almond(s):
    and blueberry muffins, 161
    in Chinese-cabbage salad, 260
    filling and frosting, 263
    in marshmallow Bavarian cream, 103
    wafers, 165
"Along the Creek" (Hopping), 105
"America" (Riley), 109
"The American Flag" (Drake), 16
Anadama bread, 56–57
Andersen, Hans Christian, 71
Ann's early peach ice cream shortcake, 138–39
apple(s):
    brown Betty, 232
    and carrot cookies, easy-to-make raw, 91
    in Chinese-cabbage salad, 260
    in cider applesauce, 90
    cottage cheese pie with butter pastry crust, old-fashioned, 116–17
    crisp, 89
    pie
        cottage cheese, 116–17
        Mabel Reiss's, 196
        sour cream, with butter-cinnamon topping, 50–51

        sour cream pie with butter-cinnamon topping, Red June, 50–51
        turnovers with a simple powdered-sugar glaze, 218–19
apple festival, 86–89
applesauce, cider, 90
apricot nectar ice cubes, 192
"Art" (Hall), 27
Ashland Park, 173–74
Aunt Clary's plain gingerbread, 245
Aunt El's strawberry pie, 30–31
Aunt Irene's stuffed tomatoes, 107
Aunt Mabel's braised chilled chicken, 207
Aunt Mabel's cider applesauce, 90
Aunt Mabel's Flag Day cake, 17
Aunt Mae's bath buns, 23
Aunt Sue's chicken croquettes served with mustard-horseradish sauce, 11–12
Aunt Sue's salmon macaroni salad, 106–107
Aunty's honey-glazed carrots, 12–13
Austin, Mary, 256
"An Autumnal Tonic" (Riley), 254

B

baby beets in vinegar, 259
baby's breath, 142
bachelor's buttons, 142–43
bacon and footlong beans salad, hot, 149
baked beans, ham with, 22–23
baked butternut squash, 260–61
balm teas, 34
baptism in Cow Creek, 19–20
basil tea, 34
Bates, Will, 118, 218
beach, a day at the, 206
beans, footlong:
    and bacon salad, hot, 149
beans, green:
    and bacon salad, hot (substitute), 149

beans, green (*cont'd*)
dish, 160–61
and gold snap beans, 100–101
in harvest salad, 241
medley, garden-fresh, 83
in three-bean salad, a simple, 224
beans, kidney:
in three-bean salad, a simple, 224
beans, lima:
in green bean medley, garden-fresh, 83
salad, 208
beans, navy:
baked, ham with, 22–23
beans, wax:
and green snap beans, 100–101
in three-bean salad, a simple, 224
Beecher, Henry, 181
beef:
ground
in ham loaf, old-fashioned, 82
in summer garden casserole, 131
round steak, in sour cream Swiss steak,
244
beets, baby:
in vinegar, 259
"Beneath the Hollyhocks" (Hopping), 32
beverages:
blackberry cordial, wild, 128
iced cider punch, summertime, 70
picnic punch, easy-to-make, 44
strawberry pineapple punch, 8
see also tea
blackberries, wild:
cordial, 128
crunch with vanilla wafer topping, deep-dish,
126–27
illustrated, 105
pie with flaky lattice crust, 125–26
blackberry social, 123–24
blue mountain tea: *see* goldenrod tea
blueberry:
and almond muffins, 161
pie with double-crust egg pastry, 118–
19

Boston brown bread tea sandwiches with assorted
fillings, 64–66
The Boston Cooking-School Cook Book (Farmer), 53
"The Boy 'At Lives on Our Farm" (Riley), 133
a boy's favorite peanut butter cookies, 198
bran:
in hermits, old-fashioned, 97
muffins, deluxe, 69
brandy-flavored powdered-sugar glaze,
251
breads:
Anadama, 56–57
Boston brown, 64–65
graham, homemade, 191
see also buns; muffins; rolls
bride's orange-blossom cake, 74–75
brine, for dill pickles, 243
broth, chicken:
freezing, 180
homemade, 180
for Yorkshire country captain, 25
buns:
bath, 23
sweet, with fruit filling, 252
see also muffins; rolls
butter:
cinnamon topping, 51
crust pastry, 116–17
frosting
creamy chocolate, 77
orange, 211
tinted, 63
icing, creamy orange, 79
Butterfield, J. A., 230
buttermilk rolls, our favorite, 208–209
butternut squash, baked, 260–61

C

cabbage:
Chinese
salad, our favorite, 260
Golden Acre
about, 101
salad, 101

red
    and spinach salad dressed with homemade
        French dressing, 14
    salad, Golden Acre, 101
cakes:
    bride's orange-blossom, 74–75
    coconut angel, 108
    fig, ginger-flavored, 232–33
    Flag Day, 17
    gingerbread
        gossamer, 54–55
        plain, 245
    groom's, with creamy chocolate butter
        frosting, 76–77
    light-yellow, 63
    orange-blossom, bride's, 74–75
    orange chiffon, with creamy orange butter
        icing, 78–79
    poppyseed pound, with tangy lemon-orange
        glaze, 26–27
    rainbow, 62–64
    raisin, with brandy-flavored powdered-sugar
        glaze, 250–51
    sour cream raisin, 262–63
    sponge, 138–39
    sweetheart, with lemon-flavored seven-minute
        frosting, 176–77
    tea
        light-yellow, 63
        orange rainbow, 64
        orange, with orange butter frosting, 210–11
        velvet, white or pink, 62
    velvet, white or pink, 62
candied red rose petals, 144–45
candies:
    candied red rose petals, 144–45
    divinity, luscious, 197
Candy Tuft, 142
canners, boiling-water-bath, 128
cantaloupe: see melons
caper bush (illus.), 27
capers, mock, 145
carrots:
    and apple cookies, easy-to-make raw, 91

    in harvest salad, 241
    honey-glazed, 12–13
"The Cat in the Window" (Reiss),
        172
cherry crunch, sweet, 43
chicken:
    braised chilled, 207
    broth
        homemade, 180
        for Yorkshire country captain, 25
    croquettes served with mustard-horseradish
        sauce, 11–12
    filling, for Boston brown bread tea sandwiches,
        65
    fried spring, 40
    and rice filling, for stuffed red bell peppers,
        136–37
    salad with homemade curried French dressing,
        curried, 68–69
    in stuffed red bell peppers, 136–37
    in Yorkshire country captain, 24–
        25
chilled baked salmon, 111
Chinese cabbage: see cabbage
chocolate:
    butter frosting, creamy, 77
    in economical surprise pie with vanilla wafer
        crust, 117–18
    in groom's cake with creamy chocolate butter
        frosting, 76–77
    pecan dollars, 188
cider:
    applesauce, 90
    punch, summertime iced, 70
cinnamon:
    butter topping, 51
    pie, 7
    topped oatmeal muffins, 253
"Cinnamon Pie" (Reiss), 7
Clare, John, 6
"Climbing Trees, Catching Butterflies"
        (Kingston), 156
"Cloud Nocturne" (Reiss), 247
cobbler, peach, 183

coconut:
   angel cake, 108
   in Flag Day cake, 17
confections:
   candied red rose petals, 144–45
   yellow rose-petal sugar, 144
   see also candies
cookies:
   almond wafers, 165
   apple and carrot, easy-to-make raw, 91
   chocolatey pecan dollars, 188
   dried fig and honey, 96
   ginger, easy-to-make refrigerator, 251
   hermits, old-fashioned, 97
   jeweled, 205
   peanut butter, 198
   sand tarts, 187
   Scottish fancies, 53
   sour cream, 35
   spice drops with creamy orange icing, 202–
      203
   sugar, old-time soft, 170–71
   vanilla walnut, slice-and-bake, 189
Coonley, Lydia A., 18
corn:
   in green bean medley, garden-fresh, 83
   mid-season, 160
   pudding, old-fashioned, 135
cornmeal:
   in Anadama bread, 56–57
cottage cheese:
   apple pie with butter pastry crust, old-
      fashioned, 116–17
   lemon cucumber salad, 148
   in stuffed tomatoes, 107
country-fried sweet potatoes, 243
cream cheese:
   and marmalade filling, for Boston bread tea
      sandwiches, 66
   mayonnaise, 151
   in sliced tomato salad, 223
   in watercress sandwiches, 164
creamy chocolate butter frosting, 77
creamy orange butter icing, 79

creamy orange icing, 203
croquettes, chicken, 11
cucumber(s):
   cottage cheese salad, lemon, 148
   dill pickles, easy-to-make, 242–43
   in ruby and butter-crunch lettuce salad with
      herbed vinaigrette, 21
   salad, jellied, 132
   and sweet onions in sour cream, dilled,
      112
curried chicken salad with homemade curried
      French dressing, 68–69

D

"The Dandelion" (Riley), vii
date, peanut butter and honey filling, for Boston
      bread tea sandwiches, 66
deep-dish wild blackberry crunch with vanilla
      wafer topping, 126–27
deluxe bran muffins, 69
desserts:
   apple brown Betty, 232
   apple crisp, 89
   apple turnovers with a simple powdered-sugar
      glaze, 218–19
   apricot nectar ice cubes, 192
   blackberry crunch with vanilla wafer topping,
      deep-dish wild, 126–27
   cherry crunch, sweet, 43
   cider applesauce, 90
   cinnamon pie, 7
   doughnuts, New England, 217
   fruit pockets, 94–95
   marshmallow Bavarian cream, 103
   orange sponge, luscious, 226
   peach cobbler, Georgia Belle, 183
   peach ice cream
      old-fashioned, 169
      shortcake, early, 138–39
   peaches, poached fresh, 130–31
   raspberries topped with chilled heavy cream,
      vine-ripened red, 113
   strawberries dipped in sugar, sun-ripened, 6
   strawberry custard, luscious frozen, 170

strawberry mousse, 29

see also cakes; cookies; pies; pudding; sauces, dessert

Dickinson, Emily, 33

dill:

  cucumbers and sweet onions in sour cream, 112

  pickles, easy-to-make, 242–43

  vinegar, 22

"A Discouraging Model" (Riley), 61

divinity, luscious, 197

"Dixieland Jazz" (Reiss), 182

double-crust egg pastry, 119

double-crust flaky pastry, 15

double-crust plain pastry, 31

doughnuts, New England, 217

Drake, Joseph Rodman, 16

E

easy-to-make dill pickles, 242–43

easy-to-make picnic punch, 44

easy-to-make potato salad, 222

easy-to-make raw apple and carrot cookies, 91

easy-to-make refrigerator ginger cookies, 251

economical surprise pie with vanilla wafer crust, 117–18

Effie's Boston brown bread tea sandwiches with assorted fillings, 64–66

Effie's homemade graham bread, 191

Effie's jellied cucumber salad, 132

Effie's poppyseed rolls, 102

Effie's preserved whole strawberries, 166

Effie's strawberry mousse, 29

Effie's stuffed red bell peppers, 136–37

Effie's sweetheart cake with lemon-flavored seven-minute frosting, 176–77

Effie's watercress sandwiches, 164

eggplant:

  about, 137

  with tomatoes, 137

"Elanoy" (song), 240

English peas: see pea(s)

F

Fannie Merritt Farmer's gossamer gingerbread, 54–55

Farmer, Fannie Merritt, 53

fashion show, 60–61

Father's Day outing, 38–39

Field, Eugene, 46

fig(s):

  cake, ginger-flavored, 232–33

  and honey cookies, 96

fish:

  boning, 111

  salmon

    chilled baked, 111

    macaroni salad, 106–107

    with tartar sauce, 99

    wiggle, 159

  sea bream, oven-fried, 214–15

  trout, pan-fried mountain, 47

Flag Day, 16

Flag Day cake, 17

flowers, drying, 142–43

fluffy orange frosting, 75

folk songs, Southern, 235–38

Fourth of July picnic, 105–06

Free, Spencer Michael, 124

fresh spinach salad, 225

fried spring chicken, 40

frostings:

  almond, 263

  butter, tinted, 63

  chocolate butter, creamy, 77

  lemon-flavored seven-minute, 177

  orange butter, 211

  orange, fluffy, 75

  seven-minute, 18

    lemon-flavored, 177

  see also glazes; icings

fruit:

  filling, sweet buns with, 252

  pockets, 94–95

fruit (*cont'd*)

    salad platter with honey-lemon mayonnaise, old-fashioned, 81–82

    see also individual names

"A Fruit-Piece" (Riley), 139

G

game: *see* venison

garden-fresh grabbled potatoes with herbs, 112–13

garden-fresh green bean medley, 83

"The Gazebo" (Reiss), 162

gazebo, Effie's, 163

Georgia Belle peach cobbler, 183

geranium (pelargonium) tea, 34

ginger:

    cookies, easy-to-make refrigerator, 251

    flavored fig cake, 232–33

    icing, 233

gingerbread:

    gossamer, 54–55

    plain, 245

glazes:

    brandy-flavored powdered-sugar, 251

    lemon-orange, tangy, 27

    powdered-sugar

        brandy-flavored, 251

        simple, 219

        thin, 109

    see also frostings; icings

"Goals" (Hall), 100

Golden Acre cabbage salad, 101

goldenrod tea, 35

grabble, 13

graduation, eighth-grade, 9–10

graham bread, homemade, 191

"Grandfield" (Reiss), 194

Grandpa's grabbled baked red potatoes, 13

grapefruit juice:

    in picnic punch, 44

green and gold snap beans, 100–101

green beans: *see* beans, green

Grimm, Jacob and Wilhelm, 71

groom's cake with creamy chocolate butter frosting, 76–77

grower's market, 140–41

Gurney, Dorothy Frances, 143

H

Hall, Grace E., 27, 80, 100, 228, 234

ham:

    with baked beans, 22–23

    loaf, old-fashioned, 82

heavy cream:

    chilled, vine-ripened red raspberries topped with, 113

    soured, in sour cream raisin cake, 262–63

    whipped, sweetened, 118

helichrysum, 143

herbed vinaigrette, 21

hermits, old-fashioned, 97

hibiscus (illus.), ix

hollyhock (illus.), 162

homemade chicken broth, 180

homemade curried French dressing, 69

homemade French dressing, 225

homemade sweet French dressing, 224

homemade tomato French dressing, 14

honey:

    and dried fig cookies, 96

    lemon mayonnaise, 82

    peanut butter date filling, for Boston bread tea sandwiches, 66

    rice pudding, 84

honeydew melon: *see* melons

Hopping, Colleen, 255–56

Hopping, Jane and Raymond (photo), 147

Hopping, Jane Watson, 255–56

    poems by, 32, 90, 105

Hopping, Randy, 255–56

Hopping, Raymond, 152, 255–56

    photo of, 98

Hopping, Walter, 152

horseradish-mustard sauce, 12

hot footlong beans and bacon salad, 149

housewarming party, 77

"The Human Touch" (Free), 124

"Hummingbirds" (Reiss), 147

hunter's moon venison roast, 258
"Hunting Weather" (Austin), 256

I

"I Don't Want to Play in Your Yard" (Petrie),
190
ice cream:
peach, old-fashioned, 169
peach shortcake, 138–39
strawberry topping for, 30
ice cream freezers, churning instructions for,
171–72
ice cream social, 167–68
icings:
ginger, 233
orange butter, creamy, 79
orange, creamy, 203
see also frostings; glazes

J

Jacksonville, Oregon, 154
"Jacksonville: Pigeons" (Reiss), 67
Johnson, George W., 230
"Judith" (Riley), 75
"June" (Aiken), 37

K

Kamping, Herman (photo), 249
Kamping, Herman and Vera, 249–50,
253
"Katrina" (Stern), 204
Keats, John, 110
kidney beans: *see* beans, kidney
Kingston, Courtney, 156
Knipe, Alden Arthur, 4

L

lamb (shoulder or breast):
in New England hot pot, 179
larkspur (illus.), 56
lemon:
batter rolls, 42
flavored seven-minute frosting, 177
honey mayonnaise, 82

orange glaze, tangy, 27
vinaigrette, 146
lemon cucumber cottage cheese salad, 148
lettuce, leaf:
in nasturtium salad, 146
salad with herbed vinaigrette, ruby and butter-
crunch, 21
light crispy pie crust, 126
light-yellow cake, 63
lima beans: *see* beans, lima
"A Little Way With Me" (Hall), 80
"Lonesome Valley" (song), 236, 237
"The Lord God Planted a Garden" (Gurney),
143
luscious frozen strawberry custard, 170
luscious orange sponge, 226

M

Mabel Reiss's apple pie, 196
Mabel's luscious divinity, 197
macaroni salad, salmon, 106–107
McCord, Jewel, 238
magnolia (illus.), 181
marshmallow Bavarian cream, 103
mayonnaise:
cream cheese, 151
honey-lemon, 82
meat: *see* beef; ham; lamb; venison
medley of watermelons, 150–51
"The Melon Man" (Reiss), 130
melons:
cantaloupe, in fruit salad platter with honey-
lemon mayonnaise, 81–82
honeydew, in fruit salad platter with honey-
lemon mayonnaise, 81–82
watermelons, medley of, 150–51
"Memory" (Aldrich), 51
mid-season corn, 160
"The Mighty Blacksmith" (Riley), 216
Missus Upjohn, 33–34
mock capers, 145
Mother's cloverleaf rolls, 261
Mother's coconut angel cake, 108
Mother's potato salad, 41

Mother's red cabbage and spinach salad
    dressed with homemade tomato French
        dressing, 14
"The Mountains" (Hall), 234
mousse, strawberry, 29
muffins:
    blueberry and almond, 161
    bran, deluxe, 69
    oatmeal, cinnamon-topped, 253
    see also buns; rolls
Mulhollen, Brian, 44
mustard-horseradish sauce, 12
"My Dancin'-Days is Over" (Riley), 238
"My Shadow" (Ripley), 185

N

nasturtium:
    in mock capers, 145
    salad, 146
navy beans: *see* beans, navy
New England doughnuts, 217
New England hot pot, 179
"A Nonsense Calendar" (June), viii
nuts: *see* individual names

O

oatmeal:
    in jeweled cookies, 205
    muffins, cinnamon-topped, 253
    in Scottish fancies, 53
    in spice drops with creamy orange icing, 202–
        203
"Oh, Her Beauty" (Riley), 174
old-fashioned corn pudding, 135
old-fashioned cottage cheese apple pie with
        butter pastry crust, 116–17
old-fashioned Elberta peach pie, 231
old-fashioned fruit salad platter with honey-
        lemon mayonnaise, 81–82
old-fashioned ham loaf, 82
old-fashioned hermits, 97
old-fashioned peach ice cream, 169
"An Old Friend" (Riley), 120
"The Old Lady From Dover" (Wells), 218

old Missus Upjohn's sour cream cookies, 35
"The Old Swimmin' Hole" (Riley), 151
old-time soft sugar cookies, 170–71
"On Learning My Mother Has Cherokee Blood"
        (Reiss), 195
"On the Grasshopper and the Cricket" (Keats),
        110
onions:
    and cucumbers in sour cream, dilled, 112
    in green bean medley, garden-fresh, 83
"Only a Fiddler" (Andersen), 71
orange:
    blossom cake, bride's, 74–75
    butter frosting, 211
    butter icing, creamy, 79
    chiffon cake with creamy orange butter icing,
        78–79
    frosting, fluffy, 75
    icing, creamy, 203
    lemon glaze, tangy, 27
    marmalade and cream cheese filling, for Boston
        bread tea sandwiches, 66
    in picnic punch, 44
    rainbow tea cakes, 64
    sponge, luscious, 226
    tea cakes with orange butter frosting, 210–11
our favorite buttermilk rolls, 208–209
our favorite Chinese-cabbage salad, 260
oven-fried sea bream, 214–15

P

pan-fried mountain trout, 47
pastry:
    butter-crust, 116–17
    cinnamon pie, 7
    double-crust egg, 119
    double-crust flaky, 15
    double-crust plain, 31
    light crispy, 126
    single-crust flaky, 50–51
pea(s):
    in harvest salad, 241
    salad, English, 48
    in salmon wiggle, 159

peach(es):
  and checking for ripeness of, 130
  cobbler, Georgia Belle, 183
  Elberta, about, 231
  in fruit salad platter with honey-lemon
    mayonnaise, old-fashioned, 81–82
  Georgia Belle, about, 183
  ice cream, old-fashioned, 169
  ice cream shortcake, early, 138–39
  pie, old-fashioned Elberta, 231
  poached fresh, 130–31
peanut butter:
  cookies, 198
  date and honey filling, for Boston bread tea
    sandwiches, 66
peanuts, Spanish:
  in divinity, luscious, 197
pears:
  in fruit salad platter with honey-lemon
    mayonnaise, old-fashioned, 81–82
pecan(s):
  dollars, chocolatey, 188
  in economical surprise pie with vanilla wafer
    crust, 117–18
pelargonium tea: see geranium tea
peppers, stuffed red bell, 136–137
"Perseids" (Reiss), 264
Petrie, H. W., 190
pickles, dill, 242–43
pies:
  apple, 196
  blackberry, with flaky lattice crust, 125–26
  blueberry, with double-crust egg pastry, 118–
    19
  cottage cheese apple, with butter pastry crust,
    116–17
  economical surprise, with vanilla wafer crust,
    117–18
  peach, old-fashioned Elberta, 231
  rhubarb, rosy, 15
  sour cream Red June apple, with butter-
    cinnamon topping, 50–51
  strawberry, 30–31
  see also pastry

pineapple:
  in marshmallow Bavarian cream, 103
  in picnic punch, 44
  strawberry punch, 8
pink velvet cakes, 62
"The Pixy People" (Riley), 71
  verses from, 72
plums:
  in fruit salad platter with honey-lemon
    mayonnaise, old-fashioned, 81–
    82
poached fresh peaches, 130–31
poetry, children's, 155–56
poppyseed:
  pound cake with tangy lemon-orange glaze,
    26–27
  rolls, 102
pork: see bacon; ham
Porter, Mabel Meekins (photo), 109
Porter, Orvil and Mabel (photo), 18
portulaca moss rose (illus.), xviii
potato(es):
  baked red, 13
  butter horn rolls, 49
  with herbs, garden-fresh grabbled, 112–
    13
  in New England hot pot, 179
  salad
    easy-to-make, 222
    Mother's, 41
potatoes, sweet:
  country-fried, 243
poultry: see chicken
pound cake: see cakes
powdered-sugar glaze:
  brandy-flavored, 251
  simple, 219
  thin, 109
"Pretty Saro" (song), 236
"The Prince, After the Rain" (Reiss), 199–
    200
produce stands, roadside, 129
prunes:
  in fruit filling, for sweet buns, 252

pudding:
  corn, old-fashioned, 135
  rice, honey, 84
punch: *see* beverages

R

"The Raggedy Man" (Riley), 86
rainbow cakes, 62–64
raisin(s):
  cake with brandy-flavored powdered-sugar
      glaze, 250–51
  in Chinese-cabbage salad, 260
  in fruit pockets, 94–95
  in hermits, old-fashioned, 97
  sour cream cake, 262–63
  in spice drops with creamy orange icing, 202–
      203
raspberries topped with chilled heavy cream,
      vine-ripened red, 113
"The Red Shoes" (Andersen), 71
Reiss, Alvin, 193
  photo of, 193
  poems by, 7, 56, 67, 115, 130, 147, 162, 172,
      179, 182, 185, 194, 195, 199–200, 215,
      221, 247, 248, 264
Reiss, Mabel, 198
  photo of, 193
"Remembering" (Reiss), 115
rhubarb pie, rosy, 15
rice:
  and chicken filling, for stuffed red bell
      peppers, 136–137
  pudding, honey, 84
Riley, Alice C. D., vii, 186, 203, 216
Riley, James Whitcomb, xvii, 25, 57, 61, 71, 72,
      75, 86, 109, 120, 121, 133, 139, 151,
      158, 168, 174, 211, 238, 254
rolls:
  buttermilk, 208–209
  cloverleaf, 261
  lemon-batter, 42
  poppyseed, 102
  potato butter horn, 49
  see also buns; muffins

rose-petals:
  candied red, 144–45
  sugar, yellow, 144
ruby and butter-crunch lettuce salad with herbed
      vinaigrette, 21
runaway boy, 92
Russian tea with preserved strawberries, 166

S

"Salad Days" (Reiss), 221
salad dressings:
  cream cheese mayonnaise, 151
  French, 225
    curried, 69
    sweet, 224
    tomato, 14
  herbed vinaigrette, 21
  honey-lemon mayonnaise, 82
  lemon vinaigrette, 146
  vinaigrette
    herbed, 21
    lemon, 146
salads:
  cabbage
    Chinese, 260
    Golden Acre, 101
    red, and spinach, 14
  Chinese-cabbage, 260
  cucumber
    cottage cheese, lemon, 148
    jellied, 132
    and sweet onions in sour cream, dilled,
      112
  curried chicken, with homemade curried
      French dressing, 68–69
  footlong beans and bacon, hot, 149
  fruit, with honey-lemon mayonnaise, 81–82
  harvest, 241
  lemon cucumber cottage cheese, 148
  lima bean, 208
  macaroni, salmon, 106–107
  nasturtium, 146
  orange sponge, luscious, 226
  pea, English, 48

potato
    easy-to-make, 222
    Mother's, 41
    red cabbage and spinach, dressed with
        homemade tomato French dressing, 14
    ruby and butter-crunch lettuce, with herbed
        vinaigrette, 21
    salmon macaroni, 106–107
    spinach, fresh, 225
    three-bean, a simple, 224
    tomato, sliced, 223
    watermelons, medley of, 150–51
salmon:
    boning, 111
    chilled baked, 111
    macaroni salad, 106–107
    with tartar sauce, 99
    wiggle, 159
"The Same Blest Thing" (Reiss), 56
sand tarts, 187
Sanders, Gene, 152
"The Sandpiper" (Thaxter), 209
sandwiches, tea:
    Boston brown bread, 64–66
    chicken filling for, 65
    cream cheese and marmalade filling for, 66
    peanut butter, date and honey filling for, 66
    watercress, 164
sauces:
    mustard-horseradish, 12
    tartar, 99
    white
        medium, 159
        thick, 12
sauces, dessert:
    strawberry, for ice cream, 30
Schuler, Katie, 153
Scottish fancies, 53
sea bream, oven-fried, 214–15
seven-minute frosting, 18
    lemon-flavored, 177
shortcakes:
    peach ice cream, early, 138–39
simple powdered-sugar glaze, 219

simple three-bean salad, 224
single-crust flaky pastry, 50–51
slice-and-bake vanilla walnut cookies, 189
sliced tomato salad, 223
snacks: *see* desserts
snap beans: *see* beans, green; beans, wax
snapdragon (illus.), 8
"The Snow Queen" (Andersen), 71
"A Song for Flag Day" (Coonley), 18
sour cream:
    cookies, 35
    dilled cucumbers and sweet onions in, 112
    raisin cake, 262–63
    Red June apple pie with butter-cinnamon
        topping, 50–51
    Swiss steak, 244
"Sourwood Mountain" (song), 236
spice drops with creamy orange icing, 202–203
spinach:
    and red cabbage salad dressing with homemade
        tomato French dressing, 14
    salad, fresh, 225
sponge cake, 138–39
squash: *see* butternut squash; zucchini
"The Squirt-Gun Uncle Maked Me" (Riley), 151
Stanley, Shauna, 156
statice, 142
Stebbins, Stephanie, 155
Stern, Stella George, 204
Stevens, Johnnie, 155
stock: *see* broth, chicken
strawberries:
    custard, luscious frozen, 170
    dipped in sugar, sun-ripened, 6
    mousse, 29
    pie, 30–31
    pineapple punch, 8
    preserved whole, 166
    topping for ice cream, 30
strawflowers, 143
sugar:
    cookies, old-time soft, 170–71
    yellow rose-petal, 144
"Summer" (Knipe), 4

"Summer" (Reiss), 185
"Summer" (Taft), 155
"A Summer Afternoon" (Riley), 121
"A Summer Afternoon" (Stebbins), 155
"Summer Apple" (Hopping), 90
"Summer Evening Sounds" (Stanley), 156
summer garden casserole, 131
"Summer in Stockbridge" (Reiss), 179
"Summer is Here, Hooray!" (Mulhollen), 44
"A Summer Sunrise" (Riley), 57
summertime iced cider punch, 70
"Summertime in the Valley" (Stevens), 155
sun-ripened strawberries dipped in sugar, 6
sweet buns with fruit filling, 252
sweet-cherry crunch, 43
sweet potatoes: *see* potatoes, sweet
sweetened whipped cream, 118
swimming hole, 152–53
Swiss steak, sour cream, 244

T

Taft, Ben, 155
tangy lemon-orange glaze, 27
tartar sauce, 99
tea:
    balm, 34
    basil, 34
    geranium (pelargonium), 34
    goldenrod (blue mountain), 35
    Russian, with preserved strawberries, 166
    Wellesley, 54
tea cakes: *see* cakes
Thaxter, Celia, 209
thin powdered-sugar glaze, 109
three-bean salad, simple, 224
"The Thrush's Nest" (Clare), 6
"Tidewaters" (Reiss), 215
"The Tinder-Box" (Andersen), 71
tinted butter frosting, 63
"To a Boy Whistling" (Riley), 168
tomato(es):
    eggplant with, 137
    French dressing, homemade, 14
    in harvest salad, 241

    peeling, 223
    in ruby and butter-crunch lettuce salad with
        herbed vinaigrette, 21
    salad, sliced, 223
    stuffed, 107
    in summer garden casserole, 131
trout, pan-fried mountain, 47
turnovers, apple, 218–19

U

Uncle Bill's sour cream raisin cake, 262–63
Uncle Bud's favorite dried fig and honey cookies,
    96
Upjohn, Missus, 33–34
"The Used-to-Be" (Riley), 211

V

vanilla wafer:
    crust, 118
    topping, 127
Vanilla walnut cookies, slice-and-bake, 189
vegetables:
    green bean medley, garden-fresh, 83
    harvest salad, 241
    in summer garden casserole, 131
    see also individual names
velvet cakes, white or pink, 62
venison roast, hunter's moon, 258
Vera's raisin cake with brandy-flavored
    powdered-sugar glaze, 250–51
vinaigrettes: *see* salad dressings
vine-ripened red raspberries topped with chilled
    heavy cream, 113
vinegar, dill, 22
"A Vision of Summer" (Riley), 25

W

walnut vanilla cookies, slice-and-bake, 189
"A Warm Summer Day" (Schuler), 153
Warren, Thomas Rupert, 216
watercress sandwiches, 164
watermelons, medley of, 150–51
wax beans: *see* beans, wax
Webster, Johnny, 157

Wellesley tea, 54
Wells, Carolyn, 218
"When the Little Boy Ran Away" (poem), 93–94
"When You and I Were Young, Maggie" (Johnson and Butterfield), 230
whipped cream: *see* heavy cream
White, Ann, 203
White, Elizabeth, xvii–xviii
    photo of, xvii
white sauce:
    medium, 159
    thick, 12
white velvet cakes, 62
Whiteman, Dick, 152
wild blackberry cordial, 128

wild blackberry pie with flaky lattice crust, 125–26
Willie's favorite fruit pockets, 94–95
"Wooden Spoons" (Reiss), 248
"The Woods in Autumn" (Hall), 228
"A Wraith of Summer-Time" (Riley), xvii
"Wynken, Blynken, and Nod" (Field), 46

Y

yellow rose-petal sugar, 144
Yorkshire country captain, 24–25
young Martha's strawberry topping for ice cream, 30

Z

zucchini, in summer garden casserole, 131

About the Author

EARLY EACH MORNING, IN the heart of summer, you can find JANE WATSON HOPPING in her made-over bedroom office working on one book or another. On the corner of the old oak library table on which she now works are her first, second, and third books, *The Pioneer Lady's Country Kitchen, The Pioneer Lady's Country Christmas,* and *The Country Mothers Cookbook,* the sight of which inspire her to further efforts.

Afternoons are spent making bread-and-butter pickles, peach and apricot jam for winter use, and loaves of sweet bread—to freeze—for her husband, Raymond, who thinks he has to have a little treat with his coffee at his ten o'clock break.

In the cool of the evening she takes a walk about the farm, snipping off faded blossoms to encourage more rosebuds, and looking under the prickly leaves in the cucumber patch to see if there will be enough cucumbers to make another batch of pickles on the morrow.